Crime and Punishment in America

PRIMARY SOURCES

Crime and Punishment in America

PRIMARY SOURCES

Sharon M. Hanes
Sarah Hermsen, Project Editor

U·X·L
An imprint of Thomson Gale,
a part of The Thomson Corporation

THOMSON
™
GALE

Detroit • New York • San Francisco • San Diego • New Haven, Conn. • Waterville, Maine • London • Munich

Crime and Punishment in America: Primary Sources

Sharon M. Hanes

Project Editor
Sarah Hermsen

Rights Acquisitions and Management
Ann Taylor

Imaging and Multimedia
Leitha Etheridge-Sims, Lezlie Light, Dan Newell

Product Design
Michelle Dimercurio

Composition
Evi Seoud

Manufacturing
Rita Wimberley

storage retrieval systems—without the written permission of the publisher.

For permission to use material from this product, submit your request via Web at http://www.gale-edit.com/permissions, or you may download our Permissions Request form and submit your request by fax or mail to:

Permissions Department
Thomson Gale
27500 Drake Rd.
Farmington Hills, MI 48331-3535
Permissions Hotline:
248-699-8006 or 800-877-4253, ext. 8006
Fax: 248-699-8074 or 800-762-4058

Cover photographs of Al Qaeda and AMBER Alert reproduced by permission of AP/Wide World Photos; Prohibition
photo courtesy of the Library of Congress. Courtroom, fingerprints, and police car reproduced by permission of ©Corbis Images.

While every effort has been made to ensure the reliability of the information presented in this publication, Thomson Gale does not guarantee the accuracy of the data contained herein. Thomson Gale accepts no payment for listing; and inclusion in the publication of any organization, agency, institution, publication, service, or individual does not imply endorsement by the editors or publisher. Errors brought to the attention of the publisher and verified to the satisfaction of the publisher will be corrected in future editions.

Library of Congress Cataloging-in-Publication Data

Hanes, Sharon M.
  Crime and punishment in America. Primary sources / Sharon M. Hanes ; Sarah Hermsen,
project editor.
    p. cm. — (Crime and punishment in America reference library)
  Includes bibliographical references and index.
  ISBN 0-7876-9168-2 (hardcover : alk. paper)
1. Crime—United States—History—Sources. 2. Punishment—United States—History—Sources. I. Hermsen, Sarah. II. Title. III. Series.
HV6779.H35 2005
  364.973—dc22   2004017068

Printed in the United States of America
10 9 8 7 6 5 4 3

Contents

Reader's Guide

Crimes are forbidden acts considered harmful or danger-ous. They fall outside society's rules of proper behavior. Some acts—such as murder, robbery, and rape—violate the behavioral codes of almost every society. Other acts may be considered crimes in one culture but not in another. In crim-inal law both society and the individual victim, when there is one, are considered harmed by crimes. Each crime threat-ens some aspect of society; for example, white-collar crime—business-related crimes such as fraud or embezzlement—threatens the economy, and the illegal dumping of waste threatens the quality of the environment. For this reason, a victim's approval is not necessary for the government to pros-ecute a crime and punish the offender.

Over the past four centuries, crime and punishment in America have steadily changed as society has changed. Some types of behavior considered criminal in colonial times, such as idleness and heresy, have ceased to be treated as crimes, while other behaviors, such as computer hacking and toxic-waste dumping, have since been added to the list of prohib-ited acts. Technological advances have improved the abilities of criminals to commit crimes and avoid detection, but such advances have also aided law enforcement officials in their work. The rise of the automobile in the early twentieth century resulted in an increase in interstate crime and faster get-aways for the criminals, but with their new patrol cars police were able to respond more readily to calls for help. At the end of the twentieth century, advances in telecommunications introduced new methods of breaking the law but also gave law enforcement officials many new ways to catch criminals and expanded crime-fighting to an international stage.

In a democratic society, the rules of behavior that maintain social order come from citizens, not from a church or from a royal head of state such as a king. These rules are set through judicial decisions, legal history, and cultural tradition. Rules are also established by legislatures, or law-making bodies, acting through democratic principles by passing laws of government based on the beliefs, opinions, and desires of the citizens. The rules and consequent punishments for violations are organized in sets and written down. Those who break the codes of criminal law in the United States are subject to the U.S. criminal justice system—arrest by law enforcement authorities, court trial, and punishment.

As English colonists established settlements in the New World beginning in the early seventeenth century, they brought English common law with them. This law included the well-known process of accusation, arrest, decision to prosecute or to dismiss, trial, judgment, and punishment. However, in colonial America rigid social order had to be maintained for survival of the first settlements and the colonists had to modify the English legal system to accommodate their unique situation in the New World. For example, there were often too few people residing in a given area for jury trials to be practical. In addition, many areas lacked a person with the proper law training to serve as a judge. Often an officer of the colony or a respected member of the community made legal decisions. Another difference between English courts and the developing American legal system involved the death penalty—the punishment of death to those convicted of serious crimes. American criminal courts applied the death penalty to fewer crimes than English courts. Colonists were also more respectful of individual civil liberties, believing the accused had a legal right to fairness.

With independence from England following the American Revolution (1775–83), a new American criminal justice system came into being. The common-law crime system gradually gave way to statutory criminal law. In contrast to common law, in statutory law acts are deemed criminal when the legislative body responds to a changing society's needs and passes a law prohibiting some activity or behavior. During the nineteenth century other basic changes in criminal justice arrived, such as professional policing and penitentiaries, or prisons.

Although fairness in the criminal justice system is a trait traditionally valued by American citizens, it has not always been evident. Throughout much of American history political power was held by one segment of society—white Protestant males. As a result black Americans, immigrant minorities, women, and other segments of society felt the full weight of law for much of American history. For example in the early twentieth century women could be arrested for voting and blacks could be convicted and executed simply because they were accused of a crime, regardless of the evidence available. The march for equality before the law and fairness in criminal justice procedures as guaranteed by the U.S. Constitution made steady progress through the late twentieth century.

The criminal justice system today is composed of many parts and numerous players. Legislatures, usually under pressure from society, make laws defining crime. Police and detectives apprehend offenders. Courts, prosecutors, defense lawyers, and judges determine the offenders' guilt. Prison wardens and guards, probation officers, and parole board members carry out the sentences. Criminal justice can be found in many varied settings, ranging from street community policing on bicycles to high-tech forensic laboratories; from isolation cells in a maximum-security prison to the historic chamber of the U.S. Supreme Court.

For an action to be considered a crime, not only does a loss or injury have to occur, but there must typically be a proven willful "intent" to commit the act. A harmful action that is an accident and did not occur from irresponsible behavior is not usually considered a crime. Crimes defined in the codes of law are either felonies or misdemeanors. Felonies are major crimes resulting in prison sentences of longer than one year. For certain felonies, namely murder cases, and in certain states, the punishment might be the death penalty, also known as capital punishment. Other felonies include robbery and rape. Misdemeanors are minor crimes punishable by fines or short periods of time, up to one year, in a local jail. Misdemeanors are sometimes called "petty" crimes, including such acts of petty theft as stealing a lawnmower from a shed or a compact disc player from a car.

Academics search for reasons why social deviance grew during the twentieth century. Criminologists and other professionals attempted to find the causes of crime in the hope of finding a cure for crime. Even though crime can be highly predictable—despite a seeming randomness at times—progress has been slow in isolating the causes.

Even less clear than the root cause of crime is the effect of the justice system on criminal activity. Crime seems to increase even as efforts to combat crime are intensified. Crime impacts millions of people, and the prevention, control, prosecution, rehabilitation, and punishment of criminals result in extraordinary expenses—not to mention the losses resulting from the crimes themselves. By the end of the twentieth century, operation of the criminal justice system at federal, state, and local levels cost $130 billion a year in addition to the $20 billion a year in losses to crime. On the other hand, industries related to crime and punishment create thousands of jobs, and the various forms of crime-related entertainment bring in many millions of dollars.

Features

Crime and Punishment in America: Primary Sources tells the story of the criminal justice system in the words of the people who shaped the field and the laws that contributed to its development. Eighteen excerpted documents touch on a wide range of topics related to crime and punishment. The excerpts in *Crime and Punishment in America: Primary Sources* are divided into seven chapters. Each of the chapters focuses on a specific theme: A Basis for Justice, Foundations of Criminal Justice, Moral Offenses, Capital Punishment, White-Collar and Organized Crime, Protection of Minorities and Youth, and Terrorism. Every chapter opens with a historical overview, followed by reprinted documents.

Each excerpt (or section of excerpts) includes the following additional features:

- **Introductory material** places the document and its author in a historical context.

- **Things to remember while reading** offers important background information about the featured text.

- **Excerpt** presents the document in its original spelling and format.

- **What happened next** . . . discusses the impact of the document and/or relevant historical events following the date of the document.

- **Did you know** . . . provides interesting fact about the document and its author.

- **Consider the following** . . . poses questions about the material for the reader to consider.

- **For More Information** offers resources for further study of the document and its author as well as sources used by the authors in writing the material.

Other features of *Crime and Punishment in America: Primary Sources* include numerous sidebars highlighting people and events of special interest. Nearly fifty black-and-white photos illustrate the text. In addition, each excerpt is accompanied by a glossary running in the margin alongside the reprinted document that defines terms, people, and ideas. The volume begins with a timeline of events and a "Words to Know" section, and concludes with a general bibliography and subject index of people, places, and events discussed throughout *Crime and Punishment in America: Primary Sources.*

Crime and Punishment in America Reference Library

Crime and Punishment in America: Primary Sources is only one component of the three-part Crime and Punishment in America Reference Library. The set includes two other titles:

Crime and Punishment in America: Almanac (two volumes) presents a comprehensive overview of the development of the American justice system. The two-volume set covers in twenty-five chapters various topics including violent crime, crimes against property, cyber crime, terrorism, environmental crime, organized crime, public order crime, school violence, and white-collar crime, from the first European settlements of the seventeenth century to the early twenty-first century. The *Almanac* also describes elements of the criminal justice system including courts, policing, forensic science, corrections, military justice, American Indian criminal justice systems, and juvenile justice. Additional chapters address the influences of moral and religious values as well as the media on crime and punishment.

Crime and Punishment in America: Biographies (one volume) presents the life stories of twenty-six individuals who have played key roles in the history of crime and punishment. People from all walks of life are included. Some held prominent national roles in developing or influencing the U.S. criminal justice system; others were defendants in key court trials that contributed significantly to the field. Profiled are well-known figures such as former Federal Bureau of Investigation (FBI) director J. Edgar Hoover, authors Charles Dickens and Truman Capote, Supreme Court justice Felix Frankfurter, domestic terrorists Ted Kaczynski and Timothy McVeigh, and social reformer Jane Addams. A number of lesser-known individuals are included as well, such as early female lawyers Belva Ann Lockwood and Arabella Mansfield, criminal defendants Daniel McNaughtan and Ernest Miranda, New York City police chief George Washington Walling, and political radical Emma Goldman.

A cumulative index of all three titles in the Crime and Punishment in America Reference Library is also available.

Comments and Suggestions

We welcome your comments on *Crime and Punishment in America* and suggestions for other topics to consider. Please write to: Editor, *Crime and Punishment in America: Primary Sources,* U•X•L, 27500 Drake Road, Farmington Hills, Michigan 48331-3535; call toll-free: 1-800-877-4253; fax to 248-699-8097; or send e-mail via http://www.gale.com.

Timeline of Events

1215 King John signs the Magna Carta in England, recognizing certain fundamental liberties and rights of landowners.

1609 English and other European colonists begin settling the East Coast of North America, adapting the English common-law criminal justice system to the New World. One such adaptation is establishing the position of sheriff.

1611 The colony of Virginia issues "Lawes Divine, Morall and Martiall" to maintain a strict control over the settlement's residents during its infancy.

1692 A series of witchcraft trials, including Sarah Good's, occurs in Massachusetts, leading to the conviction and execution of several supposed witches.

1775 The American Revolution (1775–83) erupts, driven partly by the colonists' desire to gain fairness and legal protections in the criminal justice system.

1787 The U.S. Constitution is adopted, establishing a new national governmental system that includes a

Supreme Court and gives Congress authority to make laws and establish other federal courts as needed.

1787   The first prison reform organization is established in Philadelphia, the Philadelphia Society for Alleviating the Miseries of Public Prisons, promoting rehabilitation over punishment.

1789   Congress passes the Judiciary Act, establishing the Supreme Court and various levels of federal courts, such as district and appellate (where district court decisions are appealed or reviewed) courts, and identifies their jurisdictions (the geographic area over which a court has legal authority). The act also created the U.S. attorney, attorney general, and marshal offices.

June 8, 1789 James Madison, principal author of the U.S. Constitution and future U.S. president, delivers a speech to Congress proposing the Bill of Rights.

1790   Congress passes the Crimes Act, establishing seventeen federal crimes.

1790   Philadelphia opens the Walnut Street Jail, introducing a four-tier prisoner system based on type of offender. The system includes isolation for some prisoners.

1791   The first ten amendments to the U.S. Constitution, known collectively as the Bill of Rights, are adopted. The amendments contain several sections concerning crime and punishment, including freedom of unreasonable search and seizure, freedom from self-incrimination, the right to legal counsel, and freedom from cruel and unusual punishment.

1794   The Pennsylvania legislature becomes the first in the United States to define the crime of first-degree murder and eliminates the death penalty for all crimes other than first-degree murder.

1819   The state of New York opens the Auburn maximum security prison for men, an institution that becomes the model for prison industry programs.

1829   Sir Robert Peele establishes a professional police force in London, England, becoming a model for future policing developments in U.S. cities.

1829   Pennsylvania opens the Eastern State Penitentiary, also known as Cherry Hill, which becomes the model for the Separate System, in which inmates are place in solitary confinement around the clock.

1842   Charles Dickens tours America, including Philadelphia's Cherry Hill Prison, and publishes his accounts in *American Notes.*

1844   New York City establishes the first city police force to address the rising crime rate.

1846   Michigan becomes the first state to abolish the death penalty.

1850   Allan Pinkerton establishes a private detective agency, known as the Pinkerton National Detective Agency, to provide security services for railroads and others.

1873   Congress passes the Comstock Law prohibiting the distribution of "obscene" materials in the U.S. mail, including birth control information and devices.

1890   Congress passes the Sherman Antitrust Act to prohibit large corporations from unfairly controlling competition in particular industries.

August 6, 1890 William Kemmler becomes the first person to be executed by an electric chair at the Auburn State Prison in New York.

1899   Illinois creates the nation's first juvenile court system.

1905   Pennsylvania creates the nation's first state police force.

1906   Congress passes the Pure Food and Drug Act, requiring companies to label the contents of foods, particularly of addictive ingredients. Congress also bans the importation of opium.

1908   The Bureau of Investigation is created in the U.S. Department of Justice to conduct investigations. It becomes the Federal Bureau of Investigation (FBI) in 1935.

1910   Congress passes the Mann Act, which prohibits taking women across state lines to engage in prostitution.

1911   Alice Stebbins Wells becomes the nation's first full-time professional policewoman, serving on the Los Angeles police force.

1914 The U.S. Supreme Court in *Weeks v. United States* rules that evidence illegally obtained by a federal law enforcement officer cannot be used in a federal criminal trial.

1914 Congress passes the Harrison Narcotic Drug Act, regulating the distribution of opium, cocaine, and other narcotics. This law serves as a model for future drug laws.

1920s Adoption of the police car revolutionizes policing, increasing responsiveness but reducing contact between police and citizens.

January 16, 1920 The Eighteenth Amendment to the U.S. Constitution goes into effect, prohibiting the production, sales, and transportation of alcoholic beverages.

1923 August Vollmer establishes the nation's first modern crime laboratory in Los Angeles.

1924 J. Edgar Hoover becomes head of the Bureau of Investigation and builds it into a model professional police organization.

1924 Famous defense attorney Clarence Darrow gives his eloquent plea against the death penalty in the murder trial of Nathan Leopold and Richard Loeb.

1927 The first women's federal prison is established, in West Virginia.

1929 President Herbert Hoover becomes the first U.S. president to identify crime as a key national issue in his inaugural address. Hoover appoints George Wickersham as head of the National Commission on Law Observance and Enforcement to examine all aspects of the U.S. criminal justice system. The commission issues fourteen reports by 1931.

May 1929 Leaders of several major crime organizations meet in Atlantic City, New Jersey, dividing the nation into nine territories and forming a national organized crime coalition with cooperation among the organizations.

1930 The Bureau of Investigation begins the Uniform Crime Reporting (UCR) program, the first national crime statistics system.

1931 George Wickersham delivers an address to the Cincinnati, Ohio, Regional Crime Committee titled "The Problem of Law Enforcement."

1932 Congress responds to the kidnapping and murder of the infant son of famous aviator Charles Lindbergh by passing the Lindbergh Act, defining as a federal crime the transporting of kidnapped victims across state lines.

1932 The U.S. Supreme Court rules in one of the Scottsboro cases, *Powell v. Alabama,* that states must provide defense lawyers for those defendants too poor to afford lawyers who are charged with capital crimes. In 1938 the Court extends this requirement to all defendants facing possible incarceration. In 1963 the Court rules that all indigent defendants are entitled to free legal counsel.

December 1933 Prohibition ends with the adoption of the Twenty-first Amendment to the Constitution, repealing the Eighteenth Amendment.

January 1936 The trial of Haywood Patterson, one of seven defendants in the Scottsboro rape trials, goes to the jury.

1937 The American Bar Association recommends that all motion picture and still cameras be banned from courtrooms. Congress adopts the recommendation in 1944, banning radio broadcasting, cameras, and, in 1962, television from federal courtrooms.

1939 Indiana passes the first law prohibiting driving while intoxicated.

1941 The American Society of Criminology, originally called the National Association of College Police Officials, is founded.

1941 Hervey Cleckley publishes *The Mask of Sanity,* which introduces the ideas of psychopathic behavioral disorders that contribute to criminal activity.

1951 Congress enacts the Uniform Code of Military Justice (UCMJ) for military services.

1961 The U.S. Supreme Court, in its *Mapp v. Ohio* ruling, establishes criteria for preventing illegal search and seizure.

1966 The U.S. Supreme Court rules in *Miranda v. Arizona* that criminal suspects must be advised of their legal rights before interrogation. This rule becomes known as the Miranda warning.

1966 The U.S. Supreme Court, in *Kent v. U.S.,* extends some due process guarantees to juveniles.

1966 Author Truman Capote introduces the first true-crime book when *In Cold Blood* is published. The book becomes a popular Hollywood movie.

1967 The president's Commission on Law Enforcement and Administration of Justice issues a report on organized crime and other findings of the U.S. criminal justice system after a two-year study.

1968 As part of President Lyndon B. Johnson's war on crime, Congress establishes the Law Enforcement Assistance Administration (LEAA) to provide funding assistance to states for fighting crime.

October 15, 1970 Congress passes the Racketeer Influenced and Corrupt Organizations (RICO) Act, giving law enforcement greater legal power to combat organized crime.

1972 The FBI opens its new academy in Quantico, Virginia, and adds the Behavioral Science Unit.

1972 The Bureau of Justice Statistics begins the National Crime Victimization Survey (NCVS), collecting data on both attempted and successful crimes.

1972 Congress passes the Juvenile Delinquency Prevention Act, establishing general rules for state juvenile justice systems, including the separation of juveniles from adults during custody and incarceration.

1972 The U.S. Supreme Court, in *Furman v. Georgia,* declares that the manner in which most states apply death penalty sentencing decisions violates the Constitution's protection from cruel and unusual punishment. In 1976, with *Gregg v. Georgia,* the Court upholds a new process for deciding on the death penalty using a separate sentencing trial.

1975 The National Organization for Victim Assistance (NOVA) is established to coordinate the victim rights movement.

1976   Congress passes the Resource Conservation and Recovery Act (RCRA), making it a crime to dispose of waste in a way that could cause harm to public health and the environment.

1978   Congress passes the Foreign Intelligence Surveillance Act to increase law enforcement's counterterrorism capabilities, including greater surveillance authority.

1978   Ted Kaczynski, known as the Unabomber, begins an eighteen-year period of domestic terrorism by mailing bombs to various targeted individuals. He is arrested in 1996 after killing three people and injuring twenty-three others with his bomb devices.

1980s White-collar crime captures headlines as scandal erupts around a number of savings and loans corporations.

1980   Wisconsin is the first state to pass a crime victims' bill of rights.

1980   The victims' rights group Mothers against Drunk Driving (MADD) is formed to lobby Congress and states for tougher laws.

1982   The Broken Windows theory is introduced, emphasizing that community disorder breeds criminal activity. This theory leads to a reorientation of policing, focusing on petty crimes in order to curb major crimes. Foot patrols take the place of car patrols as community policing techniques are adopted around the nation.

1982   Texas executes the first prisoner by lethal injection in the nation. Lethal injection becomes the primary method of execution in the United States.

1982   Congress passes the Victim and Witness Protection Act to provide protection for victims involved in the criminal justice system as well as witnesses and informants of federal crimes.

1984   Congress passes the Victims of Crime Act (VOCA), which provides funding to states for victim assistance programs.

1984   Congress passes the first law addressing computer-related crime, the Computer Fraud and Abuse Act, which prohibits interference with computer systems involved in interstate communications and economic trade.

1986 The War on Drugs begins with passage of the Anti-Drug Abuse Act, which leads to a major increase in arrests, court cases, and prison population. The act also makes money laundering a federal crime.

1988 Gang violence continues to escalate in the nation's cities as Los Angeles County reports 452 gang-related deaths for the year.

1989 The U.S. Supreme Court rules that execution of offenders as young as sixteen years of age does not violate the Constitution's Eighth Amendment barring cruel and unusual punishment.

1990 Congress passes the Victims' Rights and Restitution Act, confirming that victims had a right to compensation and use of federal services offering help to crime victims.

1990 California passes the first law criminalizing stalking. Other states soon follow.

1992 The acquittal of Los Angeles police officers who had been videotaped beating black motorist Rodney King triggers extensive rioting for several days in the city, leaving some sixty people dead, twenty-three hundred injured, and six thousand arrested.

1993 Islamic terrorists set off a car bomb in the underground parking garage of New York's World Trade Center, killing six and injuring one thousand.

1994 In its "get tough on crime" push, Congress passes the Violent Crime Control and Law Enforcement Act, which increases the number of federal capital crimes from two to fifty-eight, provides $4 billion for new prison construction, adds 100,000 new police officers in police departments across the nation, and adopts a "three-strikes" sentencing guideline for repeat offenders of federal crimes.

1994 Congress passes the Violence against Women Act, providing funding for assistance to women who are the victims of crime.

1995   The murder trial of former football star O. J. Simpson is televised around the world, drawing attention to the U.S. criminal justice system, including forensic science.

June 1995 In a domestic terrorist attack, Timothy McVeigh bombs the federal building in Oklahoma City, Oklahoma, killing 168 people. McVeigh is executed by lethal injection in 2001, the first person convicted of a federal crime to be executed in thirty-eight years.

1996   Congress passes the Antiterrorism and Effective Death Penalty Act, enhancing law enforcement capabilities in terrorism cases and banning U.S. citizens and companies from doing business with or supporting organizations designated as foreign terrorist organizations by the U.S. State Department.

March 4, 1997 FBI Director Louis J. Freeh delivers a speech on the rise of cyber terrorism at the 1997 International Computer Crime Conference in New York.

1998   Congress passes the Identity Theft and Assumption Deterrence Act, making identity theft a federal crime.

1998   Congress passes the Digital Millennium Copyright Act, protecting video and computer game manufacturers from Internet sales of pirated software.

October 1998 Ecoterrorists set fire to a Vail, Colorado, resort, causing extensive damage. The perpetrators allege that the resort damaged wildlife habitats.

2000   Congress passes the Religious Land Use and Institutionalized Persons Act, recognizing a prisoner's rights to practice religion while incarcerated.

September 11, 2001 Terrorists of Middle East origin crash three hijacked airliners into New York's World Trade Center and the Pentagon in Washington, D.C. A fourth hijacked airliner crashes in rural Pennsylvania on its way to a target. Almost 3,000 people are killed in the attacks.

October 2001 Congress passes the USA Patriot Act, giving law enforcement officials more power to combat the threat of terrorism.

2002   Criminal investigation of the bankruptcy of Enron, one of the nation's largest corporations, begins, leading to several convictions over the next few years on securities fraud violations.

2003 The U.S. State Department releases the document "Patterns of Global Terrorism—2002," which gives a post–September 11, 2001, accounting of global terrorism trends.

2003 The U.S. government publishes "The Al Qaeda Training Manual," a guide for international terrorists discovered in an apartment building in Great Britain.

March 2003 The U.S. Department of Homeland Security begins operation to combat terrorist threats.

Words to Know

A

Adjudication: The process of resolving an issue through a court decision.

Aggravated assault: An attack by one person upon another with intent to inflict severe bodily injury, usually by using a weapon.

AMBER Alert: (America's Missing: Broadcast Emergency Response) A national communications network for alerting the public immediately after the abduction of a youth under eighteen years of age has been reported and when the child is considered in danger. The alerts bring in the assistance of the local public in spotting the missing child or his or her abductor.

Appellate: Courts that do not hear original cases but review lower trial court decisions to determine if proper legal procedures were followed. Appeals are heard in front of a panel of judges without a jury.

Arraignment: A part of the criminal justice process during which the formal charges are read to the defendant. The defendant is advised of his or her rights, enters a plea of guilty or not guilty, and has bail and a trial date set.

Arson: Any intentional or malicious burning or attempt to burn a house, public building, motor vehicle or aircraft, or some other personal property of another person.

Assault: An attack that may or may not involve physical contact. Intentionally frightening a person or shouting threats could be considered assault.

B

Bail: Money paid for the temporary release of an arrested person to guarantee that the accused will appear for trial.

Beyond reasonable doubt: A phrase referring to the need to determine a defendant's guilt with certainty. This level of certainty is required for criminal convictions.

Bill of Rights: The first ten amendments to the U.S. Constitution, adopted in 1791. The Bill of Rights includes various protections of civil liberties in the criminal justice system, including protection from cruel punishment, unreasonable search, and self-incrimination.

Biohazard: Any biological material that has the potential to cause harm to human beings or to the environment.

Black market: The illegal sale of goods in violation of government regulations, such as selling illegal liquor at very high prices.

Blasphemy: A colonial-era crime of showing a lack of reverence toward God.

Bootlegger: A person who illegally transports liquor.

Bullying: Behavior such as teasing and threats, exclusion from social activities, and more physical intimidation; a common form of behavior among juveniles.

Burglary: Forcefully entering a home to commit a crime.

C

Capital punishment: The execution of a criminal offender; also known as the death penalty.

Capitalism: An economic system in which private business and markets determine the prices, distribution, and production of goods largely without government intervention.

Child abuse: Causing physical or emotional harm to a child.

Child labor laws: Laws restricting the type of work children can do and the number of hours they can work. These laws are designed to protect children from dangerous, unsanitary factory and farm conditions and from long hours of work at low pay. Such laws also enable them to pursue an education.

Child neglect: A failure to provide a child's basic needs, including adequate food or shelter.

Child pornography: A felony criminal offense often involving photographing and videotaping nude children or children being sexually abused.

Chop shop: A place where stolen cars are taken apart and the parts individually sold.

Civil disobedience: Challenging rules of public behavior in a nonviolent manner.

Civil law: Laws regulating ordinary private matters, in contrast to criminal law.

Civil liberties: Certain basic protections from government interference offered by the U.S. Constitution, such as freedom from self-incrimination and freedom from unreasonable searches.

Common law: A legal system in use for several centuries in England that provides a set of judicial rules "commonly" applied to resolve similar disputes. Common law is built on a history of judge's decisions rather than relying on codes, or laws, passed by a legislature. The decisions are written down and compiled annually in legal volumes available for judges to refer to.

Communism: A political and economic system where a single party controls all aspects of citizens' lives and private ownership of property is banned.

Community-based corrections: Facilities, often located in neighborhoods, that allow convicted offenders to maintain normal family relationships and friendships while receiving rehabilitation services such as counseling, work training, and job placement.

Constable: A colonial policing figure who delivered warrants, supervised the volunteer night watchmen, and carried out the routine local government functions of the community.

Copyright: The legal right of an author, publisher, composer, or other person who creates a work to exclusively print, publish, distribute, or perform the work in public.

Coroner: A public official who investigates deaths that have not clearly resulted from natural causes.

Counterterrorism: A coordinated effort among many government agencies to fight and stop terrorism.

Court-martial: A court consisting of military personnel trying a case of another military person accused of violating military law.

Crime: A socially harmful act that is prohibited and punishable by criminal law.

Crime syndicate: A group of people who work together in an illegal business activity.

Criminal justice system: The loose collection of public agencies including the police, courts, and prison officials responsible for catching and arresting suspected criminals, determining their guilt, and imposing the sentence.

Criminology: The scientific study of criminal behavior to aid in preventing and solving crimes.

Cycle of violence: The tendency of people abused during childhood to commit abuse or other crimes as adults.

D

Defendant: A person accused of a crime.

Defense attorney: A lawyer who represents a defendant to provide him or her the best possible defense from the time of arrest through sentencing and, later, appeals of the case. The defense attorney is responsible for seeing that the constitutional rights of the defendant are protected.

Delinquents: Juveniles who commit acts considered adult crimes.

Democracy: A system of government that allows multiple political parties, the members of which are elected to various government offices by popular vote of the people.

Desertion: The military crime of abandoning a military post or assignment without approval.

Disposition: The legal term for a sentence in the criminal justice system; sentences may range from fines to imprisonment in a large, tightly guarded correctional facility.

Dissident: A person with opposing political views to those in power or the government.

DNA: DNA is deoxyribonucleic acid, the substance that chromosomes are made of. Chromosomes, long connected double strands of DNA that have a structure resembling a twisted ladder, contain an individual's genetic code, which is unique to every person (except identical twins, who share the same genetic code).

Double jeopardy: A rule stating that a person cannot be tried for the same offense twice.

Drug cartel: An organized crime group that grows and sells narcotics.

Drug trafficking: The buying or selling of illegal drugs.

E

Ecoterrorism: Terrorist activities that target businesses or other organizations that are thought to be damaging the environment. The term can also refer to terrorist actions designed to harm the environment of a political enemy.

Embezzlement: The stealing of money or property by a trusted employee or other person.

Encryption: The use of secret codes that can be translated into meaningful communications only by authorized persons who have knowledge of the code.

Environmental crime: To commit an act with intent to harm ecological or biological systems for the purpose of personal or corporate gain; actions that violate environmental protection laws.

Espionage: Spies acquiring information about the activities of another country.

Exclusionary rule: Evidence obtained illegally by the police cannot be used—will be excluded from consideration—in a court of law.

Extortion: Threats to commit violence or other types of harm with the intent of obtaining money or property from another person or group.

F

Felony: A serious crime that can lead to imprisonment or execution.

First-degree murder: A deliberate and planned killing; or, a murder in connection with the commission of another felony crime such as robbery or rape.

Forensic science: The application of a wide range of scientific knowledge within a court of law. Forensic science is used to analyze a crime scene, including weapon identification, fingerprinting, document analysis, chemical identification, and trace analysis of hair and fibers.

Forgery: The signing of a false name on a legal document such as a check, and the cashing of such a check at a store or bank using false identification.

Fraud: Intentionally deceiving another for personal economic benefit.

G

Grand jury: A group of citizens chosen from the community who determine in a hearing closed to the public if there is sufficient evidence to justify indictment of the accused and a trial. Only prosecutors present evidence in grand jury hearings, not attorneys representing the defendant.

Grand larceny: Theft of money or property of great value.

H

Habitual offender: A criminal who repeatedly commits crimes, often of various types.

Hacker: Someone who gains unauthorized access to a specific computer network system and reads or copies secret or private information.

Halfway house: Rigidly controlled rehabilitation homes for offenders who have been released early from prison or are on parole. Halfway houses were created to relieve prison overcrowding. Services can include counseling, treatment, and education programs, or halfway houses can simply be a place to live under supervision.

Hate crime: A violent attack against a person or group because of race, ethnicity, religion, or gender.

Hazardous waste: Any solid or liquid substance that because of its quantity, concentration, or physical or chemical properties may cause serious harm to humans or the environment when it is improperly transported, treated, stored, or disposed of.

Heresy: Holding a belief that conflicts with church doctrine. In some societies, during certain eras—such as colonial America—heresy has been prosecuted as a crime.

Hung jury: A circumstance wherein a jury cannot agree on a verdict; in such cases the defendant may face a retrial.

I

Identity theft: The theft of an individual's identifying information—including credit card numbers, social security number, or driver's license number—to allow a criminal to use another person's identity in making purchases or for other unauthorized activities.

Impartial jury: The notion that the members of jury will regard all evidence presented with an open mind.

Incarceration: Confining a person in jail or prison.

Indictment: A written accusation of criminal charges against a person.

Insider trading: Buying and selling securities based on reliable business information not available to the general public.

Insubordination: A military crime involving the disobeying of an authority, such as a military commander.

Intake worker: A person trained to work with youthful offenders, such as a probation officer.

Intellectual property (IP) theft: The theft of material that is copyrighted, the theft of trade secrets, and violations of trademarks.

Involuntary manslaughter: A homicide resulting from negligence or lack of regard for safety.

J

Jail: A facility operated by a city or county for short-term detention of defendants awaiting trial or those convicted of misdemeanors.

Jim Crow: State and local laws in the United States that enforced legal segregation in the first half of the twentieth century, keeping races separated in every aspect of life from schools to restrooms and water fountains. Such laws were particularly common in the South.

Jurisdiction: The geographic area or type of crime over which certain branches of law enforcement or courts have legal authority.

Juvenile courts: A special court system that has jurisdiction over children accused of criminal conduct, over youthful victims of abuse or neglect, and over young people who violate rules that apply only to juveniles.

L

Labor racketeering: The existence of a criminal organization that works its way into a position of power in a labor union in order to steal from the union's retirement and health funds.

Landmark decision: A ruling by the U.S. Supreme Court that sets an important precedent for future cases and can influence daily operating procedures of police, courts, and corrections.

Larceny: Theft of property, either with or without the use of force.

Loan sharking: Charging very high interest rates on loans.

M

Mafia: A crime organization originating in Sicily, Italy, that is thought to control racketeering in the United States.

Magistrate: In colonial times the magistrate was the key judicial official in local courts, often a key member of the community. In modern times, a magistrate is an official with limited judicial authority who issues arrest and search warrants, sets bail, conducts pretrial hearings, and hears misdemeanor cases.

Mail fraud: Using the mail system to make false offers to or otherwise defraud recipients.

Malice: The intent to inflict serious bodily harm.

Mandatory sentence: A specific penalty required by law upon conviction for a specific offense.

Manslaughter: A homicide not involving malice, or the intent to inflict serious harm.

Martial law: A legal system through which the military exerts police power in place of civilian rule in politically unstable areas to protect safety and property.

Mass murderer: A person who kills many people in a single crime episode.

Mediation: A process for resolving disputes in which both the victim and offender must agree to meet and attempt to settle their dispute in a face-to-face manner, under the guidance of a neutral party.

Midnight dumping: The illegal disposal of hazardous wastes under cover of darkness in a remote area.

Miranda rights: The rights of a defendant to obtain legal counsel and refrain from self-incrimination.

Misdemeanor: A minor crime usually punishable by brief jail time or a fine.

Mistrial: A circumstance whereby a trial is discontinued because of a serious mistake or misconduct on the part of attorneys, court officials, or jury members.

Money laundering: To make the tracking of crime profits very difficult by placing money gained from crime into legitimate financial institutions, often banks outside the United States; placing such money into accounts of bogus companies; or mixing such funds with legally obtained money in the bank accounts of legitimate companies owned or operated by organized crime groups.

Moral values: The commonly accepted standards of what is right and wrong.

Multiple homicide: A crime in which a person kills more than one person on a single occasion.

Murder: Killing another person with malicious intent.

N

Narcotic: Habit-forming drugs that relieve pain or cause sleep, including heroin and opium.

Neighborhood watch: A crime prevention program in which residents watch out for suspicious activity in their neighborhoods and notify the police if they spot criminal activity.

O

Obscene: Material that has no socially redeeming value and is considered offensive according to community standards of decency.

Organized crime: People or groups joined together to profit from illegal businesses.

Organized labor: A collective effort by workers and labor organizations in general to seek better working conditions.

P

Page-jacking: A fake Web site using the same key words or Web site descriptions as a legitimate site with the intention of misdirecting Internet traffic to another site such as a pornography site.

Paraphilia: Sexual behavior considered bizarre or abnormal, such as voyeurism (spying on others for sexual pleasure) or pedophilia (sexual desire involving children).

Parens patriae: The concept that the government has the right to become the parent of children in need—to save them from terrible living conditions or protect them from criminal influences.

Parole: The release of an inmate before the end of his or her sentence.

Pedophilia: Receiving sexual pleasure from activities that focus on children as sex objects.

Penitentiary or prison: A state or federal facility for holding inmates convicted of a felony.

Perjury: Intentionally making a false statement or lying while under oath during a court appearance.

Petition: Requesting to be heard by the courts on some dispute.

Petty larceny: Theft of small amounts of money.

Pillory: A form of colonial-period punishment consisting of a wooden frame that has holes for heads and hands.

Plea bargain: A guilty plea offered by the defendant in return for reduced charges, a lighter sentence, or some other consideration.

Pollutant: A man-made waste that contaminates the environment.

Pornography: Materials such as magazines, books, pictures, and videos that show nudity and sexual acts.

Prejudice: A judgment or opinion formed without sufficient information.

Preponderance of evidence: A sufficient amount of evidence to indicate the guilt of the accused. The term also refers to the level of evidence used in civil cases and juvenile courts.

Price-fixing: Governments or companies artificially setting the price for particular goods rather than letting the market determine pricing.

Probable cause: Sufficient evidence to support an arrest.

Probation: A criminal sentence other than jail or prison time for persons convicted of less serious crimes; those sentenced with probation are usually placed under court supervision for a specific period of time.

Prohibition: Prohibiting the production, sale, transport, and possession of alcoholic beverages resulting from the adoption of the Eighteenth Amendment to the U.S. Constitution in 1919 and the resulting Volstead Act of 1920; this amendment was repealed by the Twenty-first Amendment to the Constitution in December in 1933.

Property crimes: Theft where no force or threat of force is directed toward an individual; such crimes are usually driven by the prospect of financial gain.

Prosecutor: Public officials who represent the government in criminal cases. Prosecutors are often known as district attorneys or prosecuting attorneys in federal courts and are commonly elected or appointed to their positions.

Prostitution: A person offering sexual acts in return for payments, generally payments of money.

Public defender: A state-employed attorney who provides free legal counsel to defendants too poor to hire a lawyer.

Public order crime: Behavior that is banned because it threatens the general well-being of a community or society.

R

Racism: To be prejudiced against people of a different race.

Racketeering: The act of participating in a continuing pattern of criminal behavior.

Rape: Having sexual relations by force or the threat of force.

Rehabilitation: Providing treatment to an offender to prevent further criminal behavior.

Restitution: Compensation or payment by an offender to a victim; restitution may involve community service work rather than incarceration or payments.

Restraining trade: An effort to inhibit business competition through illegal means, such as fixing prices of goods and services artificially low.

Robbery: Taking money or property by force or the threat of force.

S

Sabotage: To destroy military or industrial facilities.

Second-degree murder: An unplanned or accidental killing through a desire to cause serious bodily harm.

Securities: Stocks or bonds.

Securities fraud: An individual or organization falsely manipulating the market price of a stock or commodity by deliberately providing misleading information to investors.

Self-incrimination: Offering damaging information about oneself during a trial or hearing; a person cannot be made to testify against him or herself and has the right to remain silent during a trial or interrogation.

Serial killer: A person who kills multiple people over a period of time.

Shield laws: Legislation prohibiting rape victims from being questioned about their prior sexual history unless specific need for the information is identified.

Shoplifting: A common form of petty larceny; taking merchandise from a store without paying for it.

Slave patrols: Groups of white volunteers assembled in the 1740s to police the black slave populations with the intent of protecting white citizens from slaves, suppressing slave uprisings, and capturing runaway slaves. Slave patrols are considered an early form of organized policing.

Sociopathic: A personality disorder characterized by antisocial, often destructive, behavior with little show of emotion.

Sovereignty: A government largely free from outside political control.

Speakeasy: A place where alcoholic beverages were illegally sold during Prohibition.

Stalking: The act of repeatedly following or spying on another person or making unwanted communications or threats.

Status offenses: Rules that apply only to juveniles such as unapproved absence from school (truancy), running away from home, alcohol and tobacco use, and refusing to obey parents.

Statutory rape: Rape without force involving an adult and teenager under the age of consent who has apparently agreed to the act; it is a crime because it is established by statute, or law.

Stranger violence: A crime in which the victim has had no previous contact with his or her attacker.

Strike: A work stoppage intended to force an employer to meet worker demands.

Subversive: Political radicals working secretly to overthrow a government.

Supermax prisons: Short for super-maximum-security prisons. Supermax prisons are designed to keep the most violent or disruptive inmates separated from other prisoners and correction staff, often in a special area within an existing prison.

T

Temperance: The use of alcoholic beverages in moderation or abstinence from all alcohol.

Terrorism: The planned use of force or violence, normally against innocent civilians, to make a statement about a cause. Terrorist attacks are staged for maximum surprise, shock, and destruction to influence individuals, groups, or governments to give in to certain demands.

Three-strikes laws: Laws that dictate that a criminal convicted of his or her third felony must remain in prison for an extended period of time, sometimes for life.

Toxicity: The degree to which a substance is poisonous.

Toxicology: The study of toxic or poisonous substances that can cause harm or death to any individual who takes them, depending on the amount ingested.

Trace evidence: Microscopic or larger materials, commonly hairs or fibers, transferred from person to person or object to object during a crime; examples include human or animal hair as well as wood, clothing, or carpet fibers.

Treason: An attempt to overthrow one's own government.

True crime: Stories in books, magazines, or films or on television programs that are based on actual crimes.

Trusts: Organizations formed by combining several major industries together to stifle competition and run smaller companies out of business.

V

Victim compensation: Payment of funds to help victims survive the financial losses caused by crimes against them.

Victimization: The physical, emotional, and financial harm victims suffer from crime, including violent crime, property crime, and business corruption.

Victimless crime: Crimes often between two persons who agree to the activity, leaving no immediate victims to file charges; such crimes are considered crimes against society and are defined by law or statute.

Victims' rights: A guarantee that victims of crime be treated with dignity and fairness by police, prosecutors, and other officials and be protected from threats and harm; victims may be notified about the progress of their case and informed of upcoming court dates such as parole hearings.

Vigilantes: A group of citizens assembled on their own initiative to maintain order.

Violent crime: Crimes against the person including murder, robbery, aggravated assault, rape, sniper attacks, crimes of hate, and stalking.

Virus: A computer program that disrupts or destroys existing computer systems by destroying computer files. Viruses often cost companies and individuals millions of dollars in downtime.

W

Warrant: An order issued by a judge or magistrate to make an arrest, seize property, or make a search.

White-collar crime: A person using a position of authority and responsibility in a legitimate business organization to commit crimes of fraud and deceit for his or her personal financial gain.

Work release: The release of selected inmates from a prison or community residential center for work during the day, returning at night.

Text Credits

Following is a list of the copyright holders who have granted us permission to reproduce excerpts from primary source documents in *Crime and Punishment in America: Primary Sources.* Every effort has been made to trace copyright; if omissions have been made, please contract us.

Copyrighted excerpts reproduced from the following books:

Dickens, Charles. From "Chapter the Seventh: Philadelphia, and its Solitary Prison," in *American Notes for General Circulation.* Edited by Patricia Ingham. Penguin Books, 2000. Introduction and Notes copyright © Patricia Ingham 2000. A Dickens Chronology copyright © Stephen Wall, 1995. All rights reserved. Reproduced by permission of Penguin Books, Ltd.

Madison, James. From "Amendments to the Constitution, June 8, 1978," in *The Papers of James Madison.* Edited by Charles F. Hobson and Robert A. Rutland. University Press of Virginia. Copyright © 1979 by the Rector and Visitors of the University of Virginia. Reprinted by permission of the University of Virginia Press.

Crime and Punishment in America

PRIMARY SOURCES

A Basis for Justice

Individuals living in England in the early thirteenth century lived in a feudal society. The king granted favors to his subjects in return for their loyalty and obedience. His subjects and, most of all, the king himself believed the Almighty God gave him the right to rule. The king's law was the law of the land. No earthly document or written law was above what the king declared as lawful and just.

King John, who reigned from 1199 through 1216, abused his power. He demanded of his land barons (wealthy noblemen) unreasonably high payment fees, took away their property and possessions, and imprisoned anyone who did not cooperate with him. By 1215 the land barons had quite enough of King John. Threatening civil war, the barons wrote down their grievances and the remedies they demanded. King John reluctantly signed the document on June 15, 1215, in Runnymede Meadow on the banks of the River Thames.

The document signed at Runnymede was never intended to be a grand and sweeping new declaration of English principles of law. It was a quick agreement to end a political crisis between the king and land barons. For the first time in

1

King John of England signing the Magna Carta, which became the basis for political and personal liberty. (© Bettmann/Corbis)

history, however, a king had agreed in writing that he was not above the rules of the land and that his actions could be controlled by a written document. The document came to be known as the Magna Carta. Two of its clauses, numbers 39 and 40, became the basis for English and later American justice. The wording in clauses 39 and 40 became the seeds for due process of law and trial by jury.

These three concepts—the king was not above the law, due process of law, and trial by jury—were brought to the New World by the first English settlers at the beginning of the 1600s. The first excerpt is from the Magna Carta and gives a sample of the clauses written at Runnymede on the River Thames. The excerpt is surrounded by explanations of this most historic document.

The path to American representative government was not a straight one. By 1611 the English colonists barely survived year to year. Back in England the Virginia Company, in charge of overseeing the colonists, issued a harsh set of rules called the "Lawes Divine, Morall and Martiall," by which every colonist was to live day to day. The company hoped to set a moral foundation and strict adherence to rules that would allow the colony to survive and prosper.

One of the laws required every colonist "upon the . . . tolling of the bell" to enter the church to hear a "divine" sermon. The bell tolled twice each day. Another law stated, should a man or woman "willfully pluck up" any root, herb, flower, or grape from another's garden the punishment was death.

The second excerpt is a sampling from the "Lawes Divine, Morall and Martiall." The "Lawes" were hardly examples of due process and trial by jury. Fortunately the colony began to prosper and by 1619 the first elected assembly of colonists met in the Jamestown (Virginia) church and, among other topics, discussed the radical idea of crafting laws themselves. The harsh "Lawes" were done away with.

From the time of the first settlements up until the Revolutionary War (1775–83), colonial law had changed a great deal. Following the war, the distinctly new American legal system that emerged was rooted in basic principles of the Magna Carta and in the experiences of those early colonists. As colonists struggled to shape their legal system, the darkest and perhaps most infamous of legal episodes occurred in Salem-town, Essex County, Massachusetts, from May through October 1692. Known as the Salem Witchcraft Trials, 154 individuals were accused of witchcraft. Of the 154 accused, 42 were actually prosecuted and 19 executed. Read about these early extreme violations of civil liberties in the third excerpt, the "Examination of Sarah Good."

Magna Carta

Excerpt from the Magna Carta
Original Magna Carta published in 1215
Reprinted from *Magna Carta: Manuscripts and Myths* by Claire Breay
Published in 2002

"No free man shall be seized or imprisoned, or stripped of his rights or possessions, or outlawed or exiled, or deprived of his standing in any other way, nor will we [English royalty] proceed with force against him or send others to do so except by the lawful judgment of his equals or by the law of the land." An English document drawn up in 1215, the Magna Carta became known as the first written guarantee of basic civil liberties and was held up as a protection for Englishmen against excessive royal power for centuries. Clauses 39 and 40 of the Magna Carta, quoted above, evolved into the cornerstone of the American criminal justice system—due process of law, meaning legal procedures must be followed fairly, and trial by jury. These basic legal concepts were later incorporated into the U.S. Constitution and Bill of Rights in order to protect and uphold the civil liberties of U.S. citizens.

Surprisingly, the original purpose of the Magna Carta was neither grand nor visionary. It was a practical agreement negotiated over many months between the English land barons (wealthy noblemen) and King John (1167–1216), the tyrannical ruler of England from 1199 to 1216. The only intent of

"For no one will we sell, to no one deny or delay right or justice."

the Magna Carta was to resolve the longstanding grievances of the barons against the king, and its clauses were not issued as principles of law. Threatened by the rebellious barons with civil war in spring 1215, King John reluctantly agreed to the demands of the barons that were in the Magna Carta.

Events leading to the Magna Carta

Throughout his reign, and despite employing a powerful army of mercenaries, King John suffered repeated defeat in a series of wars to defend Britain's land in western France. The wars were disastrous; not only was warfare expensive but King John also lost income that had been generated from the French lands for the British crown. King John demanded increasing payments from his barons to pay military costs and make up for lost income.

King John and his subjects lived in a feudal society. In accordance with feudal custom the king granted barons land in return for an oath of loyalty, obedience, and military service. The barons provided knights for the king's military whenever required instead of paying rent to the king. Barons received control over their land but it was still owned by the king. In turn, the barons granted smaller parcels of their land to individuals chosen to serve as knights. This arrangement was known as holding land "in fee" from the king. For their loyalty, the king was obliged to treat his barons and knights with fairness and respect.

In addition to military service, a king was allowed to charge and collect a variety of taxes or fees from barons to support the crown. Customary fees included reliefs, aids, scutage, and county court fines. Reliefs were collected when a baron died and the baron's heir inherited the baron's land and other property. If the heir was underage, the king could take guardianship over the land and all of its profits. The king could sell the guardianship to anyone who could pay the worth of the land. When the heir came of age, he had to pay a relief to get his land back. The king also had the right to sell widows and daughters into marriage for the price of the land. With regard to reliefs, King John dealt unsympathetically and for maximum profit.

For special occasions, the king collected fees called aids from the barons. There were three such occasions: when the king's eldest son was knighted, when his eldest daughter married, and for ransom money should the king be captured and a ransom required. A scutage was a cash payment to the king instead of providing knights for military service. The payments allowed the king to hire men to serve in his army.

By King John's reign, excessively high scutage payments were commonly demanded to fulfill a baron's military obligation. Further, King John appointed all of the judges of England's county courts. The fines imposed on those who ran afoul of the courts were extreme, often taking an individual's property and possessions.

In the 1200s the pope was still the spiritual overseer of the Catholic Church. King John continually struggled over power with Pope Innocent III (1160–1216). He strenuously fought the 1206 election of Stephen Langton (d. 1228) as archbishop of Canterbury, the most powerful church position in England. King John even refused Langton entry into England until 1213. In 1215 Langton became a key negotiator between the king and his barons during negotiations over issues addressed in the Magna Carta.

Around 1210 King John's fee demands had become unreasonable, breaking all rules of customary fairness. He acted impulsively and with no regard to justice. Having had enough of this uncontrolled use of power, in January 1215 the rebellious land barons wrote down their complaints against the king. They demanded a document be drawn up guaranteeing justice in taxation, respect for ancient feudal customs of mutual obligation and fairness, and limits on King John's power.

On June 10 the barons, dressed in full armor, met the king's representatives in Runnymede meadow on the banks of the River Thames to continue negotiations. Faced with losing the barons' loyalty and a probable civil war, King John reluctantly agreed to the demands listed in a document called the "Articles of the Barons." King John placed his seal on the articles on June 15, 1215; the barons renewed their allegiance to the king on June 19.

In the days immediately following June 15, officials at the royal chancery (records office) formally drafted the full text of the points agreed to at Runnymede in the form of a legal letter. The document eventually became known as the Magna Carta (Latin for the "Great Charter"). The royal chancery then

King John of England, whose tyrannical rule led to the creation of the Magana Carta. *(© Corbis)*

distributed copies to county sheriffs and bishops to be read to the people.

The Magna Carta contained sixty-three clauses. The first guaranteed the rights and liberties of the Catholic Church free from royal interference. Nearly two-thirds of the clauses addressed the king's abuses of feudal fees and wrote down what the king could and could not charge according to customs. Other clauses dealt with justice and limited fines the king's judges could charge those taken to court.

Clauses 39 and 40, given no special significance at the time, addressed civil liberties, halted unjust imprisonment, and introduced the idea of trial by "equals," meaning trial by one's peers. Ultimately these two clauses would be key to the Magna Carta's legacy of creating fundamental principles of law. The most radical clause provided for the election of twenty-five barons to a commission to enforce the rules set down in the document. The commission had the power to seize property from the king if he did not follow the charter's rules.

As sealed in 1215 the Magna Carta was simply an agreement between the king and barons to help defuse a political crisis. It was not intended to be the foundation of democratic civil liberties or set legal principles. For the first time in history, however, a king agreed in writing that he was not above the rules of the land and that his authority could be limited by a written document. The deceptive King John had no real intention of abiding by the charter, he only hoped to buy time until he could overpower the barons. That the Magna Carta did become a basis for democracy was due to the way it was handled after the king's death and to the practical use of its clauses, which spoke to the needs of people who desired to live freely.

The following excerpt from the Magna Carta as reprinted in *Magna Carta: Manuscripts and Myths* provides a sampling of clauses as written in 1215.

Things to remember while reading excerpts from the Magna Carta:

- Clause 1 addressed freedom of the church. Influenced by Archbishop of Canterbury Langton, it promised that the church could elect its officials free of royal interference and sought to halt King John's challenges to the church. This clause was not in the Articles of Barons sealed at Runnymede but apparently was added at the royal chancery.

- Clauses 2, 7, and 12 limited the power of the king in demanding extremely high fees and in controlling the personal lives of his subjects.

- Clause 13 is an example of a clause directed at a special interest group, the citizens of cities, rather than land barons.

- Clause 20 limited court fines.

- Clauses 39 and 40 are considered to be what helped set apart the Magna Carta over time. With these words they introduce the idea of trial by jury and due process.

- Clause 52 provided "redress" or compensation for a wrong.

- Clause 61 provided a way to enforce the Magna Carta.

- Note that anytime "we" is used it refers to the king and the royal officers.

Excerpt from the Magna Carta

*1. First that we have granted to God, and by this present charter have confirmed for us our heirs **in perpetuity** that the English Church shall be free, and shall have **its rights undiminished, and its liberties unimpaired**. . . .*

In perpetuity: Forever.

Its rights undiminished, and its liberties unimpaired: The right to operate in England without royal interference.

*2. If any **earl**, baron, or other person that holds lands directly of the Crown, for military service, shall die, and at his death his heir shall be of full age and owe a "relief," the heir shall have his inheritance on payment of the ancient scale of "relief." That is to say, the heir of heirs of an earl shall pay £100 for the entire earl's barony, the heir or heirs of a knight, 100 [shillings], at most for the entire knight's "fee", and any man that owes less shall pay less, in accordance with the ancient usage of "fees." [Clause 2 restated: When a landholder dies, his heir must pay a fee to inherit the property. The customary fee for the heir of an earl was 100 pounds, for a knight 100 shillings or 5 pounds.]*

*7. At her husband's death, a widow may have her marriage portion and inheritance at once and without trouble. She shall pay nothing for her **dower**, marriage portion, or any inheritance that she and her husband held jointly on the day of his death. She may remain in her husband's house for forty days after his death, and within this period her dower shall be assigned to her. . . .*

*12. No "scutage" or "aid" may be levied in our kingdom without its **general consent**, unless it is for the ransom of **our person**, to make our eldest son a knight, and (once) to marry our eldest daughter. For these purposes only a reasonable "aid" may be levied. "Aids" from the city of London are to be treated similarly.*

13. The city of London shall enjoy all its ancient liberties and free customs, both by land and by water. We also will and grant that all other cities, boroughs, towns, and ports shall enjoy all their liberties and free customs. . . .

*20. For [a] **trivial offence**, a free man shall be fined only in proportion to the degree of his offence, and for a serious offence correspondingly, but not so heavily as to deprive him of his livelihood.*

*39. No free man shall be seized or imprisoned, or stripped of his rights or possessions, or outlawed or exiled, or deprived of his **standing** in any other way, nor will we proceed with force against him, or send others to do so, except by the lawful judgement of his equals or by the law of the land.*

40. To no one will we sell, to no one deny or delay right or justice. [Individuals shall expect an orderly process in hearing legal matters. The king could not delay or deny justice.]

52. To any man whom we have deprived or dispossessed of lands, castles, liberties, or rights, without the lawful judgement of his equals, we will at once restore these. In cases of dispute the matter shall be

Earl: British nobleman higher in status than a baron.

Dower: Deceased husband's property or money due to her rightly as his widow.

General consent: Agreement by the barons.

Our person: The king.

Trivial offence: Misdemeanor, or minor infraction.

Standing: Social standing, as in earl, baron, etc.

resolved by the judgement of the twenty-five barons referred to below in the clause for securing the peace.

61. Since we have granted all these things for God, for the better ordering of our kingdom, and to **allay** the discord that has arisen between us and our barons, and since we desire that they shall be **enjoyed in their entirety**, with lasting strength, forever, we give and grant to the barons the following security:

The barons shall elect twenty-five of their number to keep, and cause to be **observed with all their might**, the peace and liberties granted and confirmed to them by this charter.

If we, our chief, justice, our officials, or any of our servants offend in any respect against any man, or **transgress** any of the articles of the peace or of this security, and the offence is made known to four of the said twenty-five barons, they shall come to us—or in our absence from the kingdom to the chief justice—to declare it and claim immediate **redress**. If we, or in our absence abroad the chief justice, make no redress within forty days, **reckoning** from the day on which the offence was declared to us or to him, the four barons shall refer the matter to the rest of the twenty-five barons, who may **distrain upon and assail us in every way possible**, with the support of the whole community of the land, by seizing our castles, lands, possessions, or anything else saving only our own person and those of the queen and our children, until they have secured such redress as they have determined upon. . . .

The twenty-five barons shall swear to obey all the above articles faithfully, and shall cause them to be obeyed by others to the best of their power. . . .

63. It is accordingly our wish and command that the English Church shall be free, and that men in our kingdom shall have and keep all these liberties, rights, and concessions, well and peaceably in their fullness and entirety for them and their heirs. . . .

Both we and the barons have sworn that all this shall be observed in good faith and without **deceit** . . . .

Given by our and in the meadow that is called Runnymede, between Windsor and Staines, on the fifteenth day of June in the seventeenth year of our reign [June 15, 1215].

Allay: Halt.

Enjoyed in their entirety: Enforced.

Observed with all their might: Enforced with all of their power.

Transgress: Violate.

Redress: Compensation for the wrong.

Reckoning: Beginning.

Distrain upon and assail us in every way possible: Right the wrong.

Deceit: Trickery.

The Magna Carta limited the power of the English royalty and laid the foundation for what became the fundamental principals of law.

(© Bettmann/Corbis)

What happened next . . .

Although King John had promised to abide by the clauses of the Magna Carta forever, on August 24, 1215, he had the pope issue a document declaring it null and void. That document reached England in late September. Technically, the Magna Carta was valid for only ten weeks. Disputes and confrontations continued between King John and the barons until the king's death from a sudden attack of dysentery (an infection of the lower intestines) in October 1216.

When King John died, his son and heir Henry III (1207–1272) was only nine-years-old. The earl of Pembroke, William Marshal, was appointed to govern until Henry III came of age to assume the throne. Marshal, to restore peace, revised and reissued the Magna Carta on November 12, 1216 and again on November 6, 1917. In 1225 King Henry III further revised and reissued the charter under his own "Great Seal." This version of the Magna Carta maintained the core of the clauses agreed to at Runnymede and, in 1297, it was written onto the first statute (law) roll and officially became part of English law. The Magna Carta was read twice yearly in both county courts and cathedrals as the affairs of government and church were interwoven together. Anyone who broke the laws of the Magna Carta could be excommunicated (forced to leave the church). In the mid-fourteenth century the portion of Clause 39 that read "by the lawful judgement of his equals" evolved into trial by "peers," or trial by jury.

A strong test of the Magna Carta occurred in the 1600s when King James I, who ruled from 1603 to 1625, and Charles I, who ruled from 1625 to 1649, both of the House of Stuart, tried to rule with absolute power. They believed God gave them the right to rule rather than any earthly document. Parliament, a government body made up at the time of various English noblemen, continued to uphold the ideas of the Magna Carta and it came to be seen as a check or safeguard on royal power.

Sir Edward Coke (1552–1634), chief justice under King James I, became a leader in Parliament in opposition to King Charles I and wrote extensively on civil liberties. Key guarantees defended by Parliament were trial by jury and the assurance that individuals would not be unfairly imprisoned or their possessions seized. The most important aspect of the Magna Carta's creation was its impact on the New World. Brought by English settlers in the 1600s to the future United States of America, the Magna Carta planted the seeds for our future justice system.

The Magna Carta impacted the New World from the start; early colonists, echoing Sir Coke's teachings in the first half of the seventeenth century, presumed they had the same rights and liberties of those in England. Leaders of colonies, such as William Penn (1644–1718) who founded Pennsylvania in 1681, developed legal codes that included liberties directly based on guarantees in the Magna Carta.

In the eighteenth century future U.S. presidents John Adams (1735–1826; served 1797–1801) and Thomas Jefferson (1743–1826; served 1801–08) studied Coke's writings on civil liberties and the Magna Carta. Just before armed conflict broke out between the American colonies and England in 1775, the colony of Massachusetts adopted a seal depicting a soldier holding a sword in one hand and the Magna Carta in the other.

The Declaration of Independence, written in 1776, listed the American colonists' grievances against the British royalty just as the Magna Carta in 1215 addressed grievances of the English land barons against King John. The preamble of the U.S. Constitution makes it clear that government's power comes from the people.

In more modern times, Eleanor Roosevelt (1884–1962), American humanitarian and wife of President Franklin D. Roosevelt (1882–1945; served 1933–45) used wording similar to that in the Magna Carta when she authored the 1948 Universal Declaration of Human Rights for the United Nations. At the beginning of the twenty-first century, echoes of Clauses 39 and 40 were still heard in U.S. court proceedings.

Did you know . . .

- When written, the Magna Carta's clauses applied only to those persons at the highest levels of feudal society. It was meant to protect the rights and property of England's most powerful families. It did not apply to the common folk or peasants who made up the majority of England's population. Only after many centuries was it applied to all.

- The Magna Carta was not actually called the Magna Carta until after the November 6, 1217, revision. At that time clauses of the charter relating to the royal forest were put into a shorter document known as the Charter of Forest. The remaining clauses became known as the Magna Carta.

- At the beginning of the twenty-first century, four copies of the Magna Carta originally produced by the royal chancery in June 1215 still survived. Two were held by the British Library in London, one was archived at Lincoln Cathedral in Lincoln, and one was at Salisbury Cathedral in Salisbury. All were written using a quill (feather) pen and parchment (treated sheepskin).

- Only four clauses remained part of the English legal system at the start of the twenty-first century: Clauses 1, 13, 39, and 40.

- At the beginning of the twenty-first century, a 1297 version of the Magna Carta was displayed in the National Archives Rotunda in Washington, DC. The U.S. Declaration of Independence and Bill of Rights were also displayed.

- In 1957 the American Bar Association erected a monument at Runnymede in recognition of the Magna Carta's influence on American law.

Consider the following . . .

- Look up Amendments 5 and 6 in a copy of the Bill of Rights. Compare the amendments with Clauses 39 and 40 of the Magna Carta. What wording supports the idea that the amendments were patterned after Clauses 39 and 40?

- Why do you suppose clauses 39 and 40 were hidden deep in the Magna Carta? Remember that there was no such thing as a jury trial in 1215. What form might a "lawful judgement" of one's "equals" have looked like in the thirteenth century?

- Cite examples of countries in today's world where single leaders are or recently have been above the law. Choose one country and research what civil liberties do or do not exist for its citizens.

For More Information

Books

Breay, Claire. *Magna Carta: Manuscripts and Myths*. London: The British Library, 2002.

Holt, James C., ed. *Magna Carta and the Idea of Liberty*. Malabar, FL: R. E. Krieger, 1982.

Pallister, Anne. *Magna Carta: The Heritage of Liberty*. Oxford: Clarendon Press, 1971.

Web Sites

The British Library. http://www.bl.uk/collections/treasures/magna.html (accessed on August 24, 2004).

"Featured Documents." *National Archives and Records Administration.* http://www.archives.gov/exhibit_hall/featured_documents/magna_carta/legacy.html (accessed on August 24, 2004).

Lawes Divine

Excerpt from "Lawes Divine, Morall and Martiall"
Original "Lawes Divine" published in 1611
Reprinted from *Tracts and Other Papers Relating Principally to Origin, Settlement, and Progress of the Colonies of North America from the Discovery of the Country to the Year 1776,* **edited by Peter Smith**
Published in 1947

The Magna Carta officially became part of English law in 1297 and was used to defend against abuse of power by English royalty. The Magna Carta was put to its strongest test in the first half of the 1600s during the rule of King James I from 1603 to 1625 and Charles I, who ruled from 1625 to 1649. Both were from the House of Stuart and reasserted a king's right to absolute power over his subjects. Each believed his ruling power came directly from God, not from the consent of the people and certainly not from a written document like the Magna Carta.

In 1606 it was King James who granted the Virginia Company of London a charter to recruit individuals for settlement of the new land called Virginia. The officers of the Virginia Company ruled over the Virginia settlements until 1624 when King James revoked their charter for not making enough money. From the initial settlement at Jamestown in 1607, the Church of England, overseen by King James, was the official church of the English settlements.

The English church was led by the pope and the Catholic Church until 1534 when Parliament passed the "Act of

"No man shall use traitorous words against his Majesty's person or royal authority, upon pain of death."

Supremacy," declaring the king of England and not the pope as head of the Church of England, commonly called the Anglican Church. The royal government and the Anglican Church became tightly interlocked. When in 1609 the Virginia Company in London made plans to spread the settlers out along the James River in Virginia, they included plans for a church at each site. To maintain order and strict obedience to the Anglican Church and therefore to King James, the company prepared and imposed the "Lawes Divine, Morall and Martiall" upon its settlers in 1611.

The "Lawes Divine" were a harsh set of rules by which all Virginia colonists were supposed to live. The rules addressed aspects of settlement life from daily church attendance to the consequences of stealing a plant from another's garden. The ultimate punishment associated with violating most of the rules was death. The concept of individual rights and liberties put forth in the Magna Carta found no place in "Lawes Divine."

Foreshadowing the "Lawes"

The first permanent English settlers, approximately one hundred men, arrived on the Virginia shore in April 1607 and began settling a marshy peninsula they named Jamestown. Instead of allowing themselves time to recuperate from the difficult four-month journey across the Atlantic, the men immediately started clearing trees, building shelters, and recklessly devouring the food and ale brought from England. Later, with little food and after drinking the salty marsh water, the settlers began to sicken and die.

Even though wildlife and fish were abundant, few settlers had any idea how to hunt or fish. To make matters worse, their leaders constantly bickered and quarreled among themselves over how to improve their dire situation. By January 1608 when more settlers and supplies arrived from England only thirty-eight men were still alive. One of the survivors was Captain John Smith (1580–1631) who took over leadership of Jamestown in September 1608 when other men proved incapable of the task.

Twenty-eight-year-old Smith demanded the Virginia Company not send him gentlemen but rather individuals who were carpenters, farmers, fishermen, and those with strong backs capable of the arduous work needed to build a settlement. Smith instituted strict military-like discipline and reverence of the Almighty from which he, like all Anglicans, believed all power and success came. After resorting to these measures, the Virginia settlement got back on track. Smith's organizational approach foreshadowed the severe regulations of "Lawes Divine."

Quoted in Philip Alexander Bruce's 1910 book *Institutional History of Virginia in the Seventeenth Century*, the gallant persevering Smith attributed the Jamestown settlement's preservation "to the direct intervention of the almighty [God], whose providence [divine guidance] however dark the hour, never failed them." Yet after being injured in a gunpowder explosion in the summer of 1609, Smith left for England in October and never returned.

John Smith took leadership of Jamestown in 1608 and instituted strict military-like discipline. *(The Library of Congress)*

The settlers left behind, including four hundred more who arrived in August, were left without Smith's leadership through the harsh winter of 1609–10. So many starved to death that winter it became known as the "starving time." Of five hundred settlers alive in the fall, only sixty survived until spring. Just as the Jamestown settlers were strongly considering a return to England, a new governor, Thomas West (1577–1618), and ships laden with supplies arrived in late spring 1610.

West, known as Lord De la Warr, immediately gave orders to repair the Jamestown church and stabilize the settlement. During his administration prayers were read daily at ten o'clock in the morning and four o'clock in the afternoon. Two sermons continued to be preached on Sunday plus one on Thursday. Surviving records of early Jamestown clearly illustrate how loyalty to the familiar religious observances back home in England had become a required part of the settlers' daily life.

In early 1611 Lord De la Warr fell deathly ill and hastily returned to England. He reported to the Virginia Company that settlement troubles continued, including the death of more colonists, difficulties with neighboring Indians, and few if any prospects for profitable operations to make the colony pay off. Nevertheless, the Virginia Company refused to give up on its struggling venture.

The company sent Sir Thomas Gates and Sir Thomas Dale to Virginia in May 1611. Gates was appointed governor to replace Lord De la Warr and Dale served in a new position called marshal. Marshals maintained discipline in English armies under rules of martial law—discipline maintained by military authority. Dale was charged with maintaining discipline in Virginia but had no real military force, just various appointed officers. Instead the Virginia Company armed Dale with the "Lawes Divine, Morall and Martiall."

Both Gates and Dale demanded strict adherence to the lawes. Dale considered his work at Jamestown as laying a solid foundation of morality and piety that would allow the colony to prosper. He thought the "Lawes Divine" were absolutely necessary to repress all disorder, wrongdoing, and to assure respect for religion and the church's rules. Every leader or "officer" in the colony was ordered to set an example by attending daily prayers, both Sunday sermons and one weekday sermon.

Dale required punctuality (being on time). Together with input from four religious and dependable settlers of their choosing, church officials (known as clergy) observed and reported to Dale any colonist who failed to attend services. As set in the "Lawes Divine," punishment for not following the rules was severe—loss of pay and food for a specified period, whipping, loss of one's ears, and even death.

The following excerpt contains only "lawes" directed toward the colonists. Following those thirty-seven or so laws were extensively detailed instructions to the colony officials comprising the "Martiall" part of the "Lawes."

Despite the death and chaos, new settlers continued to arrive in America. Eventually due to the strict laws order was restored and the colonies flourished. *(© Bettmann/Corbis)*

Things to remember while reading excerpts from "Lawes Divine, Morall and Martiall":

- King James I believed he ruled by the divine (guided by God) right of kings. Therefore all laws, although written by royal representatives, such as the officers of the Virginia Company, directly came through God and the king.

- Because the laws were "divine," punishment for disobedience was extreme.

- Analysis of each word in the title of the excerpt reveals much about the nature of the Lawes: "Lawes"—laws; "Divine"—guided by God and also used as a name or title of an individual clergy member as "the reverend Divine"; "Morall"—morals (the rights and wrongs of behavior as approved by the ruling authority, and overseen by God);

"Martiall"—martial law, or law enforced by military authority—in the case of the English settlements the marshal and his appointed officers enforced the "Lawes."

- The Lawes Divine illustrate how the first settlers in America lived under laws granting no liberty or civil rights.

Excerpt from "Lawes Divine, Morall and Martiall"

Note: Lawes 1 through 10 are a modern English translation. To serve as an example, the remainder of the excerpt is in the original Old English wording. Reading at a careful pace, it is relatively easy to understand.

Whereas his Majesty . . . has in his own realms a principal care of true religion and reverence to God and has always strictly commanded his generals and governors, with all his forces wheresoever, to let their ways be, like his ends, for the glory of God. . . .

1. First, Since we owe our highest and supreme duty, our greatest, and all our allegiance to Him for whom all power and authority is derived and flows as from the first and only fountain, and being especial soldiers impressed in this sacred cause, we must alone expect our success from Him, who is only the blesser of all good attempts, the king of kings, the commander of commanders, and lord of hosts, I do strictly command and charge all captains and officers, of what quality or nature soever, whether commanders in the field or in town or towns, forts or fortresses, to have a care that the Almighty God be duly and daily served and that they call upon their people to hear sermons, as that also they diligently frequent morning and evening prayer themselves by their own exemplar and daily life and duty herein, encouraging to the martial law in the case provide. . . . [All power, success, and good comes from the Lord. He is the supreme commander. All officers of the colony owe their allegiance to the Lord. All officers must set an example for the settlers by faithfully attending all sermons and morning and afternoon prayer. If officers fail to set a proper example they will receive appropriate punishment.]

3. That no man **blaspheme** God's holy name upon pain of death, or use unlawful oaths, taking the name of God in **vain**, curse, or **bane** upon pain of severe punishment for the first offense so committed and for the second to have a **bodkin** thrust through his tongue; and if he continue the blaspheming of God's holy name, for the third time so offending, he shall be brought to a martial court and there receive censure of death of his offense. [No one may curse or mock the name of the Lord, which is blasphemy. Punishment for the first offense is not specified but would involve severe pain; punishment for the second offense was a pierced tongue; and for the third offense, death.]

4. No man shall use any traitorous words against his Majesty's person or royal authority, upon pain of death. [No settler may betray the trust or refuse to carry out a duty demanded by an officer of the settlement; officers are appointed by the king. Punishment is death.]

5. No man shall speak any word or do any act which may tend to the **derision or despite** of **God's holy word** upon pain of death; nor shall any man unworthily **demean** himself unto any preacher or minister of the same, but generally hold them in **all reverent regard and dutiful entreaty**; otherwise he the offender shall openly be whipped three times, and ask public forgiveness in the assembly of the congregation three several **Sabbath** days.

6. Every man and woman duly, twice a day upon the first tolling of the bell, shall upon the **working days** repair unto the church to hear divine service upon pain of losing his or her day's allowance for the first omission, for the second to be whipped, and for the third to be condemned to the galleys for six months. Likewise, no man or woman shall dare to violate or break the Sabbath by any gaming, **public or private abroad** or at home, but duly **sanctify** and observe **the same**, both himself and his family, by preparing themselves at home with private prayer that they may be the better fitted for the public, according to the commandments of God and the orders of our church. As also every man and woman shall repair in the morning to the divine service and sermons preached upon the Sabbath day in the afternoon to divine service and **catechizing**, upon pain for the first fault to lose their provision and allowance for the whole week following, for the second to lose the said allowance and also to be whipped, and for the third to suffer death. . . .

8. He that, upon **pretended malice**, shall murder or take away the life of any man, shall be punished with death. [No man shall murder another.]

Blaspheme: Show lack of reverence toward something holy.

Vain: A disrespectful or rude manner.

Bane: With an intent to ruin or harm.

Bodkin: A long sharp instrument for making holes in cloth.

Derision or despite: Show contempt for or defiance and ridicule.

God's holy word: Words from the Bible.

Demean: Behave disrespectfully.

All reverent regard and dutiful entreaty: Have only the utmost respect for the clergymen.

Sabbath: Sunday.

Working days: Monday through Saturday.

Public or private abroad: Outside the home.

Sanctify: Make holy.

The same: Sabbath.

Catechizing: Teaching.

Pretended malice: Intent to cause injury.

9. *No man shall commit the horrible and detestable sins of* **sodomy**, *upon pain of death, and he or she that can be lawfully convicted of* **adultery** *shall be punished with death. No man shall* **ravish** *or force any woman, maid or Indian or other, upon pain of death; and know that he or she that shall commit* **fornication**, *and evident proof made thereof, for their first fault shall be whipped, for their second they shall be whipped, and for their third they shall be whipped three times a week for one month and ask public forgiveness in the assembly of the congregation.*

10. *No man shall be found* **guilty of sacrilege**, *which is a trespass as well committed in violating and abusing any sacred ministry, duty, or office of the church irreverently or prophanely, as by being a church robber to* **filch**, *steal, anything out of the church appertaining thereunto or unto any holy and consecrated place to the divine service of God which no man shall do upon pain of death. Likewise, he that shall rob the store of any* **commodities** *therein of what quality soever, whether provisions of* **victuals**, *or of arms, trucking stuff, apparel, linen, or woolen, hose or shoes, hats or caps, instruments or tools of steel, iron, etc., or shall rob from his fellow soldier or neighbor anything that is his, victuals, apparel, household stuff, tool, or what necessary else soever, by water or land, out of boat, house, or knapsack shall be punished with death. . . . [(a) No one may disrespect or abuse church sacraments like baptism, taking communion, or marriage; (b) no one may steal or destroy items belonging to the church or ministry; (c) no one may steal from the supply house or from anyone else's property—food, weapons, clothes, material, tools, etc.; (d) punishment for all could be death.]*

15. *No man of what condition soeuer shall barter, trucke, or trade with the Indians, except he be thereunto appointed by lawful authority, vpon paine of death. . . .*

23. *No man shall* **imbezell**, *lose, or willingly breake, or fraudulently make away, either Spade, Shovell, Hatchet, Axe,* **Mattocke**, *or other toole or instrument vppon paine of whipping.*

24. *Any man that hath any edge toole, either of his owne, or which hath heretofore beene belonging to the store, see that he bring it instantly to the storehouse, where he shall receive it againe by a particular note, both of the toole, and of his name taken, that such a toole vnto him apperaineth, at whose hands, vpon any necessary occasion, the said toole may be required, and this shall he do, vpon paine of seuere punishment [anyone who has borrowed a tool must return it, then sign it out again when needed by using his name]. . . .*

Sodomy: Homosexual activities or certain forms of sexual activity.

Adultery: Sexual relations between a married person and someone other than his or her spouse.

Ravish: Rape.

Fornication: Sex between two people not married to one another.

Guilty of sacrilege: Showing disrespect for the church or its sacraments [acts of faith].

Filch: Take.

Commodities: Supplies.

Victuals: Food.

Imbezell: Old English for embezzle; when someone steals property entrusted to his or her care by another.

Mattocke: A digging tool.

31. What man or woman soeuer, shall rob any garden, publike or priuate, beingset to weed the same, willfully pluck vp therein any roote, herbe, or flower, to spoile and wast or steale the same, or robbe any vineyard, or gather vp the grapes, or steale any eares of the corne growing, whether in the ground belonging to the same fort or towne where he dwelleth, or in any other, shall be punished with death [no stealing from another's garden or vineyard; punishment is death]. . . .

All such Bakers are appointed to bake bread, or what else, either for the store to be giuen out in generall, or for any one in particular, shall not steale nor imbezell, loose, or defraud any man of his due and proper weight and measure nor vse any dishonest and deceipt-full tricke to make the bread weigh heavier, or make it courser vpon purpose to keepe back any part or measure of the flower or meale committeed vnto him [bakers must follow a strict recipe for baking bread and use a set amount of ingredients]. . . .

All such cookes as are appointed to seeth [i.e., boil], bake or dresse any manner of way, flesh, fish, or what else, of what kind soeuer, either for the generall company, or for any private man, shall not make lesse, or cut away any part or parcel of such flesh, fish, etc. [cooks must prepare food without holding back any for them-selves]. . . .

*All fishermen, dressers of **Sturgeon** or such like appointed to fish, or to cure the said Sturgeon for the vse of the Colonie, shall giue a just and true account of all said fish as they shall take by day or night . . . the first time offending heerein, of losing his eares, and for the second time to be condemned a yeare to the Gallies, and for the third time offending, to be condemned to the Gallies for three yeares [fish-ermen must accurately report all fish they catch; punishment for bak-ers, cooks, and fishermen: first offense—loss of ears; second offense—a year in a ship galley; third offense—three years in a gal-ley]. . . .*

Sturgeon: Large, bony fish.

What happened next . . .

The strict enforcement of the "Lawes Divine" by Gates and Dale worked. The behavior of colonists generally fell into line. The governor and marshal were able to increase the number of settlements along the James River and encouraged crop experimentation. Colonist John Rolfe found that a West Indian species of tobacco, *Nicotiana tabacum*, grew easily on the Virginia land. In 1614 Gates took four barrels of the dried tobacco back to England. The English clamored to purchase it.

The settlements soon realized they had a crop, tobacco, to sustain them. Back in London, however, the Virginia Company was financially strapped after years of investing in the settlements with no profits. Sir Edwin Sandys assumed leadership of the company in 1618. Sandys promised liberal land grants and replacement of the Lawes Divine with a more representative government arrangement for the settlements. Sandys appointed Sir George Yeardley as the new governor of Virginia and sent him across the Atlantic with supplies and new settlers.

As soon as Yeardley arrived in April 1619, he announced the martial law of the Lawes Divine would end. He told the colonists to elect two citizens from each settlement and come to Jamestown in late July to decide on new laws with which to rule the colonies. On July 30, 1619, an assembly convened in the Jamestown church. The meeting lasted six days. First, after approving the "Great Charter" that allowed the assembly to exist, the members decided on laws prohibiting drunkenness, idleness, and gambling. They discussed land issues, planting, and relations with Indians.

Discussions led to the idea of having the colonists draft some laws themselves. John Pory, a colonist, went so far as to suggest that he and his fellow settlers should be able to "allowe or disallowe" orders from the Virginia Company back in London. At the time, the Virginia Company had complete veto power over anything passed by the assembly. For the Virginia Company's officers in London—who were considered representatives of King James—this suggestion was radical. They still believed themselves messengers from God since all laws came from God's guidance through the British crown. Nevertheless, the seeds of law and independence for the colonists had been planted.

Did you know . . .
- The assembly that met on July 30, 1619, at the church in Jamestown, Virginia, was the first legislative (lawmaking) body in America.

- The Jamestown assembly gave itself a very British name, the House of Burgesses. A burgess was a citizen of a British borough. In England, a borough was any community that could send a representative to Parliament, England's legislative body.

- The assembly approved the first tax in America on August 4, 1619. The burgesses decreed that every man in the Virginia colony must give one pound of his very best tobacco to those who met at Jamestown in payment for their services.

Consider the following . . .

- List traits of character individuals who volunteered to go to Virginia must have possessed. Based on the characteristics you list, do you think the severe "Lawes" prepared by the Virginia Company were justified for colony survival? Why or why not?

- Use your imagination to write about a day in the life of a settler living under the Lawes. How well or how poorly does your settler adapt to the rules?

- Obtain a copy of the U.S. Bill of Rights written in 1791. Study amendments 1, 5, and 6. Compare and contrast the basic liberties and rights in these amendments with the regulations set in the Lawes.

- Review the names of the early governors of the Jamestown settlement. For whom was the colony of Delaware named?

For More Information

Books

Billings, Warren M., John E. Selby, and Thad W. Tate. *Colonial Virginia: A History.* White Plains, NY: KTO Press, 1986.

Bruce, Philip A. *Institutional History of Virginia in the Seventeenth Century.* New York: Knickerbocker Press, 1910.

Davis, Burke. *Getting to Know Jamestown.* New York: Coward, McCann, and Geoghegan, 1971.

Force, Peter, ed. *Tracts and Other Papers, Relating Principally to the Origin, Settlement, and Progress of the Colonies in North America, From the Discovery of the Country to the Year 1776.* Vol. 3. New York: Peter Smith, 1947.

Lacy, Dan M. *The Colony of Virginia*. New York: F. Watts, 1973.

Web Sites

Excerpts from the "Lawes Divine, Morall, and Martiall." *Le Projet Albion.*
http://puritanism.online.fr/puritanism/sources/valaws1611.html
(accessed on August 24, 2004).

First Legislative Assembly at Jamestown, Virginia. http://www.nps.gov/colo/
Jthanout/1stASSLY.html (accessed August 24, 2004).

Sarah Good

Excerpt from the "Examination of Sarah Good"

Reprinted from *The Salem Witchcraft Papers: Verbatim Transcripts of the Legal Documents of the Salem Witchcraft Outbreak of 1692,* **edited by Paul Boyer and Stephen Nissenbaum**

Published 1977

Seventeenth century colonists believed in witches, as did their European ancestors. The Great European Witch Hunt occurred from the fifteenth through the seventeenth centuries. Belief in magic and witchcraft was widespread in the American colonies. It was normal to profess a strong faith in the Almighty God and at the same time to employ magical charms and potions to ward off witches and the devil. Relatively few individuals, however, were accused of witchcraft and fewer still were prosecuted and executed. Accusations were often dismissed, or those convicted received light sentences. The exception played out in New England in the early 1690s. The most famous American witch hunt occurred from May through October 1692 in Salem Town, Essex County, Massachusetts.

> "No creature [do I imploy] but I am falsely accused."
>
> *Sarah Good*

Witch hunting

The English began successful colonization of the New World in 1607 with other Europeans following by the 1630s and 1640s, bringing with them their belief in witchcraft. Since everyday survival preoccupied most colonists, between the 1620s and the end of the seventeenth century there were only

A woman faints while testifying in court during the Salem Witchcraft trials. *(The Library of Congress)*

nineteen accusations of witchcraft that made it into court. One resulted in conviction with the individual being whipped and banished. Sporadic witchcraft trials were held in New York, New Jersey, Pennsylvania, and Maryland, where only one case ended in an execution.

During the 1600s witchcraft accusations were more prevalent in New England. A total of 250 individuals were formally accused of witchcraft. Before the Salem horrors of 1692, some 100 New England colonists were charged, twenty convicted, and sixteen executed. In 1692 in Salem, Massachusetts, 150 additional witchcraft trials took place.

Legalities and the crime of witchcraft

Seventeenth century laws on witchcraft in New England paralleled those in England, based on a verse from the King

James translation of the Bible. The verse, from Exodus 22:18, read "Thou shalt not suffer a witch to live." The King James version of the Bible was ordered by King James I (ruled 1603–25) in the early 1600s. By 1647 all New England colonies had made witchcraft a capital crime, punishable by death.

The actual witchcraft laws reflected the church's view that convictions required proof of contact between the accused and the devil. This made the crime difficult to successfully prosecute. On the other hand, most colonists were concerned with the supernatural skills of witches such as casting a spell to cause harm to another. It was on this basis that most all charges were made.

The surest path to conviction was getting a confession from the accused; few individuals, however, were willing to confess. So under seventeenth century New England laws, in order to convict an alleged witch, at least two witnesses had to give evidence that the accused had a pact with the devil. The most common attempt was to show signs of "witches' teats" on the body of the accused. Supposedly witches nourished their "familiars" at these teats. "Familiars" were evil spirits with which witches had close relationships. Both preachers and magistrates (judges) demanded a physician confirm findings of a witch's teat on the accused individual.

Another type of proof was spectral evidence, or seeing visions. People believed an evil spirit could assume the identity of an individual who had signed a pact with the devil and visions of that individual would appear to victims and torment them. The witnesses would testify that menacing visions of the accused individual had indeed appeared to them.

Proof of witch's teats or spectral visions was difficult. When New England laws were applied properly, and they usually were, convictions were few. This explains why only twenty convictions were achieved out of one hundred cases prosecuted in New England up until 1692. Yet in 1692 New Englanders were so distraught over what they perceived as their failing to achieve a successful and perfect God-fearing colony that they embarked on a major witch-hunt. They convinced themselves the devil and his witches were to blame. When charges against individuals were made during this time, witchcraft laws were not properly applied—instead, prosecution and conviction relied on spectral and suggested but unproven evidence.

God's wrath

The most intense periods of witch hunting in Europe came when a country experienced a particularly stressful time such as civil war, famine, or spreading disease. Why the American colonies had only one large witch-hunt, occurring in Massachusetts in 1692, was most likely the result of extreme stress in the New England colonies.

The Puritans of New England, English Protestants who opposed the Church of England, believed they had been chosen by God to establish a holy land in the New World. Massachusetts governor John Winthrop (1588–1649) told his colony's residents that if they failed to establish communities of holy, reverent people they would feel the wrath or anger of God and be punished.

In the second half of the seventeenth century more and more residents moved away from a rural New England setting where the land was rocky and difficult to farm, and into Boston and surrounding areas where jobs in crafts and manufacturing were available. Many people in the newer urban areas had strayed from regular church attendance. Political disagreements involving the rule of England over the colonies dominated town meetings. Soon preachers called on the people to mend their ways and get back to godliness and disciplined lives or divine punishment would be coming.

Sure enough, in the 1670s, one catastrophe after another came to the New England area. War with the Indians called the King Philips War in 1675 and 1676 killed between six hundred and one thousand New Englanders and many towns were destroyed or damaged. Approximately three thousand Indians were killed, villages destroyed, and hundreds of captives sold into slavery to the West Indies. Matters only worsened as Boston experienced devastating fires in 1676 and 1679. Smallpox epidemics struck in 1677, 1678, and again in 1690. New Englanders looked for something to blame for their misfortunes. Anxiety and frustrations grew as the colonists feared they had indeed failed in their mission and were feeling God's anger.

In 1679 the Massachusetts General Court called for a general synod [meeting] of New England's clergy to consider what

An accused witch going through the judgement trial, where she is dunked in water to prove her guilt of practicing witchcraft.

(© Bettmann/Corbis)

was causing the terrible events of the 1670s. The synod cited God's displeasure with New Englanders for their immoral behavior, argumentative ways, love of worldly goods, interest in profits, and not working cooperatively with their neighbors. Another problem was belief in magic, with clergymen believing those who used potions and charms and held magic powers were displeasing an all-powerful God. Those who attempted to practice magic, they believed, were being tempted by the devil. The synod gatherings continued throughout the 1680s.

Salem

Reverend Samuel Parris from Salem village attended one of the synod gatherings in 1690. In January and February

1692, just before the Salem witch-hunt started, he was preaching that people had failed God and God had abandoned them. Parris insisted all men were evil by nature.

Rather than console his congregation in these difficult times, Parris constantly stirred up trouble in Salem. Yet he claimed the work of the devil was causing all the problems. Villagers were determined to find and punish those responsible; under these circumstances the 1692 Salem witch-hunt began.

Both men and women and occasionally children were accused of witchcraft, but the vast majority were women. The women accused were often poor, widowed, perhaps childless, particularly quarrelsome, or bad tempered. Most were between the ages of forty and sixty, did not attend church, and were in conflict with family friends or neighbors. Those whose lifestyles were outside what was considered normal and proper came under close scrutiny. Examples of deviant life patterns included those who cursed, had questionable morals like prostitutes, and those who wandered the streets, homeless.

Sarah Good

The case of Sarah Good serves as an example of one witchcraft prosecution. Sarah Good was well known in Salem. Penniless, she wandered the streets with her children begging from door to door and sleeping in neighborhood barns. Whether she received a handout or not she would leave a house grumbling and mumbling indistinguishable words. New Englanders believed such utterances, especially if they came from someone dealing with the devil, could cast spells and curses causing physical harm.

Frequently, as in Sarah's case, the sudden death of livestock or crop failure was blamed on a spell cast by a suspected witch. Contact with a witch could also cause an individual to see visions of the supposed witch. The vision would harass and hurt its victim.

In January 1692 Elizabeth Parris, the nine-year-old daughter of Reverend Parris, and Abigail Williams, eleven years old, began exhibiting odd behavior—screaming, having seizures, and going into trance-like states. Unable to find a physical cause, the town doctors attributed the behavior to the influ-

A terrified woman stands pressed against a door as an angry town mob accuses her of witchcraft. *(© Baldwin H. Ward & Kathryn C. Ward/Corbis)*

ence of the devil. Other girls began to show similar behavior. Pressed to say who had afflicted them, they named Sarah Good, a slave/maid of Reverend Parris named Tituba, and another town woman Sarah Osborne.

On March 1, 1692, Sarah faced examination by magistrates John Hathorne and Jonathan Cowin. In the following excerpt Sarah says that she is "falsely accused." During the examination, the girls were made to look at Sarah, causing them to be "tormented." Sarah claimed that the words she mumbled leaving houses were words of a Psalm and that she served only God.

Through the next few months depositions were taken from many townspeople including Sarah and Thomas Gadge and seventeen-year-old Elizabeth Hubbard. Sarah and Thomas Gadge claimed after Sarah Good appeared begging at their door, some of their "cowes [cows] died in a sudden, terible [terrible] and strange, unusuall [unusual] maner." Elizabeth Hubbard claimed Sarah Good had appeared in a vision to her and "most greviously afflect and tortor [torture] me." She also claimed to have seen the apparition of Sarah Good hurt Elizabeth Parris, Abigail Williams, and Ann Putnam. In most of the testimonies, witnesses claimed a vision of Sarah Good urged them to "write in hir [her] book." It was believed if someone wrote in a witch's book they too had made a pact with the devil.

Sarah Good was found guilty at her trial and was later sentenced to hang. She showed no remorse and was hanged on July 19, 1692.

Things to remember while reading excerpts from the "Examination of Sarah Good":

- The Great European witch-hunt began in France in the 1420s. Peaking between 1580 and 1640, witch-hunts spread across Europe particularly to Germany, Switzerland, Poland, Scotland, and England. Thousands were accused and executed for devil worship.

- Believing in the supernatural, witches, evil spirits, and magic was common among colonists who came from England and Europe.

- Salem residents believed in witches, but the community was also split into quarreling factions that accused each other of moral failings. Bitter resentment of one family toward another was not uncommon.

- Most all accusations of witchcraft occurred when one neighbor or family accused another of causing them harm.

Excerpt from the "Examination of Sarah Good"

The examination of Sarah Good before the worshipfull Assts John Harthorn Jonathan Curren

*(H) Sarah Good what evil spirit have you **familiarity** with*

(S G) none

(H) have you made no contract with the devil,

Good answered no

(H) why doe you hurt these children

(g) I doe not hurt them. I scorn it.

(H) who doe you imploy then to doe it

(g) I imploy no body,

(H) what creature do you imploy then,

(g) no creature but I am falsely accused

(H) why did you go away muttering from mr Parris his house

(g) I did not mutter but I thanked him for what he gave my child

(H) have you made no contract with the devil

(g) no

(H) desired the children all of them to look upon her, and see, if this were the person that had hurt them and so they all did looke upon her and said this was one of the persons that did torment them—presently they were all tormented.

(H) Sarah good doe you not see now what you have done why doe you not tell us the truth, why doe you thus torment these poor children

(g) I doe not torment them,

(H) who do you imploy then

(g) I imploy nobody I scorn it

(H) how came they thus tormented,

(g) what doe I know you bring others here and now you charge me with it

(H) why who was it

(g) I doe not know but it was some you brought into the meeting house with you

(H) wee brought you into the meeting house

*(g) but you brought in **two more***

(H) Who was it then that tormented the children

Familiarity: A close relationship.

Two more: Tibuta and Sarah Osburn.

(g) it was osburn

(H) what is it that you say when you goe muttering away from persons houses

(g) if I must tell I will tell

(H) doe tell us then

(g) if I must tell I will tell, it is the commandments I may say my commandments I hope

(H) what commandment is it

(g) if I must tell you I will tell, it is a psalm

(H) what psalm

After a long time shee muttered over some part of a psalm

(H) who doe you serve

(g) I serve god

(H) what god doe you serve

*The god that made heaven and earth though shee was not willing to mention the word God her answers were in a very wicked, **spitfull manner reflecting and retorting aganst the authority** with **base and abusive words** and many lies shee was taken in. it was here said that her housband had said that he was afraid that shee either was a witch or would be one very quickly the worsh mr Harthon [Magistrate Hathorne] asked him his reason why he said so of her whether he had ever seen any thing by her he answered no not in this nature but it was her **bad carriage** to him and indeed said he I may say with tears that shee is an enimy to all good.*

(Salem Village March the 1t 1691/2

Written by Ezekiell Chevers

Salem Village March the 1t 1691/2)

(Essex County Archives, Salem—Witchcraft Vol. 1, page 6). . . .

(Sarah Gadge v. Sarah Good)

*The **deposition** of Sarah Gadge the wife of Thomas Gadge aged about 40 years this **deponent** testifieth and saith that about two years & an halfe agone; Sarah Good Came to her house & would have come into the house, but s'd Sarah Gadge told her she should not come in for she was afraid she had been with them that had the Smallpox: & with that she fell to mutring [muttering] & scolding extreamly & soe: told s'd Gadge if she would not let her in she should*

Spitfull manner reflecting and retorting aganst the authority: Disrespectful, rebellious manner.

Base and abusive words: Filthy language; cursing.

Bad carriage: The evil manner in which they acted toward her husband.

Deposition: Testimony taken in writing under oath outside of a trial setting.

Deponent: One who gives evidence in a deposition.

give her something; & she answered she would not have any thing to doe with her & the next morning after to s'd Deponents best remembrance one of s'd Gadges Cowes Died in A Sudden, terible & Strange, unusuall maner soe that some of the neighbors & said Deponent did think it to be done by witchcraft. . . .

(Essex County Archives, Salem—Witchcraft, Vol. 1, page 8)

(Ann Putnam, Jr. v. Sarah Good)

The Deposition of Ann Putnam Ju'r who testifieth and saith, that on the 25th of February 1691/92 I saw the **apperishtion** of Sarah good which did tortor [torture] me most greviously but I did not know hir name tell the 27th of February and then she tould me hir name was Sarah good and then she did prick me and pinch me most greviously: and also sense severall times urging me **vehemently to writ in hir book** and also on the first day of march being the day of hir Examination Sarah good did most greviously tortor me and also severall times sence: and also on the first day of march 1692 I saw the Apperishtion of Sarah Good goe and afflect and tortor the bodys of Elizabeth parish Abigail Williams and Elizabeth Hubburd. . . .

Salem Witch Trials Statistics

In 1692 alone, legal actions were taken in Massachusetts against 154 individuals accused of the crime of witchcraft. While the cases were located throughout Massachusetts, a large number occurred in Salem, so the trials as a whole have come to be called the Salem Witch Trials. Of the 154 prosecutions, 19 ended in execution, 13 of which were women and 6 were men. Four individuals died while in prison and one man was crushed to death under rocks during his interrogation. Of the 154, 42 prosecutions took place in Salem resulting in 10 of the 19 executions. Forty-one occurred in Andover, resulting in three of the 19 executions. Towns where prosecutions also took place were Amesburg (1 executed), Beverly, Gloucester, Haverhill, Lynn, Malden, Marblehead (1 execution), Reading, Rowley, Topsfield (2 executed), Wenham, plus a few others. One execution occurred in Wells, Maine, and records show that the location of one execution is uncertain.

What happened next . . .

By late August some colonists were dismayed by the gruesome hangings taking place in their communities. Many began to wonder if innocent people were dying and there was growing opposition to the trials. On October 8, 1692 Thomas Brattle, a successful, wealthy Boston merchant wrote a widely

Apperishtion: An apparition; a vision of a spirit-like figure.

Vehemently to writ in hir book: Strongly urged Ann to write in her (Sarah's) book; anyone who signed in a witch's book was making a pact with the devil.

distributed public letter stating that the chief judge in the trials, William Stoughton, had been overzealous and unwise in his prosecutions.

Brattle called the spectral evidence and supposed ceremonies that witches participated in with the devil mere concoctions of imagination and fantasy. A considerable number of other Massachusetts ministers also spoke out against the witch trials. Having grown skeptical, Massachusetts governor William Phips, who had commissioned the court on May 27 to begin the trials, dissolved the witchcraft court on October 29.

Phips also began to release those still held in jail, including children accused of witchcraft—Abigail and Dorothy Faulkner, Abigail and Stephen Johnson, and Sarah Carrier—all aged from eight to thirteen years. Even those who were in jail after confessing to witchcraft were released. Amazingly, the witnesses who had been afflicted by the released witches suffered no further harm. Although a few charges continued to be made they slowed to a trickle with most dismissed.

In December the Massachusetts General Court passed a new law that better defined precisely what infractions would have to occur for a person to be convicted of being an agent of evil or a wicked spirit. For example, anyone who raised a dead person from the grave or used part of a dead person's body in a ritual of witchcraft could be condemned to death. If anyone used witchcraft-like spells to destroy another's property, they could be imprisoned. The court heard more cases in early 1693 but dismissed nearly all of them.

In Salem, Reverend Parris continued to be involved in community disputes. In July 1697 Parris left Salem for Stowe, Massachusetts. The new reverend, Joseph Green, took immediate action to restore harmony among Salem's residents.

Did you know . . .

- Only one actual witch-hunt of any size took place in America before 1692. It occurred in Hartford, Connecticut, in 1662. The Hartford hunt resulted in eight prosecutions and four executions.

- Salem village had about six hundred residents and was part of the larger Salem town. It was known as a community full of disputes and quarreling citizens.

- If an individual accused of witchcraft confessed, he or she was often spared execution. The public shame and ridicule that came with the confession was usually considered enough of a punishment.

Consider the following . . .

- Make a list of various happenings that by 1692 caused the Salem residents to begin accusing fellow townspeople as witches.

- Until 1692 there was great difficulty in legally proving a person was a witch. Do you think judges in the 1692 witchcraft trials felt pressured by their community members to quickly prosecute and convict?

- What do you think the Salem colonists hoped would result from the conviction and execution of witches?

- Develop a skit around the witch trial excerpts and present it to the class.

For More Information

Books

Aronson, Marc. *Witch-Hunt: Mysteries of the Salem Witch Trials.* New York: Atheneum Books for Young Readers, 2003.

Boyer, Paul, and Stephen Nissenbaum, eds. *The Salem Witchcraft Papers: Verbatim Transcripts of the Legal Documents of the Salem Witchcraft Outbreak of 1692.* Vol. 2. New York: Da Capo Press, 1977.

Hill, Frances. *Delusion of Satan: The Full Story of the Salem Witch Trials.* New York: Da Capo Press, 1997.

Le Beau, Bryan F. *The Story of the Salem Witch Trials.* Upper Saddle River, NJ: Prentice Hall, 1998.

Norton, Mary Beth. *In the Devil's Snare: The Salem Witchcraft Crisis of 1692.* New York: Alfred A. Knopf, 2002.

Taylor, Alan. *American Colonies.* New York: Viking, 2001.

Web Sites

Salem Witch Museum. http://www.salemwitchmuseum.com (accessed on August 24, 2004).

"What About Witches." *Salem, Massachusetts, City Guide.* http://www.salemweb.com/guide/witches.shtml (accessed on August 24, 2004).

Foundations of Criminal Justice

From the birth of the nation at the time of the American Revolution (1775–83) until the early part of the twentieth century, the various parts of the American criminal justice system, including courts, policing, and prisons, gradually developed at the federal and state levels. These loosely coordinated segments of the criminal justice system have been responsible for apprehending, investigating, determining guilt, imposing sentences, and carrying out punishments of criminal offenders.

Prior to the American Revolution, no distinct American legal system existed. Each colony operated independently. Criminal codes, punishments, and courts varied from colony to colony. By the time of the Revolution, reformers wanted to establish a more unified and professional legal system. With the country's founders crafting a constitution for the new nation, a unique opportunity was presented to not only provide uniformity, but also to make sure the colonists' hard won liberties would not be lost to the new federal and state governments.

The U.S. Constitution gave the federal government specific powers. The founders believed that by limiting the pow-

The Bill of Rights, adopted in 1791, spelled out the protections in the criminal justice system for citizens. *(National Archives and Records Administration)*

ers of the government, individual liberties would be adequately protected. As the various states met to vote on adopting the drafted constitution, people demanded their liberties and protections in the criminal justice process be specifically listed. They feared that as the federal government grew over time, individual liberties would gradually disappear.

To ensure adoption of the hotly debated constitution, it was decided to draft a series of amendments that would spell out the protections for citizens. This document would consist of ten amendments and become known as the Bill of Rights. James Madison (1751–1836; served 1809–17), a key author of the constitution and later the fourth president of the United States, was an energetic campaigner for its adoption. He joined in writing the Bill of Rights. The first excerpt in this chapter is an address by Madison to the newly formed Congress on June 8, 1789, simply titled "Amendments to the Constitution." Madison spells out what he envisioned the Bill of Rights should include.

The Bill of Rights was adopted in 1791. One key element was the Eighth Amendment protecting citizens from cruel and unusual punishment. Incarceration was becoming the preferred method of punishment rather than public whippings or more brutal measures as branding, cutting off ears, and piercing tongues with hot irons. The growth of new prison systems in the early nineteenth century brought experiments in how inmates should be treated. One form of imprisonment emphasized total isolation. Inmates were placed alone in their cells, often with a Bible, to think about their crimes and hopefully decide to live their lives in a more socially productive manner.

While incarcerated for years, these inmates saw no one—including friends or relatives—and received no news from the outside world. The second excerpt is from a book, *American Notes,* written by world famous English author and social reformer Charles Dickens (1812–1870). It describes his travels to America in 1842 and his guided tour of the new Cherry Hill Prison in Philadelphia, Pennsylvania. Dickens was shocked about what he observed and strongly urged change in American corrections.

Another key element of the criminal justice system, policing, slowly developed throughout the nineteenth century.

Professional policing did not arrive in most major U.S. cities until the mid-1800s. Despite improvements, policing remained part of the local political process in towns and cities. As a result corruption was rampant and respect for law enforcement was low.

The introduction of Prohibition in 1919, making it a crime to sell, transport, or possess liquor, created a crime wave in the 1920s. Police agencies were overwhelmed and ineffective. By 1929 concern about the U.S. criminal justice system became a national issue for the first time. The third excerpt is a speech by former U.S. Attorney General George W. Wickersham to the Cincinnati, Ohio, Regional Crime Committee on April 16, 1931, titled *The Problem of Law Enforcement*. Wickersham, who chaired a national commission that became the first comprehensive assessment of the U.S. criminal justice system, reviewed its findings.

James Madison

Excerpt from "Amendments to the Constitution"

Delivered by James Madison on June 8, 1789, to the House of Representatives

Reprinted from *The Papers of James Madison,* edited by Charles F. Hobson and Robert A. Rutland

Published in 1979

"The people shall not be deprived or abridged of their right to speak, to write, or to publish their sentiments."

James Madison of colonial Virginia is considered the father of the U.S. Constitution. Madison fought hard for the recognition and protection of individual rights in the new nation's legal framework. He also supported the need for a strong central government. As a result, Madison sought a delicate balance between a strong and effective central federal government and the basic freedoms of citizens from potentially oppressive government rule.

Madison formed his beliefs on individual liberties from government actions while serving in various political roles during the American Revolution (1775–83). With war underway, Madison served in the 1776 Virginia Convention that drew up the state's declaration of rights and a new state constitution. From 1778 to 1779 he served on the Virginia Council of State that guided actions of the new governor.

Madison also represented Virginia in the Continental Congress from 1780 to 1783, which drafted the first constitution known as the Articles of Confederation. The Articles proved ineffective by creating a weak central government and giving most power to the states. The central government had no law enforcement powers and no central courts. Charged with creating a more effective national government, the Constitutional Convention convened in Philadelphia in 1787. Madison took the lead in drafting a new constitution. The end result provided was a constitution with a much stronger central government, but with a complex system of checks and balances between the three branches and different levels of government and an independent judicial system.

Adoption of the new constitution required the approval of at least nine of the original thirteen states. Adoption was up in the air as considerable debate centered on the strengthened central government. Many looked back at the two centuries under dominant British rule and did not wish to see such a powerful central government. They still wanted most power to rest with the individual state governments, as in the Articles of Confederation. This group was known as the anti-Federalists; they believed the new constitution threatened individual liberties, including its criminal courts of law.

James Madison. Before becoming the fourth U.S. president, Madison was one of the writers of the U.S. Constitution and Bill of Rights. *(National Archives and Records Administration)*

To help with the adoption process, Madison and John Jay, a future Supreme Court justice, and Alexander Hamilton, the first U.S. secretary of treasury, wrote a series of eighty-five essays known collectively as *The Federalist Papers*. Madison and the others explained that individual liberties would best be protected by a strong central government, not the many individual state governments.

Doubts persisted and many still demanded a stronger statement on the protection of individual rights than the Constitution offered. Madison and others relented and agreed to write the first amendments to the Constitution to satisfy those concerned. Finally by the summer of 1788, Madison and the

Federalists had prevailed and the new constitution was ratified by eleven states, two more than necessary.

Madison then began writing the Bill of Rights, the first ten amendments to the U.S. Constitution. Madison was also elected as a Virginia delegate to the new U.S. House of Representatives. Madison described the newly developing bill to the House on June 8, 1789.

Things to remember while reading excerpts from "Amendments to the Constitution":

- Citizens of the new nation did not want to find themselves once again at the mercy of a powerful court system as they had been in the king's courts of Britain. They sought fairness in how criminal justice was administered.

- Madison received a solid education at what later became known as Princeton University studying the important thinkers of Europe. He accepted the growing idea that humans fully possessed the power of reason, the basis for emphasizing individual rights over the power of government. Madison also read law but was not interested in its practice.

- Being short of stature and poor in health, Madison tackled revolutionary politics rather than the battlefield. At twenty-five years of age Madison served as an intellectual force in the American Revolution (1775–83) war effort.

Excerpt from "Amendments to the Constitution"

*It will be a desirable thing to extinguish from the **bosom** of every member of the community any apprehensions, that there are those among his countrymen who wish to deprive them of the liberty for which they valiantly fought and honorably bled. . . .*

*It cannot be a secret to the gentlemen in this **house**, that, notwithstanding the ratification of this system of government by*

Bosom: Chest; meaning a person's emotional center.

House: U.S. House of Representatives.

*eleven of the thirteen United States, in some cases unanimously, in others by large majorities; yet still there is a great number of our constituents who are dissatisfied with it. . . . We ought not to disregard their inclination, but, on principles of **amity** and moderation, conform to their wishes, and expressly declare the great rights of mankind secured under this constitution. . . .*

But I will candidly acknowledge, that, over and above all these considerations, I do conceive that the constitution may be amended; that is to say, if all power is subject to abuse, that then it is possible the abuse of the powers of the general government may be guarded against in a more secure manner than is now done, while no one advantage, arising from the exercise of that power, shall be damaged or endangered by it. We have in this way something to gain, and, if we proceed with caution, nothing to lose. . . . But I do wish to see a door opened to consider, so far as to incorporate those provisions for the security of rights, against which I believe no serious objection has been made by any class of our constituents. . . .

*The people shall not be deprived or abridged of their right to speak, to write, or to publish their sentiments; and the freedom of the press, as one of the great bulwarks of liberty, shall be **inviolable**.*

*The people shall not be restrained from peaceably assembling and consulting for their common good; nor from applying to the legislature by petitions . . . for **redress of their grievances** . . . .*

No person shall be subject, except in cases of impeachment, to more than one punishment, or one trial for the same offence; nor shall be compelled to be a witness against himself; nor be deprived of life, liberty, or property without due process of law; nor be obliged to relinquish his property, where it may be necessary for public use, without a just compensation.

Excessive bail shall not be required, nor excessive fines imposed, nor cruel and unusual punishments inflicted.

The rights of the people to be secured in their persons, their houses, their papers, and their other property from all unreasonable searches and seizures, shall not be violated by warrants issued without probable cause, supported by oath or affirmation, or not particularly describing the places to be searched, or the persons or things to be seized.

In all criminal prosecutions, the accused shall enjoy the right to a speedy and public trial, to be informed of the cause and nature of the accusation, to be confronted with his accusers, and the witnesses

Amity: Common understanding.

Inviolable: Cannot be violated.

Redress of their grievances: To resolve political issues.

against him; to have a compulsory [required] process for obtaining witnesses in his favor; and to have the assistance of counsel [lawyer] for his defence. . . .

No state shall violate the equal rights of conscience, or the freedom of the press, or the trial by jury in criminal cases. . . .

No appeal to such court shall be allowed where the value in controversy shall not amount to ___ dollars: nor shall any fact triable by jury, according to the course of common law, be otherwise re-examinable than may consist with the principles of common law. . . .

*The trial of all crimes (except in cases of impeachments, and cases arising in the land or naval forces, or the militia when on actual service in time of war or public danger) shall be by an impartial jury . . . with the **requisite of unanimity** for conviction, of the right of challenge, and other accustomed requisites; and in all crimes punishable with loss of life or member, presentment or indictment by a grand jury, shall be an essential preliminary, provided that in cases of crimes committed within any county which may be in possession of an enemy, or in which a general insurrection may prevail, the trial may by law be authorized in some other country of the same state, as near as may be to the seat of the offence.*

In cases of crimes committed not within any country, the trial may by law be in such county as the laws shall have prescribed. In suits at common law, between man and man, the trial by jury, as one of the best securities to the rights of the people, ought to remain inviolate [sacred or unbreakable]. . . .

*Although I know whenever the great rights, the trial by jury, freedom of the press, or liberty of conscience, came in question in that body, the invasion of them is resisted by able advocate, yet their **Magna Charta** does not contain any one provision for the security of those rights, respecting which, the people of America are most alarmed. The freedom of the press and rights of conscience, those choicest privileges of the people, are unguarded in the British constitution.*

But altho' the case may be widely different, and it may not be thought necessary to provide limits for the legislative power in that country, yet a different opinion prevails in the United States. The people of many states, have thought it necessary to raise barriers against power in all forms and departments of government, and I am inclined to believe, if once bills of rights are established in all the states as well as the federal constitution, we shall find that altho' some of them

Requisite of unanimity: All jurors agree on the verdict.

Magna Charta: Early English document [also known as the Magna Carta] granting rights to citizens and limiting the power of royalty.

Civil Liberties and Criminal Justice

The 1791 Bill of Rights greatly influenced the development of the U.S. criminal justice system through the next two centuries. Of the ten amendments, the following specifically address criminal justice issues:

Fourth Amendment—the right of people to be safe from unreasonable search and seizures. Warrants for arrest and search had to be based on sufficient evidence to support an arrest, known as probable cause.

Fifth Amendment—called for grand juries (a panel of citizens convened to determine if sufficient evidence exists to charge a person with a crime) and also stated that a person could not be tried for the same offense twice, known as double jeopardy. Defendants also could not be made to testify against themselves and had the right to remain silent during questioning.

Sixth Amendment—called for speedy, public trials using impartial juries.

Eighth Amendment—banned excessive bail (money a defendant pays a court to be released while waiting for a trial) and cruel and unusual punishment.

---

are rather unimportant, yet, upon the whole, they will have a salu-tary tendency. . . .

It has been said by way of objection to a bill of rights, by many respectable gentlemen . . . that they are unnecessary articles of a republican government, upon the presumption that the people have those rights in their own hands, and that is the proper place for them to rest. It would be a sufficient answer to say that this objection lies against such provisions under the state governments as well as under the general government; and there are, I believe, but few gentlemen who are inclined to push their theory so far as to say that a declaration of rights in those cases is either ineffectual or improper. It has been said that in the federal government they are unnecessary, because the powers are enumerated, and it follows that all that are not granted by the constitution are retained: that the constitution is a bill of powers, the great residuum being the rights of the people; and therefore a bill of rights cannot be so necessary. . . .

I admit that these arguments are not entirely without foundation; but they are not conclusive to the extent which has been supposed. It is true the powers of the general government are circumscribed; they are directed to particular objects; but even if government keeps within

Salutary: Helpful; supporting a useful purpose.

Republican: Government in which the power is held by the citizens who elect their political leaders.

Residuum: The remainder.

Prison inmates making whips. Many inmates were put through hours of hard labor manufacturing goods while in prison. *(© Corbis)*

Discretionary: Left to its own judgment.

Indefinite: limited.

*those limits, it has certain **discretionary** powers with respect to the means, which may admit of abuse to a certain extent, in the same manner as the powers of the state governments under their constitutions may to an **indefinite** extent; because in the constitution of the United States there is a clause granting to Congress the power to make* *all laws which shall be necessary and proper for carrying into execution all the powers vested in the government of the United States, or in any department or officer thereof; this enables them to fulfill every purpose for which the government was established. . . .*

[Madison concedes to those critics of the U.S. Constitution who demand more explicit restrictions on the national government than the Constitution provides that the Constitution does give the national government some flexibility in making laws it sees as necessary. Through its law-making power the federal government could overstep its limits, as state governments could do with the much more sweeping powers they hold than the federal government.]

*I wish also, in revising the constitution, we may throw into that section, which **interdicts** the abuse of certain powers in the state legislatures. . . . The words, "No state shall pass any **bill of attainder, ex post facto law** . . ." were wise and proper restrictions in the constitution. I think there is more danger of those powers being abused by the state governments than by the government of the United States. . . . I should therefore wish to extend this interdiction, and add, as I have stated . . . that no state shall violate the equal rights of conscience, freedom of the press, or trial by jury in criminal cases; because it is proper that every government should be disarmed of powers which **trench upon** those particular rights. I know in some of the state constitutions the power of the government is controlled by such a declaration, but others are not. . . .*

*Having done what I conceived was my duty, in bringing before this house the subject of amendments, and also stated such as I wish for and approve, and offered the reasons which occurred to be in their support; I shall content myself for the present with moving that a committee be appointed to consider of and report such amendments as ought to be proposed by Congress to the legislatures of the states, to become, if ratified by three-fourths thereof, part of the constitution of the United States. . . . I should advocate greater dispatch in the business of amendments, if I was not convinced of the absolute necessity there is of pursuing the organization of the government; because I think we should obtain the confidence of our fellow citizens . . . as we **fortify** the rights of the people against the encroachments of the government. . . .*

Interdicts: Prohibits.

Bill of attainder: The legislature finding a person guilty of a felony rather than a court of law.

Ex post facto law: Making a new law apply to the past actions of people.

Trench upon: Abuse.

Fortify: Strengthen.

What happened next . . .

The Bill of Rights was adopted by the states in 1791. It provided important individual liberties, such as freedom from cruel and unusual punishment, freedom from self-incrimination, and freedom from illegal search and seizures. Following its adoption, Madison used his seat in the House of Representatives, which he held until 1797, to defend individual and state rights from the strong federal government he helped fashion.

Madison founded a new political party known as the Democratic-Republicans whose main focus was to ensure the federal government did not infringe on the individual liberties he had listed in the Bill of Rights. Madison and fellow party leader Thomas Jefferson fought the stronger Federalist tendencies of the George Washington (1732–1799; served 1789–97) and John Adams (1735–1826; served 1797–1801) administrations.

Thomas Jefferson won the presidency for the party in the 1800 elections and appointed Madison his secretary of state. Madison would not only follow Jefferson into the White House in 1809, but became head of the University of Virginia upon Jefferson's death. Madison died in 1836.

Did you know . . .

- James Madison became the fourth president of the United States and served for two terms from 1809 to 1817. His presidency was dominated by the War of 1812 (1812–14) with Great Britain, the first U.S. foreign war to protect its newly created governmental system.

- Madison was born in 1751 on a Virginia plantation at the base of the Blue Ridge Mountains, his official home for his entire life. Though the plantation had slaves and Madison kept slaves his entire life, following his presidency Madison was an outspoken critic of slavery and headed the American Colonization Society dedicated to relocating freed American slaves back into Africa. Little came from the effort.

Consider the following . . .

- Have the class research arguments by the Federalists and anti-Federalists regarding the federal government. Present a debate over the merits of each perspective, focusing on criminal justice concerns.

- Some claimed the liberties protected by Madison and the Supreme Court eroded in the late twentieth and early twenty-first centuries. For example, the War on Drugs initiated in the 1980s and the later USA Patriot Act (passed as an antiterrorist measure in 2001) gave law enforcement greater powers. Describe how individual liberties could be affected by these programs.

- The protections offered in the Bill of Rights would not be strongly upheld until the 1960s when the Supreme Court issued a series of rulings that revolutionized the criminal justice system. What did the Supreme Court rule and how did it support the constitutional protections in the Bill of Rights?

For More Information

Books

Hobson, Charles F., and Robert A. Rutland, eds. *The Papers of James Madison*. Vol 12. Charlottesville, VA: University Press of Virginia, 1979.

Charles Dickens

Excerpt from **American Notes**

Reprinted from *Charles Dickens: American Notes for General Circulation,*
edited by Patricia Ingham
Originally published in 1842; excerpt taken from 2000 reprint

> "The system here, is rigid, strict, and hopeless solitary confinement. I believe it, in its effects, to be cruel and wrong."

With the U.S. Constitution protecting American citizens from cruel and unusual punishment, a search for more humane forms of punishment began in the late 1800s. The idea of incarceration had been in use since the late 1700s, but by the early 1800s two different types of prison systems were being tried in the United States. One was known as the "Philadelphia" plan and the other, the "Auburn" plan. They were named after the cities where two new state prisons were located—in Philadelphia, Pennsylvania, and Auburn, New York.

Under the Philadelphia plan, also known as the Separate System, prisoners were kept isolated in their cells both day and night. They were allowed certain books, especially the Bible, and sometimes allowed to perform certain handcrafts. Most of all they were left to think about their crimes. Food was pushed into the cell through hatches. Prisoners never saw or spoke with anyone except the prison guards who did not know their names or why they were there. Prisoners exercised in their own individual yards, and very few visitors were allowed. Critics called this prolonged solitary confinement cruel and unusual punishment, especially for those serving sentences of many years.

In January 1842 thirty-year-old Charles Dickens and his wife Catherine set sail from Liverpool, England, to begin a tour of America. Internationally famous for his novels, Dickens was well received upon his arrival in the port of Boston. Given his personal interest in criminal law and prisons, U.S. officials gave him tours of several modern American prisons.

Among the prisons was the world famous Eastern Penitentiary in Philadelphia known as Cherry Hill. Opened in 1830 Cherry Hill was an international showplace for using methods of prisoner isolation. Dickens visited Cherry Hill on March 8, 1842, and denounced the Separate System as intolerably cruel in *American Notes,* published in October 1842. He was convinced the prison inflicted far more harm on its victims than other prison systems.

English author Charles Dickens. After visiting the United States in 1842, Dickens wrote an account disapproving of what he called intolerably cruel conditions in the American prison system, which relied heavily on solitary confinement. *(AP/Wide World Photos)*

Things to remember while reading excerpts from *American Notes*:

- By the 1840s Charles Dickens was the most popular author in Britain and had achieved international fame. His recent novels included *The Pickwick Papers* (1837) and *Oliver Twist* (1838).

- Books about America were very popular in England at the time. British citizens were intrigued with America's new democratic government and wanted to know more. Dickens' publishers provided him a contract to travel to America and write about his adventures. He was to compare American and British institutions.

- In contrast to the system at Cherry Hill prisoners in the Auburn plan, known as the Silent System, were allowed to be among other inmates though only to work in groups during the day and under very strict supervision. They were able to make products sold in the outside world. Like the Philadelphia plan, inmates could not speak or communicate with one another and spent their nights sleeping in separate cells. Guards stayed with the prisoners night and day to make sure they obeyed the strict silence rules, requiring a large staff. The Philadelphia plan required a more expensive building but a much smaller staff.

- Dickens strongly opposed slavery. His outspokenness on the trip met with increasing resistance from the American public. By June, when Dickens set sail back to England, his popularity in the United States had sharply declined.

Excerpt from American Notes

My stay in Philadelphia was very short, but what I saw of its society, I greatly liked. . . .

In the outskirts, stands a great prison, called the Eastern Penitentiary: conducted on a plan peculiar to the state of Pennsylvania. The system here, is rigid, strict, and hopeless solitary confinement. I believe it, in its effects, to be cruel and wrong.

*In its intention, I am well convinced that it is kind, humane, and meant for reformation; but I am persuaded that those who devised this system of Prison Discipline, and those **benevolent** gentlemen who carry it into execution, do not know what it is that they are doing. I believe that very few men are capable of estimating the immense amount of torture and agony which this dreadful punishment, prolonged for years, inflicts upon the sufferers; and in guessing at it myself, and in reasoning from what I have seen written upon their faces, and what to my certain knowledge they feel within, I am only the more convinced that there is a depth of terrible endurance in it which none but the sufferers themselves can **fathom**, and which no man has a right to inflict upon his fellow creature. I hold this slow and*

Benevolent: Having good intentions.

Fathom: Understand.

*daily tampering with the mysteries of the brain to be immeasurably more than any torture of the body; and because its ghastly signs and tokens are not so **palpable** to the eye and sense of touch as scars upon the flesh; because its wounds are not upon the surface, and it **extorts** few cries that human ears can hear; therefore I the more denounce it, as a secret punishment which slumbering humanity is not roused up to stay. I hesitated once, debating with myself, whether, if I had the power of saying "Yes" or "No," I would allow it to be tried in certain cases, where the terms of imprisonment were short; but now, I solemnly declare, that with no rewards or honors could I walk a happy man beneath the open sky by day or lie me down upon my bed at night, with the consciousness that one human creature, for any length of time, no matter what, lay suffering this unknown punishment in his silent cell, and I the cause, or I consenting to it in the least degree.*

I was accompanied to this prison by two gentlemen officially connected with its management, and passed the day in going from cell to cell, and talking with the inmates. Every facility was afforded me, that the utmost courtesy could suggest. Nothing was concealed or hidden from my view, and every piece of information that I sought was openly and frankly given. The perfect order of the building cannot be praised too highly, and of the excellent motives of all who are immediately concerned in the administration of the system, there can be no kind of question.

*Between the body of the prison and the outer wall, there is a spacious garden. Entering it, by a **wicket** in the massive gate, we pursued the path before us to its other termination, and passed into a large chamber, from which seven long passages **radiate**. On either side of each, is a long, long row of low cell-doors, with a certain number over every one. Above, a gallery of cells like those below, except that they have no narrow yard attached (as those in the ground **tier** have), and are somewhat smaller. The possession of two of these, is supposed to **compensate** for the absence of so much air and exercise as can be had in the dull strip attached to each of the others, in an hour's time every day; and therefore every prisoner in this upper story has two cells, adjoining and **communicating** with, each other.*

*Standing at the central point, and looking down these dreary passages, the dull **repose** and quiet that prevails, is awful. Occasionally, there is a drowsy sound from some lone weaver's shuttle, or shoemaker's **last**, but it is stifled by the thick walls and heavy dungeon-door, and only serves to make the general stillness more*

Palpable: Easily seen.

Extorts: Brings forth or causes, usually by pain.

Wicket: Small door within the larger entrance.

Radiate: Extend out from a central point.

Tier: Level.

Compensate: Make up for.

Communicating: Open passage.

Repose: Lack of movement.

Last: A wooden or metal model of a foot used to shape and repair shoes and boots.

profound. Over the head and face of every prisoner who comes into this **melancholy** house, a black hood is drawn; and in this dark shroud, an emblem of the curtain dropped between him and the living world, he is led to the cell from which he never again comes forth, until his whole term of imprisonment has expired. He never hears of wife or children; home or friends; the life or death of any single creature. He sees the prison-officers, but with that exception he never looks upon a human **countenance**, or hears a human voice. He is a man buried alive; to be dug out in the slow round of years; and in the mean time dead to everything but torturing anxieties and horrible despair.

His name, and crime, and term of suffering, are unknown, even to the officer who delivers him his daily food. There is a number over his cell-door, and in a book of which the governor of the prison has one copy, and the moral instructor another: this is the index to his history. Beyond these pages the prison has no record of his existence: and though he lives to be in the same cell ten weary years, he has no means of knowing, down to the very last hour, in what part of the building it is situated; what kind of men there are about him; whether in the long winter night there are living people near, or he is in some lonely corner of the great jail, with walls, and passages, and iron doors between him and the nearest sharer in its solitary horrors.

Every cell has double doors: the outer one of sturdy oak, the other of grated iron, wherein there is a trap through which his food is handed. He has a Bible, and a slate and pencil, and, under certain restrictions, has sometimes other books, provided for the purpose, and pen and ink and paper. His razor, plate, and can, and basin, hang upon the wall, or shine upon the little shelf. Fresh water is laid on in every cell, and he can draw it at his pleasure. During the day, his bed-stead turns up against the wall, and leaves more space for him to work in. His loom, or bench, or wheel, is there; and there he labors, sleeps and wakes, and counts the seasons as they change, and grows old.

The first man I saw, was seated at his loom, at work. He had been there, six years, and was to remain, I think, three more. He had been convicted as a receiver of stolen goods, but even after this long imprisonment, denied his guilt, and said he had been hardly dealt by [ignored]. It was his second offence. . . .

In another cell, there was a German, sentenced to five years' imprisonment for larceny, two of which had just expired. With colors procured in the same manner, he had painted every inch of the walls and ceiling quite beautifully. He had laid out the few feet of ground, be-

Melancholy: Gloomy.

Countenance: Face or facial expression.

hind, with exquisite neatness, and had made a little bed in the cen-
ter, that looked by the bye like a grave. The taste and ingenuity he
had displayed in everything were most extraordinary; and yet a more
dejected, heart-broken, wretched creature, it would be difficult to imag-
ine. I never saw such a picture of forlorn affliction and distress of mind.
My heart bled for him; and when the tears ran down his cheeks, and
he took one of the visitors aside, to ask, with his trembling hands ner-
vously clutching at his coat to detain him, whether there was no hope
of his dismal sentence being **commuted**, *the spectacle was really too*
painful to witness. I never saw or heard of any kind of misery that im-
pressed me more than the wretchedness of this man.

There was one man who was allowed, as an **indulgence**, *to keep*
rabbits. His room having rather a close smell in consequence, they
called to him at the door to come out into the passage. He complied
of course, and stood shading his haggard face in the unwonted sun-
light of the great window, looking as **wane** *and unearthly as if he*
had been summoned from the grave. He had a white rabbit in his
breast, and when the little creature, getting down upon the ground,
stole back into the cell, and he, being dismissed, crept timidly after
it, I thought it would have been very hard to say in what respect the
man was the nobler animal of the two. . . .

I went from cell to cell that day; and every face I saw, or word I
heard, or incident I noted, is present to my mind in all its painful-
ness. . . .

I took that opportunity of inquiring how they conducted them-
selves immediately before going out; adding that I presumed they
trembled very much.

"Well, it's not so much a trembling," was the answer—"though
they do quiver—as a complete derangement of the nervous system.
They can't sign their names to the book; sometimes can't even hold
the pen; look about 'em without appearing to know why, or where
they are; and sometimes get up and sit down again, twenty times in
a minute. This is when they're in the office, where they are taken
with the hood on, as they were brought in. When they get outside
the gate, they stop, and look first one way and then the other: not
knowing which to take. Sometimes they stagger as if they were drunk,
and sometimes are forced to lean against the fence, they're so bad:—
but they clear off in course of time.". . .

My firm convictions, that independent of the mental anguish it
occasions—an anguish so acute and so tremendous, that all imagi-
nation of it must fall far short of the reality—it wears the mind into

Commuted: Shortened.

Indulgence: A toleration of something.

Wane: Faded, through loss of strength or stature.

Emigrants heading west arrive at the Mississippi River as described by Charles Dickens in his "American Notes." *(© Bettmann/Corbis)*

---

a morbid state, which renders it unfit for the rough contact and busy action of the world. It is my fixed opinion that those who have undergone this punishment, must pass into society again morally unhealthy and diseased. There are many instances on record, of men who have chosen, or have been condemned, to lives of perfect solitude, but I scarcely remember one, even among sages of strong and vigorous intellect, where its effect has not become apparent, in some disordered train of thought, or some gloomy hallucination. What monstrous phantoms, bed of despondency and doubt, and born and reared in solitude, have stalked upon the earth, making creation ugly, and darkening the face of Heaven!. . .

It seems to me that the objection that nothing wholesome or good has ever had its growth in such unnatural solitude, and that even a dog or any of the more intelligent among beasts, would pine, and mope, and rust away, beneath its influence, would be in itself a sufficient argument against this system . . . there is surely more than sufficient reason for abandoning a mode of punishment attended by so little hope or promise, and fraught, beyond dispute, with such a host of evils.

What happened next . . .

After Dickens's 1842 journey the effectiveness of each of the two prison systems was hotly debated in the United States. Some emphasized inmate reform while others favored deterring crime through severe punishment. A major concern of the Separate System at Cherry Hill was the cost of solitary confinement. Each prisoner had to have his own cell and exercise yard, and food and other necessities were provided individually. At this time criminologists began investigating the psychological character of criminals. As a result, concern increased over the effects of such pronounced isolation on individuals, as expressed so vividly by Dickens.

Dickens remained active in social reform movements following his trip to America. He used some profits from his highly popular novels to publish a newspaper called the *Daily News* beginning in January 1846. With Dickens as editor, the newspaper promoted social issues including free public education for the poor, various forms of civil and religious liberty, low-cost housing, and equal rights legislation. The newspaper was a financial failure and lasted only until 1850.

Dickens also wrote several significant works after his trip, including *A Christmas Carol* (1843), *David Copperfield* (1850), *A Tale of Two Cities* (1859), and *Great Expectations* (1860).

Did you know . . .

- Dickens's book *American Notes* was highly unpopular in the United States. Not only did he denounce the prison system at Cherry Hill, but he was also outspoken against slavery, corrupt American politics, and the slanderous press. The U.S. press blasted the book in reviews.

- Dickens was also a strong opponent of the death penalty. He claimed justice was not fairly applied with much depending on a person's wealth. The poor and uneducated generally received harsher treatment in the criminal justice system, including punishment. In addition, he argued that judges and juries made mistakes that could not be corrected if the accused was dead.

- Dickens returned to the United States twenty-five years later in November 1867. He received a grand welcome in Boston Harbor including a shower of rockets and flares. Dickens toured sixteen eastern cities using his own writings for public readings. It was highly successful and past hard feelings over his previous trip had been forgotten.

- Dickens died suddenly of a cerebral hemorrhage at home in Kent, England, in 1870. He was buried in the Poet's Corner of London's Westminster Abbey.

Consider the following . . .

- Divide the class into two groups and debate the benefits and drawbacks of the two prison systems being tested in America at the time of Dickens's trip—the Philadelphia and the Auburn plans.

- Write an essay describing what it would be like in the Cherry Hill prison, seeing no one, hearing no one, not receiving any news from the outside. What would your thoughts be if you were mistakenly convicted of a crime and sentenced to years at Cherry Hill? Imagine the hood taken from your head after being escorted to your cell for the first time.

- Is solitary confinement still used in U.S. prisons? Under what conditions is it applied?

For More Information

Books

Collins, Philip. *Dickens and Crime*. London: Macmillan & Company, Ltd., 1962.

Dickens, Charles. *American Notes*. New York: Penguin Books, 2000.

Kaplan, Fred. *Dickens: A Biography*. New York: William Morrow & Company, Inc., 1988.

Silverman, Ira. *Corrections: A Comprehensive View*. 2nd ed. Belmont, CA: Wadsworth, 2001.

Web Sites

"Charles Dickens: Novelist." *The National Archives Learning Curve*. http://www.spartacus.schoolnet.co.uk/PRdickens.htm (accessed on August 19, 2004).

"National Institute of Corrections (NIC)." *U.S. Department of Justice*. http://www.nicic.org (accessed on August 19, 2004).

George W. Wickersham

Excerpt from **The Problem of Law Enforcement**
An address by George W. Wickersham on April 16, 1931
Published by the National Commission on Law Observance and
Enforcement, 1931

"Justice must not fall
because the agencies of
enforcement are either
delinquent or
inefficiently organized."

The 1920s were a particularly trying time for the U.S. criminal justice system. The introduction of Prohibition by passage of the Eighteenth Amendment to the U.S. Constitution in 1919 introduced a new crime wave. Prohibition meant that no longer could people legally sell, transport, or possess alcoholic beverages. A black market for liquor immediately developed as the public's thirst for alcohol did not diminish though the availability did.

With so much money to be made by supplying illegal liquor, the influence of organized crime grew. The criminal justice system seemed incapable of responding effectively as some criminals like Al Capone (1899–1947) achieved celebrity status. Much money could also be made in local law enforcement—through bribes and corruption. Public respect for the criminal justice system declined to an all-time low.

President Herbert Hoover (1874–1964; served 1929–33) won the presidential election in November 1928. In his inaugural address on March 4, 1929, Hoover became the first U.S. president to refer to crime as a national issue in an inauguration speech. He announced his desire to create a National Commission on Law Observance and Enforcement. Hoover appointed George Wickersham, a former U.S. attorney general under President William H. Taft (1857–1930; served 1909–13), to head the commission.

There were ten other members on the commission with Wickersham; some were prominent Americans such as the dean of Harvard Law School. The commission was charged with assessing the condition of criminal justice in the nation, and to investigate the problems in enforcing Prohibition. The commission was to make recommendations on how to improve the U.S. legal system including policing, the courts, and corrections.

Wickersham was a lawyer by training who practiced in New York before being named Taft's attorney general. After leaving public office in 1912, Wickersham returned to private law practice but remained very dedicated to public affairs. In 1915 as the state of New York developed a new state constitution, he chaired the judiciary committee for the constitutional convention. In the mid-1920s he also served on a commission charged with reorganizing the state's government.

By June 1930 the Wickersham Commission had completed its work and issued fourteen reports on practically every aspect of criminal justice. It was the most comprehensive assessment in the history of the United States to that time. The reports looked into Prohibition enforcement, deportation laws used to rid the country of political radicals, prison operations, police misconduct, juvenile justice, the causes of crime, and the costs of crime.

Though the Wickersham Commission reports provided a wealth of information and recommendations on many aspects of law enforcement, the judicial system, and prisons, the sections drawing the most attention were those addressing Prohibition. Unlike many of the other reports, the commission was indecisive on what to do about Prohibition. The resulting report sections were contradictory, drawing criticism from both supporters and opponents of Prohibition. The press made fun of the results and President Hoover distanced himself from the report. Wickersham gave speeches highlighting less controversial findings of the commission and on April 16, 1931, he spoke before the Regional Crime Committee of Cincinnati, Ohio.

Political cartoon criticizing the Wickersham Law Enforcement Commission for its reports, considered useless by critics, on Prohibition. The wealthy fat man in the cartoon is labeled **Commission.** *(National Archives and Records Administration)*

Things to remember while reading excerpts from *The Problem of Law Enforcement*:

- Wickersham was a short, stocky man who was very blunt in expressing his views. He was an excellent choice as a strong leader for the commission, which became known as the Wickersham Commission.

- Wickersham's primary task as attorney general in 1909 was to enforce the Sherman Antitrust Law against illegal corporate practices. He earned great respect for the large number of business monopoly cases he tackled.

- The Wickersham Commission was the first national study of criminal justice in the United States. Two previous crime commissions were the Cleveland Survey of Criminal Justice in the early 1920s and the 1926 Missouri Crime Survey.

- Competition among criminals over the lucrative bootlegging market led to bloody gangster wars in the late 1920s, drawing even greater public concern over the ability of law enforcement to make the streets safe.

- A "get tough on crime" approach in the late 1920s had decreased the use of parole (when inmates are allowed to leave prison before serving out their full sentences) and probation (when offenders are allowed to remain in their community under supervision) in criminal justice.

Excerpt from The Problem of Law Enforcement

*Since the national Commission on Law Observance and Enforcement **rendered** its report on the problem of the enforcement of prohibition under the provisions of the eighteenth amendment and the laws enacted pursuant thereto, I am constantly asked if our work is not finished and when our commission will dissolve.*

The overwhelming public interest in prohibition has obscured the fact that the commission was charged with the duty to study and report on any other subject.

But, as a matter of fact, for many months bodies of research experts and scholars have been at work for us, probing sources of information bearing upon many of the problems suggested by the title of the commission, and patiently gathering facts and formulating recommendations for our consideration. All this is being done in fulfillment of the mandate laid upon the commission by the president, to study and report upon the whole of the problems involved in criminal-law enforcement.

Rendered: Delivered.

In his inaugural address, President Hoover referred to disregard and disobedience of law as the most **malign** of the dangers confronting the State. Confidence in rigid and speedy justice, he said, is decreasing. Rigid and **expeditious** justice he declared to be "the first safeguard of freedom, the basis of all ordered liberty, the vital force of progress." And he added:

"Justice must not fall because the agencies of enforcement are either delinquent or inefficiently organized. To consider these evils, to find their remedy, is the most sore necessity of our time."

On the day of the inauguration of Mr. Hoover as President the Congress included in one of the appropriation bills an allotted sum "for the purpose of a thorough inquiry into the problem of the enforcement of prohibition together with the enforcement of other laws." The President shortly afterwards created this commission to conduct the inquiry so authorized, giving to the legislative act a broad interpretation by **enjoining** the commission to make an exhaustive study of the entire problem of the enforcement of our laws and the improvement of our judicial system, and inviting them to make the widest inquiry into the shortcomings of the administration of justice and into the causes and **remedies** for them. . . .

Abundant evidence has been spread before the American people for years past of the need of a thorough overhauling of our whole system of criminal justice. Every day furnishes examples of the absence of that wholesome respect for law which ought to be characteristic of a self-governing people. . . .

The Department of Commerce, in June 1929, stated that no authoritative or reliable statistics on crime and criminal justice are available except for limited areas in the United States, notably New York and Missouri and the cities of New York, Detroit, Chicago, and Cleveland.

"In short there is an absolute need for reliable statistics, expertly analyzed, before an intelligent diagnosis of the situation can be properly undertaken.". . . In the light of such criticism, . . . one of the first subjects which our commission assigned for study and report was that of criminal statistics. The result of careful studies made for the commission . . . recommends that the compiling and publishing of statistics of Federal administration of justice shall be committed to one bureau in the Department of Justice. . . .

If we could know just what causes men to commit crime, we should be able to better judge the fitness and value of our punitive

Malign: Harmful.

Expeditious: Speedy.

Enjoining: Directing.

Remedies: Solutions.

and reformative methods and to mold them to more effectively prevent lawless conduct. Personally, I believe there is no one cause of crime. Human nature is complex. Men yield to temptation. Some men are so constituted physically or mentally that they cannot resist temptation. Again, what would tempt one man to violate a law would not move another. But while there may be no one cause of crime, as there is no one cause of disease, there are circumstances and conditions which may readily be recognized as tending to foster and encourage lawless conduct, and which may be **mitigated** or removed by wise public action. So it appeared to the commission that a study into some of these conditions might furnish fruitful results. . . . Mary van Kleeck and Emma A. Winslow have made experimental inquiries into the influence of unemployment and occupational conditions upon crime. A preliminary review . . . of published investigations she [Winslow] found to be fairly conclusive with reference to the tendency for crimes against property and vagrancy to increase during periods of economic depression and decrease during prosperity, and for alcoholism to increase during periods of prosperity and decrease during depression. Other groups of offenses apparently are affected only slightly and irregularly. . . . It is through careful studies of this kind that reliable conclusions may be reached concerning the social and economic conditions which tend to produce or discourage criminality. As a result . . . unemployment ranks high among the factors which influence crimes against property. . . .

Any study of the causes of crime in any community must address itself to an earnest consideration of the condition and the education of the children of the community. Very slowly we have been coming to a realization of the preeminent importance of the child to the State. That importance would seem to be obvious . . . one dollar wisely invested in the care of a child; one day spent in the careful considerate study of its environment and the method of accomplishing its removal from evil influences, may result in greater profit to the State than one thousand dollars spent on the machinery of criminal justice. The New York Crime Commission has very truly said, "The ultimate crime prevention task is that of guiding the development of childhood behavior." A very challenging statement is made by that commission in its 1930 report, that a study of the life histories of 145 male inmates of the State prisons and reformatory during the months of August and September, 1929, of the age of 30 years and under, showed that a majority of these men began their delinquent careers as children. . . . The juvenile court

Mitigated: The effect lessened.

Attorney General George Woodward Wickersham. Wickersham was a lawyer who practiced in New York before being named Taft's attorney general and heading the Wickersham Law Enforcement Commission.

(© Corbis)

has been described as "America's most notable contribution to the field of criminology and penology." Its organization and functions and a study of its workings are essential to a clear understanding of its accomplishments and its possibilities. Communities should be led to realize that while juvenile courts cost money, they do not cost as much as prisons. . . .

With the great increase in number and character of Federal crimes have come new and serious additions to the jurisdiction of Federal courts which they are ill fitted satisfactorily to exercise . . . and only recently has Congress made fairly reasonable appropriations for the administration of the probation and parole laws. Under our system of punitive justice, an offender convicted of crime is liable to fine or imprisonment, or both. By virtue of probation laws in many States, and in the Federal jurisdiction, under certain conditions, the court is empowered instead of sending him to prison, to release the offender on probation, which means under official supervision and control, during the term for which he might have been imprisoned. Under parole laws, some constituted authority other than the court may release an offender, after he has served a portion of his sentence, subject to supervision and good behavior until the expiration of his original sentence. . . .

A study of 8,475 male occupants of six penal institutions in the State of New York, recently made by the American Prison Association, showed that less than half of them were normal, one-fourth were feeble-minded, and nearly one-third psychopaths or psychotic. This is believed to be fairly representative of many, if not most, prison populations. . . .

Yet much of our dealing with criminals has wholly ignored the fact of individuality and treated them wholesale. . . .

Probation laws generally have been framed upon well thought out theories. They contemplate the assembly of all available information concerning the prisoner, as a guide to the judge in determining whether or not to release him on probation instead of sending him to prison. The operation of parole laws usually is so restricted that the offender can not be released from close custody until he shall have served a definite fraction of his imprisonment sentence.

The operation of both classes of laws has been greatly impeded by inadequate appropriations, insufficient numbers or imperfectly trained probation or parole officers, and by assignment to them so large a number of offenders as to make impossible anything like adequate supervision of the probationers or parolees. . . .

In the desperate effort to compel obedience to law, experience has shown that those charged with the high function of enforcing the law sometimes stoop to attain their ends by means as illegal as the acts they seek to punish or suppress. It is time a study should be made of this phase of our civilization and that now in course of preparation for our commission will be presented as perhaps the first, or one of the first attempts to put in concrete form for public consideration this ugly side of our officialdom. . . .

There are many signs of a public awakening to the need of a radical improvement in our penal laws and in the machinery of criminal justice. The public mind is avid for concrete facts and ready to respond to effective leadership in pointing out the best way to accomplish the needed reforms. Our commission is dealing with the problems from the national standpoint. The studies which local organizations have made and are making, and the reports and recommendations already published, not only are useful in the especial communities to which they apply but are helpful to the solution of the broader problems in the national field with which our commission is dealing. The nature of our Federal system creates complications and difficulties foreign to the centralized governments of other lands. But in this, as with other problems, I am persuaded that when an informed public sentiment is aroused, the genius of the American people will find some way of removing the reproach to which our system of criminal justice so long has been justly exposed.

What happened next . . .

The commission's reports did not give the existing criminal justice system high marks. According to the commission in a volume titled *Lawlessness in Law Enforcement,* many police departments across the nation were corrupt, not well operated, and poorly trained. The reports were also critical of the nation's prison system for not adequately rehabilitating inmates. The Wickersham Commission revived the use of probation and parole in rehabilitating offenders.

Specific recommendations provided in the reports on how to improve criminal justice in America were gradually adopted through the years. A new generation of police leaders in the 1930s used the commission's findings to improve their departments, including ways for the public to report police misconduct. For example, as the commission found, prisons focused more on strict discipline and punishment than treatment. These harsh conditions fueled violence and riots within the prison walls. Using the Wickersham Commission recommendations later in the 1930s, prison systems began classifying inmates according to their level of security risk. The less serious offenders were placed in prison farms and forest camps. Prisons also placed emphasis on education and vocational training.

The commission, as indicated in Wickersham's excerpts, identified a major need to keep national crime statistics. The agency that later became the Federal Bureau of Investigation (FBI) created Uniform Crime Reports (UCR) in 1935 to help track crime. Both Wickersham and UCRs were major factors in the debate over the creation of a national crime data system.

Overall, the commission's reports greatly affected the long-term understanding of crime and punishment in the United States. It was one of the first efforts to estimate the cost of crime to society and two of its volumes explored the causes of crime and the importance of sociological studies. This was a major step in recognizing the new field of criminology, the scientific study of crime.

Did you know . . .

- Police officials at first angrily denounced the Wickersham findings on police misconduct such as forced confessions through brutal physical force and not letting suspects have access to lawyers. Wickersham reported that most police misconduct was directed toward the poor, minorities, labor activists, and political radicals. Police reform was now a national issue to be addressed throughout the following decades.

- As a result of the attention drawn to the Prohibition by the reports, many of the other meaningful recommendations had to wait until Prohibition officially ended in 1933.

- The Wickersham Commission set the foundation for the President's Commission on Law Enforcement and Administration of Justice in the mid-1960s, known as the President's Crime Commission.

Consider the following . . .

- What do you think the country learned through its decade-long experimentation with Prohibition?

- Throughout the1920s prison crowding increased due to convicted violators of Prohibition. What is the importance of probation and parole as described by Wickersham for improving prison conditions?

- Explain the reasons why growing poverty increases crime rates. Which sections of your community or region reflect this trend?

For More Information

Books

Chase, Anthony. *Law and History: The Evolution of the American Legal System.* New York: New Press, 1997.

Friedman, Lawrence M. *Crime and Punishment in American History.* New York: Basic Books, 1993.

Walker, Samuel. *Popular Justice: A History of American Criminal Justice.* 2nd ed. New York: Oxford University Press, 1997.

Web Site

"Uniform Crime Reports." *Federal Bureau of Investigation.* http://www.fbi.gov/ucr/ucr.htm (accessed on August 19, 2004).

3

Moral Offenses

Since the first European settlements in North America in the early seventeenth century, governments in America have tried to regulate morality. The early colonists equated sin with crime. Such offenses as blasphemy (showing a lack of reverence toward God), heresy (holding a belief that conflicts with church doctrine), and adultery (sex between two adults, one of whom is married to another) were considered criminal acts and dealt with by sometimes severe punishments.

Actions and behavior that do not conform to accepted standards of what is considered right or wrong are called public order crimes. Such behavior is seen as disruptive to daily life. They are also called vice crimes or moral offenses. Social standards, or morals, can change through time triggering changes in criminal law. The colonies had "blue laws," so called because they were printed on blue paper, banning certain activities such as work on Sundays.

Blue laws in Europe even enforced what people could eat or wear on Sundays according to their social status. Moral offenses decreased over time as the public accepted that certain forms of social deviation, though still perhaps offensive to

Those prosecuted for moral offenses—such as drug use, gambling, or prostitution—often contend they are victimless crimes, such as suspected madam Polly Adler, seen here in New York police custody. *(© Bettmann/Corbis)*

Gambling

The United States has long had criminal laws against certain forms of gambling. The unauthorized selling of lottery tickets has been a crime throughout U.S. history. Other offenses include the promoting of gambling, possession of gambling records, and possession of any equipment associated with gambling. There are certain forms of gambling allowed in some parts of the country, such as betting on race horses, dog racing, at casinos, and in state lotteries.

most, should not be considered a crime. Types of modern-day moral offenses include the sale of obscene materials, certain kinds of sexual activity, drug and alcohol abuse, and gambling.

Moral offenses often involve behavior between two consenting adults with no immediate victims to bring charges. This is why moral offenses are sometimes referred to as victimless crimes. The activity commonly involves one person providing goods (such as drugs) or services (gambling or prostitution) to another. With no one to file a criminal complaint claiming injury, these are crimes simply because they were outlawed. Therefore the criminal justice system must rely on informants, undercover agents, and surveillance equipment to detect or investigate such crimes.

Critics of moral offenses claim they should not be considered crimes, but rather discouraged through better parenting and the community in other ways. Critics further claim making these activities crimes creates a black market that can lead to other more serious crime including violence.

Others, however, contend that society as a whole is a victim of these deviant behaviors as well as the friends and family of those involved in the activity. For example, drug use can lead to property crime by a person trying to pay for an expensive as well as destructive habit. Prostitution can cause the spread of disease and put the prostitutes in potentially violent situations. If moral offenses were allowed to occur in a community legally, then more serious criminal activity would likely follow according to those who consider moral offenses a crime. These offenses should remain an illegal criminal activity, which in turn will protect the moral fiber of communities.

This chapter presents excerpts from three legal documents, two federal laws, and a constitutional amendment, attempting to regulate the moral behavior of U.S. citizens and protect community order. All three also demonstrate the futility in trying to enforce these laws.

By the late 1800s reformers feared that the availability of birth control information and devices was increasing sexual activity. They pressed for a ban on this and other material they considered obscene. In response, Congress took action. The first excerpt is from the resulting 1873 Comstock Law, more formally called "An Act for the Suppression of Trade in, and Circulation of, Obscene Literature and Articles of Immoral Use." The law represents the first action by the federal government to prohibit what some considered obscene material, including birth control information.

Social reformers in the late nineteenth and early twentieth centuries were also concerned with drug and alcohol use in the nation. Existing concern over opium use escalated when the process of refining opium into heroin was discovered in 1898. Heroin addiction was growing rapidly at the turn of the century. The second excerpt from Harrison Narcotic Drug Act of 1914 represents the first federal attempt to regulate the distribution of illegal drugs into and within the United States.

Increased restrictions on narcotics were followed by a total ban on alcoholic beverages. The third excerpt, Eighteenth Amendment—Prohibition of Intoxicating Liquors represents the beginning of a failed thirteen-year experiment to prohibit alcohol use in the United States. Though criminal laws concerning alcohol use would be greatly scaled back in the 1930s, drug laws would continue to multiply despite limited success in curbing drug use.

Comstock Law

Excerpt from the Comstock Law

Reprinted from *The Statutes at Large and Proclamations of the United States of America from March 1871 to March 1873*, Vol. XVII. Edited by George P. Sanger

Published in 1873

"That no obscene . . . pamphlet, picture, paper, print, or other publication of an indecent character . . . may be written or printed."

Sexual morality has long played an important role in U.S. criminal justice history even as many other Western countries have decreased emphasis on these kinds of moral offenses. Sexual crimes are those activities that the local community finds offensive. During the late 1870s a national campaign was mounted to legislate public morality. As new advances in birth control were made through the nineteenth century, interest steadily grew. By the 1870s a wide variety of birth control methods were readily available in pharmacies throughout the nation.

Abortion, too, remained free of legal restriction in many areas. The easy public access to birth control information and devices attracted the opposition of Anthony Comstock (1844–1915) and others. Believing access to birth control promoted greater sexual activity outside of marriage, they lobbied Congress to pass a bill prohibiting the mailing of birth control information and devices as well as abortion information through the U.S. mail. They also hoped to prohibit the shipment of birth control items from state to state.

Things to remember while reading excerpts from the Comstock Law:

- Anthony Comstock authored a 1868 comprehensive law in New York State that prohibited the distribution of literature and photographs that some considered immoral works. Comstock also founded the New York Society for the Suppression of Vice in 1868, for which he served as an officer until his death in 1915.

- The Comstock Law was primarily aimed at stopping trade in obscene literature and other immoral items; both birth control devices and abortion fell within this definition.

- Under the Comstock Law, the U.S. Postal Authority was responsible for deciding what was obscene; Anthony Comstock also began serving as a U.S. Post Office Inspector in 1873.

- Efforts to prohibit abortions began in the 1820s in the United States.

- As states passed laws banning abortion in 1820s, illegal abortions became increasingly frequent until passage of the Comstock Law.

Anthony Comstock (1844–1915). Comstock authored a 1868 comprehensive law in New York State that prohibited the distribution of birth control devices and obscene and immoral literature and photographs. *(The Library of Congress)*

Excerpt from the Comstock Law

Be it enacted by the Senate and House of Representatives of the United States of America in Congress assembled, That whoever, within the District of Columbia or any of the Territories of the United States, or other place within the exclusive jurisdiction of the United States, shall sell, or lend, or give away, or in any manner exhibit, or shall offer to sell, or to lend, or to give away, or in any manner to exhibit, or shall otherwise publish or offer to publish in any manner, or shall have in his possession, for any such purpose or purposes, any obscene book, pamphlet, paper, writing, advertisement, circular, print, picture, drawing or other representation, figure, or image on or of paper or other material, or any cast, instrument, or other article of an immoral nature, or any drug or medicine, or any article whatever, for the prevention of **conception,** *or for causing* **unlawful abortion,** *or shall advertise the same for sale, or shall write or print, or cause to be written or printed, any card, circular, book, pamphlet, advertisement, or notice of any kind, stating when, where, how, or of whom, or by what means, any of the articles in this section hereinbefore mentioned, can be purchased or obtained, or shall manufacture, draw, or print, or in any wise [way] make any of such articles, shall be deemed guilty of a misdemeanor, and, on conviction thereof in any court of the United States having criminal jurisdiction in the District of Columbia, or in any Territory or place within the exclusive jurisdiction of the United States, where such misdemeanor shall have been committed; and on conviction thereof, he shall be imprisoned at hard labor in the penitentiary for not less than six months nor more than five years for each offense, or fined not less than one hundred dollars nor more than two thousand dollars, with costs of court.*

SEC. 2 That section one hundred and forty-eight of the act to revise . . . the statutes relating to the Post-office Department, approved June eighth, eighteen hundred and seventy-two, be amended to read as follows:

SEC. 148. That no obscene, lewd, or lascivious book, pamphlet, picture, paper, print, or other publication of an indecent character, or any article or thing designed or intended for the prevention of conception or procuring of abortion, nor any article or thing intended or adapted for any indecent or immoral use or nature, nor any written or printed card, circular, book, pamphlet, advertisement or notice of any kind giving information, . . . or postal-card upon which indecent or **scurrilous epithets** *may be written or printed, shall be carried in the mail, and any person who shall knowingly deposit . . . any of the hereinbefore-mentioned articles or things . . . shall be deemed guilty of a misdemeanor, and, on conviction thereof, shall, for every offense, be fined not less than one hundred dollars nor more than five thousand dollars, or imprisoned at hard labor not less than one year nor more than ten years, or both, in the discretion of the judge.*

Conception: The process of becoming pregnant.

Unlawful abortion: The deliberate termination of a pregnancy.

Scurrilous epithets: Abusive or vulgar words or names.

SEC. 3. That all persons are prohibited from importing into the United States, from any foreign country, any of the hereinbefore-mentioned articles or things . . . and all such prohibited articles in the course of importation shall be detained by the officer of customs, and proceedings taken against the same under section five of this act.

*SEC. 4. That whoever, being an officer, agent, or employee of the government of the United States, shall knowingly aid or **abet** any person engaged in any violation of this act, shall be deemed guilty of a misdemeanor, and, on conviction thereof, shall, for every offense, be punished as provided in section two of this act.*

*SEC. 5. That any judge of any district or circuit court of the United States, within the proper district, before whom complaint in writing of any violation of this act shall be made, to the satisfaction of such judge, and founded on knowledge or belief, and, if upon belief, setting forth the grounds of such belief, and supported by oath or affirmation of the complainant, may issue, **conformably** to the Constitution, a warrant directed to the marshal, or any deputy marshal, in the proper district, directing him to search for, seize, and take possession of any such article or thing hereinbefore mentioned. . . .*

Abet: To support.

Conformably: Consistent with.

What happened next . . .

The Comstock Law was widely used to prosecute people distributing birth control information and devices. In 1878 a movement was attempted to repeal the Comstock Law but met with only limited success. The Comstock Law remained largely intact. Anthony Comstock was credited for destroying some 160 tons of literature and photographs he considered obscene.

The most famous case involving the Comstock Law was brought against Margaret Sanger (1879–1966) in 1936. Sanger, an American activist in the distribution of birth control information in the early twentieth century, was arrested and prosecuted for her activity on many occasions (see sidebar). Due to the efforts of Sanger and other birth control advocates, the court overturned federal efforts to stop birth control,

Margaret Sanger in a New York courtroom. Sanger founded the
National Birth Control League and established the first birth control
clinic in Brooklyn, New York. *(AP/Wide World Photos)*

essentially ending Comstock Law prosecutions concerning
birth control.

By the end of the nineteenth century most abortions had
been outlawed. In 1965 all fifty states still had antiabortion
or pro-life laws that allowed abortions only in cases of rape,
incest, or to save the mother's life.

By 1967 the federal government became an active player
in distributing birth control information, first through the
Child Health Act and then the Family Planning Services and
Population Act of 1970, which established separate govern-

Margaret Sanger

Margaret Sanger was a trained nurse who worked with poor women in the Lower East Side of New York City. Faced with the effects of unplanned pregnancies on a daily basis, in 1912 she left nursing and began distributing birth control information. Sanger founded the monthly publication *The Woman Rebel,* which included birth control information. The first issue appeared in March 1914. Upon using the mail for distributing the publication in 1913 she was indicted under the Comstock Law for mailing obscene materials. Authorities confiscated (removed) all copies of the publication.

The publication's issues over the next five months were similarly confiscated. The indictment was withdrawn and in 1917 Sanger founded the National Birth Control League. In the next few years she established the first birth control clinic in Brooklyn, New York. She was arrested and sentenced to thirty days at the Queens penitentiary in New York. In the following years she was arrested and prosecuted many times for distributing birth control information.

In 1921 the National Birth Control League became the American Birth Control League. In 1923 she opened the first permanent birth control clinic in the United States, in New York City. In 1927 Sanger helped organize the first World Population Conference and by 1942 the Birth Control League became the Planned Parenthood Federation. Through the years Sanger wrote many books and articles on birth control.

ment funds for birth control. By the late twentieth century, pro-abortion rights groups promoted birth control, sex education, and healthcare. The programs, while controversial, became part of public school curriculums. Some members of pro-life groups, however, had turned to violent measures such as bombing abortion clinics to get their point across.

In the early twenty-first century, sexual moral offenses included adultery, incest (sex with a family member), bigamy (illegally having two spouses; a person may only have one legal spouse at a time), polygamy (having multiple spouses at the same time), obscene materials, and statutory rape (sex with an underage person). Pornography was protected by the First Amendment of the Constitution as freedom of expression. This includes magazines, books, photographs, and videos. Pornography becomes obscene and illegal only when it violates existing local standards of morality and decency. It is still a criminal offense to produce and sell obscene material. What is considered obscene varies from community to community and through time. In contrast, child pornography is always illegal.

The most common sexual crime throughout the United States remained prostitution. Congress passed the Mann Act in 1910 making it illegal to transport women across state lines for the purpose of prostitution. Enforcement went beyond forced prostitution to combat prostitution in general.

Did you know . . .

- The distribution and use of contraceptives remained a crime until 1965 when the U.S. Supreme Court issued a landmark decision, ruling that the ban on birth control interfered with an individual's right to privacy.

- Another Supreme Court decision in 1969 ruled laws banning possession of obscene material in a person's home were unconstitutional.

- One of the largest morals cases before the Supreme Court was in 1973 when the Court ruled that the ban on abortion (during the first three months of pregnancy) in most states was unconstitutional, again on the grounds of invasion of privacy.

- A major international organization opposing the distribution of birth control information and devices as well as abortions in the twenty-first century is the Roman Catholic Church.

- In 1878 the first birth control clinic was opened, located in Amsterdam, in the Netherlands.

- In the late 1990s Congress attempted to control pornography on the Internet through the Communications Decency Act of 1996 and the Child Online Protection Act of 1998. Both, however, were found unconstitutional reflecting the difficulty of enforcing standards on the Internet.

Consider the following . . .

- Look up in the library or on the Internet various articles by birth control advocate Margaret Sanger. What arguments does she present in her fight against the Comstock Law? Why did she believe women should be freely provided with birth control information?

- What has been the history of sex education and birth control counseling in your school or community? Is it readily available or strictly limited?

- List the reasons provided by those who oppose making moral offenses a crime and the reasons offered by those promoting criminalization of socially deviant behavior. Which approach do you believe is most appropriate?

For More Information

Books

Hardin, G. J. *The Margaret Sanger Story and the Fight for Birth Control.* Westport, CT: Greenwood Press, 1975.

McCann, Carole R. *Birth Control Politics in the United States, 1916–1945.* Ithaca, NY: Cornell University Press, 1994.

Tone, Andrea. *Devices and Desires: A History of Contraceptives in America.* New York: Hill and Wang, 2001.

Web Sites

"Abortion Is Pro-life." *Capitalism Magazine.* http://www.abortionisprolife.com (accessed on August 19, 2004).

Planned Parenthood Federation of America, Inc. http://www.plannedparenthood.org (accessed on August 19, 2004).

Harrison Act

Excerpt from the Harrison Narcotic Drug Act of 1914

Reprinted from *The Statutes at Large and Proclamations of the United States of America from March 1913 to March 1915.* **Vol. XXXVIII, Part 1**

Published in 1915

"Any person who violates or fails to comply with any of the requirements of this Act shall, on conviction, be fined . . . or be imprisoned."

Prior to the twentieth century few restrictions were placed on drug trade and use. Opium and cocaine flowed freely into the United States. Drug abuse was considered more a public health problem than a criminal activity. Drugs such as opium and cocaine were common in medicines. Opium, which affects the brain and spinal cord, had been a painkiller and sedative for centuries. Opium and cocaine were also used to fight depression, relieve chronic pain, serve as an anesthetic, settle intestinal disorders, and relieve a variety of other afflictions.

Cocaine was even used as an ingredient in wine and Coca Cola. Other drugs were processed from opium, such as morphine, a major pain-fighting drug for the wounded in the American Civil War (1861–65; war in the United States between the Union [North], who was opposed to slavery, and the Confederacy [South], who was in favor of slavery). Drugs derived from opium are called opiates. In 1898 a process to derive heroin from opium was discovered, becoming the most additive opiate of all.

The first effort to regulate drugs came in 1906 with the Pure Food and Drug Law. The act posed few restrictions, how-

Opium den in Chinatown, New York, 1925. After the Harrison Narcotic Drug Act of 1917 restricted the use of many narcotics to prescription by doctors, illegal drug trafficking became a lucrative enterprise for organized crime. *(© Bettmann/Corbis)*

ever, as it primarily concerned the labeling of medicines by pharmaceutical companies. It did lead to a decline in the use of opiates in medicines. The next action by Congress came just three years later with the Opium Exclusion Act of 1909, which prohibited importing opium. Domestic production and the use of opiates in medicines continued.

In 1914 Congress passed the Harrison Narcotic Drug Act, the first measure to control narcotics trafficking. The act approached control through a revenue path—requiring those who transported, sold, or possessed narcotics to report it to the Internal Revenue Service (IRS) and pay taxes. The Harrison Act limited opium availability to only small amounts as prescribed by doctors, who were required to register and pay taxes on the amounts they prescribed.

Things to remember while reading excerpts from the Harrison Narcotic Drug Act of 1914:

- Opium comes from opium poppy plants native to Turkey; cocaine comes from the coca plant found in South America. Both produce a feeling of euphoria (an artificial high) but have long-term health consequences when abused.

- In 1874 the city of San Francisco banned the smoking of opium except in the Chinatown district.

- In its earliest legislation on narcotics in 1890, Congress placed a tax on opium and morphine.

- Following the discovery of heroin in 1898, heroin addiction skyrocketed over the next several years.

Excerpt from the Harrison Narcotic Drug Act of 1914

An Act To provide for the registration of, with collectors of internal revenue, and to impose a special tax upon all persons who produce, import, manufacture, compound, deal in, dispense, sell, distribute, or give away opium or coca leaves, their salts, derivatives, or preparations, and for other purposes.

Be it enacted by the Senate and House of Representatives of the United States of America in Congress assembled, That on and after the first day of March, nineteen hundred and fifteen, every person who produces, imports, manufactures, compounds, deals in, dispenses, sells, distributes, or gives away opium or coca leaves of any compound, manufacture, salt, derivative, or preparation thereof, shall register with the collector of internal revenue of the district his name or style, place of business, and place or places where such business is to be carried on: Provided, That the office, or if none, then the res-

*idence of any person shall be considered for the purposes of this Act to be his place of business. At the time of such registry and on or before the first day of July, annually thereafter, every person who produces, imports, manufactures, compounds, deals in, dispenses, sells, distributes, or gives away any of the aforesaid drugs shall pay to the said collector a special tax at the rate of $1 per **annum**. . . .*

It shall be unlawful for any person required to register under the terms of this Act to produce, import, manufacture, compound, deal in, dispense, sell, distribute, or give away any of the aforesaid drugs without having registered and paid the special tax provided for in the section.

That the word "person" as used in this Act shall be construed to mean and include a partnership, association, company, or corporation, as well as a natural person. . . .

That the Commissioner of Internal Revenue, with the approval of the Secretary of the Treasury, shall make all needful rules and regulations for carrying the provisions of this act into effect.

SEC. 2. That it shall be unlawful for any person to sell, barter, exchange, or give away any of the aforesaid drugs except in pursuance of a written order of the person to whom such article is sold, bartered, exchanged, or given, on a form to be issued in blank for that purpose by the Commissioner of Internal Revenue. Every person who shall accept any such order, and in pursuance thereof shall sell, barter, exchange, or give away any of the aforesaid drugs, shall preserve such order for a period of two years in such a way as to be readily accessible to inspection by any officer, agent, or employee of the Treasury Department duly authorized for that purpose, and the State, Territorial, District, municipal, and insular officials named in section five of this Act. . . .

(a) To the dispensing or distribution of any of the aforesaid drugs to a patient by a physician, dentist, or veterinary surgeon registered under this Act in the course of his professional practice only: Provided, That such physician, dentist or veterinary surgeon shall personally attend; and such record shall be kept for a period of two years from the date of dispensing or distributing such drugs, subject to inspection, as provided in this Act.

(b) To the sale, dispensing, or distribution of any of the aforesaid drugs by a dealer to a consumer under and in pursuance of a written prescription issued by a physician, dentist, or veterinary surgeon registered under this Act: Provided, however, That such prescription shall

Annum: Year.

be dated as of the day on which signed and shall be signed by the physician, dentist, or veterinary surgeon who shall have issued the same: And provided further, That such dealer shall preserve such prescription for a period of two years from the day on which such prescription is filled in such a way as to be readily accessible to inspection by the officers, agents, employees, and officials hereinbefore mentioned.

(c) To the sale, exportation, shipment, or delivery of any of the aforesaid drugs by any person within the United States or any Territory or the District of Columbia or any of the insular possessions of the United States to any person in any foreign country, regulating their entry in accordance with such regulations for importation thereof into such foreign country as are prescribed by said country, such regulations to be promulgated [published] from time to time by the Secretary of State of the United States.

(d) To the sale, barter, exchange, or giving away of any of the aforesaid drugs to any officer of the United States Government or of any state, territorial, district, county, or municipal or insular government lawfully engaged in making purchases thereof for the various departments of the Army and Navy, the Public Health Service, and for Government, State, territorial district, county, or municipal or insular hospitals or prisons. . . .

SEC. 3. That any person who shall be registered in any internal-revenue district under the provisions of section one of this Act shall, whenever required so as to do by the collector of the district, render to the said collector a true and correct statement or return, verified by affidavit, setting forth the quantity of the aforesaid drugs received by him in said internal-revenue district, during such period immediately preceding the demand of the collector, not exceeding three months, as the said collector may fix and determine; the names of the persons from whom the said drugs were received; the quantity in each instance received from each of such persons, and the date when received.

SEC. 4. That it shall be unlawful for any person who shall not have registered and paid the special tax as required by section one or this Act to send, ship, carry, or deliver any of the aforesaid drugs from any State or Territory or the District of Columbia, or any insular possession of the United States, to any person in any other State or Territory or the District of Columbia or any insular possession of the United States: Provided, That nothing contained in this section shall apply to common carriers engaged in transporting the aforesaid

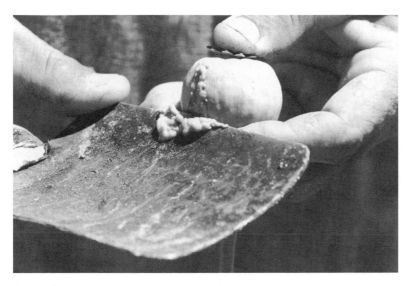

A poppy bulb being scraped to make opium or one of its derivatives, such as heroine. *(AP/Wide World Photos)*

drugs, or to any employee acting within the scope of his employment, of any person who shall have registered and paid the special tax as required by section one of this Act, or to any person who shall deliver any such drug which has been prescribed or dispensed by a physician, dentist, or veterinarian required to register under the terms of this Act, who has been employed to prescribe for the particular patient receiving such drug, or to any United States, State, county, municipal, District, Territorial, or insular officer or official acting within the scope of this official duties. . . .

*SEC. 6. That the provisions of this Act shall not be construed to apply to the sale, distribution, giving away, dispensing, or possession of preparations and remedies which do not contain more than two **grains** of opium, or more than one-fourth of a grain of morphine, or more than one-eighth of a grain of heroin, or more than one grain of codeine, or any salt or derivative of any of them in one fluid ounce, or, if a solid or semisolid preparation, in one . . . ounce; or to liniments, ointments, or other preparations which are prepared for external use only, except liniments, ointments, or . . . any of their salts or any synthetic substitute for them; Provided, That such remedies and preparations are sold, distributed, given away, dispensed, or possessed as medicines and not for the purpose of evading the intentions and provisions of this Act. The provisions of this Act shall not apply to decocainized coca leaves or preparations made therefrom,*

Grains: Small fractions of an ounce (grain is a very small unit of weight; 480 grains equal once ounce in pharmacy measurements).

or to other preparations of coca leaves which do not contain co-
caine. . . .

SEC. 9. That any person who violates or fails to comply with any
of the requirements of this Act shall, on conviction, be fined not more
than $2,000 or be imprisoned not more than five years, or both, in
the discretion of the court.

SEC. 10. That the Commissioner of Internal Revenue, with the
approval of the Secretary of the Treasury is authorized to appoint
such agents, deputy collectors, inspectors, chemists, assistant
chemists, clerks, and messengers in the field and in the Bureau of In-
ternal Revenue in the District of Columbia as may be necessary to
enforce the provisions of this Act. . . .

What happened next . . .

Many of the states also passed their own laws prohibiting the sale of opiates by 1916. A narcotics division was established in the U.S. Treasury Department that enforced the ban on all narcotics sales. The Harrison Act did have an effect on the supply of drugs; it was reflected by an increased demand for drugs on the black market by the mid-1920s. This demand led to organized crime expanding from bootlegging under Prohibition to include drug trafficking as well.

Well-known crime leaders turned away from the more competitive production and selling of rum running to drug trafficking on an international basis. The goal of organized crime was to regulate the supply of drugs into the country, therefore keeping demand and the price of narcotics high. They purchased legitimate warehouses, antique stores, and art galleries to store illegal shipments of drugs and launder drug money. What law enforcement considered a narcotics epidemic swept the country by the late 1920s.

The ban on alcohol from Prohibition followed the Harrison Act by five years. Others sought to ban tobacco, which was considered to have medicinal value in the nineteenth century. That opinion markedly changed through the twentieth century leading to the Cigarette Labeling and Advertising Act of 1965. The act required tobacco companies to place health warnings on cigarette packaging and advertising. By the 1990s tobacco smoking was becoming increasingly unacceptable though still legal.

Other drugs gained the attention of the public and legislatures. In 1915 California became the first state to criminalize marijuana use. Many other states passed similar laws over the next two decades, and Congress passed a federal law, the Marijuana Tax Stamp Act in 1937 banning marijuana use. Efforts to legalize marijuana use for medicinal purposes gained limited success in several states by the early twenty-first century.

The social upheavals of the 1960s brought greater attention to marijuana and hallucinogens that had gained popularity with the country's youth. In addition, many soldiers sent to the Vietnam War (1954–75; a controversial war in which the United States aided South Vietnam in its fight against a takeover by Communist North Vietnam) in the late 1960s were introduced to marijuana and heroin in Southeast Asia. In response, Congress passed the Comprehensive Drug Abuse Prevention and Control Act in 1970. The act created the position of a top government administrator, referred to as a "Drug Czar," charged with coordinating the anti-drug law enforcement efforts of many agencies.

Through the 1970s states passed drug laws that included tough sentencing measures, in some cases fifteen years to life in prison for selling small amounts of drugs. This trend favoring punishment over rehabilitation continued to grow as drug use expanded. In the mid-1980s President Ronald Reagan (1911–2004; served 1981–89) introduced the "War on Drugs." At the time, a rise in use of crack cocaine, an inexpensive, powerful form of the drug, was spreading quickly in the nation's inner cities. Along with crack cocaine came a rise in gang activity and violence.

Congress passed the Anti-Drug Abuse Acts of 1986 and 1988. The acts greatly increased law enforcement efforts against drug offenders including border patrols. The act also provided for a forfeiture of property associated with committing drug crimes or purchased from drug profits. Regarding punishment, the acts increased mandatory sentences, provided funding assistance for building more prisons, and established the death penalty for drug-related killings.

The courts supported this strong stance by ruling that a mandatory life sentence for selling cocaine was not cruel and unusual punishment. By the late 1990s the federal government and states were spending some $40 billion a year on the drug war. The fight even went beyond the nation's borders to Columbia, a key source for cocaine.

The United States maintained stiffer drug laws and punishment than most European countries. Despite this long and expensive fight against drug use, by the early twenty-first century some four million heavy drug users still existed in the United States and some 400,000 were in prisons convicted of drug offenses. Some drug use was down, such as cocaine, while others were up, like heroin. Drug trafficking remained very profitable despite a decrease in protection against unlawful search and seizure.

Did you know . . .

- The war on drugs dominated the criminal justice system in the 1980s and 1990s until antiterrorism measures took priority. Prisons expanded greatly to hold the large volume of drug offenders apprehended during this period.

- International drug trafficking by organized crime syndicates operating out of Asia and South America rose in prominence in the latter half of the twentieth century.

- By the 1990s many jurisdictions adopted zero-tolerance policies against drug use and trafficking, prostitution on the streets, and gambling in public places. They believed if these lesser crimes were tolerated, then more serious criminal activity would occur as well.

- In the early 2000s Afghanistan was the leading producer of opium.

Consider the following . . .

- Divide the class into two groups and discuss the long-standing debate as to whether drug use should be considered a crime or a public health issue. How do the two perspectives differ in the treatment of drug traffickers and users? Should society accept drug use as unavoidable and focus only socially disruptive behavior?

- Opium declined in use through the twentieth century, while heroin use increased with millions of addicts worldwide. Cocaine also declined in use by the twenty-first century but remained a problem for law enforcement. Describe the effects that heroin and cocaine have on the human body.

- What have been the key drug enforcement issues in your community?

For More Information

Books

Abadinsky, Howard. *Drug Abuse: An Introduction.* Chicago, IL: Nelson-Hall Publishers, 1997.

Hanson, Bill, ed. *Life With Heroin: Voices From the Inner City.* Lexington, MA: Lexington Books, 1985.

Inciardi, James A. *The War on Drugs: Heroin, Cocaine, Crime, and Public Policy.* Palo Alto, CA: Mayfield Publishing Company, 1986.

Sora, Joseph, ed. *Substance Abuse.* New York: H. W. Wilson, 1997.

Web Sites

National Institute on Drug Abuse. http://www.nida.nih.gov (accessed on August 19, 2004).

U.S. Drug Enforcement Administration. http://www.dea.gov (accessed on August 19, 2004).

Prohibition

Excerpt from the Eighteenth Amendment—Prohibition of Intoxicating Liquors

Adopted on January 29, 1919

Reprinted from the *Findlaw* Web site at http://caselaw.lp.findlaw.com/data/constitution/amendments18/

"The manufacture, sale, or transportation of intoxicating liquors . . . for beverage purposes is hereby prohibited."

Alcohol is the most frequently used drug in the United States. Rum was often present in community gatherings in the early colonial settlements. Concern began to rise over those who drank too much. Laws were passed focusing on alcohol abuse and its disruptive effects on small communities. A call for a ban on alcohol grew throughout the nineteenth century among social workers, clergy, and others part of what were called temperance movements.

By the 1870s organizations such as the Women's Christian Temperance Union crusaded around the nation promoting the prohibition of alcohol. Another key national group, the Anti-Saloon League, joined the fight for prohibition in the 1890s.

Passage of the Eighteenth Amendment to the Constitution banning the manufacture, sale, and transportation of alcoholic beverages came in January 1919. To put the amendment into effect, Congress passed the Volstead Act in October 1919. The act expanded the prohibition to include beer and wine as well as hard liquor and criminalized its possession.

Things to remember while reading excerpts from the Eighteenth Amendment— Prohibition of Intoxicating Liquors:

- Prohibition officially went into effect on January 16, 1920.

- Prohibitionists believed enforcement would be easy and inexpensive.

- Crime syndicates had previously been organized around gambling, prostitution, and other vices. It readily adapted to the new financial bonanza of bootlegging illegal liquor.

- Since the United States did not have a personal income tax until 1915, money from liquor taxes became a primary source of funding for the federal government from 1870 to 1915.

An Anti-Saloon League poster from the 1910s making the case for Prohibition. This poster questions if the benefits of alcohol tax revenues are really worth the social costs. *(The Library of Congress)*

Excerpt from the Eighteenth Amendment— Prohibition of Intoxicating Liquors

Section 1. After one year from the ratification of this article the manufacture, sale, or transportation of intoxicating liquors within, the importation thereof into, or the exportation thereof from the United States and all territory subject to the jurisdiction thereof for beverage purposes is hereby prohibited.

*Section 2. The Congress and the several States shall have **concurrent** power to enforce this article by appropriate legislation.*

Concurrent: Jurisdiction by two authorities at the same time.

*Section 3. This article shall be inoperative unless it shall have
been **ratified** as an amendment to the Constitution by the legislature
of the several States, as provided in the Constitution, within seven
years from the date of the submission hereof to the States by the
Congress.*

What happened next . . .

Prohibition did not curb America's desire to drink alcoholic beverages, but it did create a crime wave including dramatic growth in organized crime. Gangs operated their own alcohol distilleries and paid off local police and politicians to look the other way. In addition, gangsters smuggled (bootlegged) liquor into the United States from Canada and Mexico. With so much bribery and corruption, there was a significant decrease in the respect for law enforcement.

By the late 1920s gangsters had become well established and wealthy. Some gang leaders became millionaires as the cost of drinks rose significantly. The number of saloons increased from some 16,000 before Prohibition to 33,000 speakeasies (illegal drinking places) following the passage of Prohibition.

Overall, Prohibition was a disaster causing many unexpected problems. Besides leading to widespread disrespect for the criminal justice system and creating extremely wealthy criminals, Prohibition cost the lives of many police officers in shootouts with criminals, the deaths of citizens drinking bootlegged alcohol containing poisonous chemicals, thousands of lost jobs in breweries and the wine industry, and massive law enforcement expenses.

By 1930 various organizations opposed to Prohibition joined together to form the Association Against the Prohibition Amendment. Their common goal was to repeal Prohibition. They drafted the Twenty-first Amendment and submitted it to Congress in February 1933 to begin the ratification process.

With the arrival of the Democratic Party to the White House in March 1933 led by Franklin D. Roosevelt

(1882–1945; served 1933–45), the failed experiment in Prohibition officially ended. Roosevelt immediately cut government funds for Prohibition enforcement and pressed Congress to pass a bill raising the permissible alcohol content for beverages to begin beer production. The beer act was passed on April 7, 1933. Some two hundred breweries began operation.

The Twenty-first Amendment was ratified on December 5, 1933, and added to the Constitution repealing the Eighteenth Amendment. Caught in the grips of the Great Depression (1929–41), the government desperately needed the tax revenues it could earn from alcohol production and sales, the creation of jobs, and the decreased costs of law enforcement.

Organized crime leaders had to find a new means of making money. They turned to loan-sharking (charging very high interest rates on loans), labor racketeering, and drug trafficking. By the end of the twentieth century drug trafficking, a natural extension of Prohibition, was organized crime's biggest business.

A woman places a tire cover promoting the appeal of the Eighteenth Amendment over a spare tire. The Eighteenth Amendment made all alcoholic beverages illegal and created more social problems than it was intended to prevent. *(The Library of Congress)*

Did you know . . .

- Only about one-third of the adult population was willing to abstain from alcohol during Prohibition; instead, drinking became a symbol of independence and sophistication.

- In the first few years of Prohibition most illegal alcohol came from private home stills (distilleries, to distill and produce alcohol), while all necessary supplies were easily available at most stores. Organized crime groups, however, eventually took over most production.

- Public intoxication remains a crime as well as having an open container of alcohol while in public. Drinking and driving laws have steadily become more severe in enforcement and punishment.

- Intoxication cannot be used as a defense in a criminal trial for committing some other crime.

Consider the following . . .

- Given the high costs of drug enforcement and the lack of success, some want to end the prohibition on illegal drugs and regulate drugs like alcohol. What would the effects be of such an effort? How would the rate of drug use change? Would organized crime decrease? Would government taxes on drugs be helpful in funding drug treatment programs?

- What were the problems law officials faced in enforcing Prohibition? Would there be more effective ways of enforcing it today?

- What led the promoters of Prohibition to believe the nation would readily accept the ban? Research the history of your local community in the 1920s. How did it respond to Prohibition?

For More Information

Books

Behr, Edward. *Prohibition: Thirteen Years That Changed America*. New York: Arcade Publishing, 1996.

Kobler, John. *Capone: The Life and World of Al Capone*. New York: G. P. Putnam's Sons, 1971.

Kyvig, David E. *Repealing National Prohibition*. Chicago, IL: University of Chicago Press, 1979.

Pegram, Thomas R. *Battling Demon Rum: The Struggle for a Dry America, 1800–1933*. Chicago, IL: Ivan R. Dee, 1998.

Rose, Kenneth D. *American Women and the Repeal of Prohibition*. New York: New York University Press, 1996.

Web Sites

Court TV's Crime Library: Criminal Minds and Methods. http://www.crime library.com (accessed on August 19, 2004).

"Temperance and Prohibition." *Ohio State University Department of History*. http://prohibition.history.ohio-state.edu (accessed on August 19, 2004).

4

Capital Punishment

Execution as a criminal punishment has been a part of U.S. history since the early colonial days of the seventeenth century. It is a story of changing methods based on what the public considers the most effective deterrent to future criminals, as well as what is considered sufficiently humane. There is also a long history of debate over the morality of taking human lives.

Capital punishments were harsh in colonial times. Though hanging was the most common method of execution, other methods—including burning alive, beheadings, and being crushed under a stack of stones—were also used. Whipping was the most common form of noncapital punishment. All of these punishments were carried out in public places and witnessed by large crowds. By the early nineteenth century hanging became the accepted form of execution over the more brutal types since the U.S. Constitution's Eighth Amendment prohibited cruel and unusual punishment. Executions were also moved out of public viewing and into the newly built state prisons.

Execution continues to be among the most controversial moral issues in criminal justice. Many considered hanging an

Capital punishment has always been a part of U.S. history, though less brutal and more humane methods have been sought over the years.
(© Corbis)

inhumane form of execution. Depending on the nature of the rope, weight of the convict, the distance of the drop, and various other factors much could go wrong, including gruesome beheadings. A movement to abolish capital punishment began in the 1830s, and after a lull during the American Civil War (1861–65; war in the United States between the Union [North], who was opposed to slavery, and the Confederacy [South], who was in favor of slavery) gained momentum again in the 1870s.

During the 1870s scientists were experimenting with the recent discovery of electricity, which led to construction of the first power plant in 1879. For the first time a useful form of electric power was available to communities. Competition grew between Thomas Edison and George Westinghouse in early electric energy development through the 1880s. By 1888 a more reliable power supply was being delivered to cities. After witnessing accidental electrocutions of animals and people, some immediately believed electricity could be the means to painless and swift deaths to replace hangings.

New York State adopted electrocution as its means of execution and it became law on January 1, 1889. Those supporting the death penalty believed electrocution would counter opponents' arguments that the death penalty was inhumane.

The first excerpt, "Far Worse Than Hanging," gives a vivid account of the first execution by electrocution. The debate over the humaneness of execution was in the forefront of the newspaper reporter's mind in writing his account of the execution, which did not go smoothly. Despite the flaws in the execution of William Kemmler, the death penalty persisted in the United States and by the 1920s had gained renewed support.

The second excerpt, "The Plea of Clarence Darrow," provides parts from what many consider the most eloquent speech against capital punishment ever delivered. The courtroom plea was made by famous defense lawyer Clarence Darrow, who represented two young men, Nathan Leopold and Richard Loeb, at their murder trial.

William Kemmler

Excerpt from "Far Worse Than Hanging"
Reprinted from the *New York Times*
Published in the August 7, 1890, edition, on the front page

"Probably no convicted murderer of modern times has been made to suffer as Kemmler suffered."

News reporter covering Kemmler's execution

William Kemmler was a vegetable peddler in the slums of Buffalo, New York. An alcoholic, on March 29, 1888, he was recovering from a drinking binge the night before when he became enraged with his girlfriend, Tillie Ziegler. He accused her of stealing from him and preparing to runaway with a friend of his. When the argument reached a peak, Kemmler calmly went to the barn, grabbed a hatchet, and returned to the house. He struck Tillie repeatedly, killing her. He then went to a neighbor's house and announced he had just murdered his girlfriend.

Kemmler's resulting murder trial proceeded quickly. He was convicted of first-degree murder on May 10. Three days later he was sentenced to death, destined to be the first person executed in an electric chair under New York's new execution law replacing hanging with electrocution. A chair was ready at the Auburn state prison. The leading developers of electrical power, including George Westinghouse, did not want to see their new product used in this manner. A lawyer filed an appeal claiming the electric chair violated the Eighth Amendment's prohibition of cruel and unusual punishment.

At the appeal hearing on July 9, lawyers asserted that electricity was unpredictable. What might kill one person might not be enough to kill another. Attorneys for the state countered that as long as good contact with the offender's skin was made with the two electrodes, death would be swift and painless given enough voltage. Three months later on October 9 the judge ruled in favor of the state. Kemmler's lawyer then appealed to the State Court of appeals and a hearing was set for February 25, 1890. The appeals court quickly ruled in favor of the state. This decision was then appealed to the U.S. Supreme Court, which accepted the case.

On May 21 the Supreme Court heard arguments in the case as to whether electrocution was constitutionally valid or not. Two days later on May 23 Chief Justice Melville Fuller delivered the Court's opinion, denying Kemmler's appeal. In a landmark decision the Court upheld the constitutionality of the electric chair in capital punishment. The execution date was set for August 6, 1890, at 6:00 A.M.

On execution day Kemmler dressed in a suit provided for him and was escorted to the execution chamber in the basement of New York's Auburn prison where the electric chair awaited him. A group of twenty-five witnesses were assembled to view the execution, including fourteen doctors to evaluate the electrocution process. The proceedings seemed strangely casual as Kemmler took off his coat and sat in the chair after being introduced to the witnesses in the room. He was strapped into the chair with a series of leather straps around his arms, waist, and legs.

One electrode, a wooden cap with a metal plate and wet sponge in its center, was strapped on his head. The wet sponge ensured electrical current flow. A second similar electrode was

An electric chair used to execute criminals condemned to death. After its discovery, electricity was used to replace older, less humane forms of execution—though many critics today see it as cruel and unusual punishment. *(© Bettmann/Corbis)*

placed on Kemmler's spine at the lower back. The electric current would pass from one electrode to the other when the power was turned on. A black cloth was placed over his head.

As reported by the newsman, once the new Westinghouse generator had revved up to 2,000 volts, the executioner pulled a switch sending the current into Kemmler's body. Kemmler turned bright red and went into convulsions (uncontrollable seizures). After seventeen seconds the current was stopped. To the horror of all of those present, however, Kemmler was not dead. He appeared to groan and struggle to breathe. Quickly the order was given to electrocute him once more, but they had to wait briefly for the generator to power up. This time the current was turned on for over a minute. Witnesses smelled burning flesh and heard odd crackling sounds. When Kemmler appeared dead, the current was turned off.

Things to remember while reading excerpts from "Far Worse Than Hanging":

- The adoption of electrocution as a means for carrying out death penalties in New York was first introduced by the state's governor in 1885. A commission studied the proposal and issued a report recommending the adoption of electrocution in January 1888.

- A debate had been raging over the use of direct current or alternating current in homes and businesses through the 1880s. Many believed alternating current would be much more reliable and effective in killing a person. Alternating current was selected for the Auburn electric chair.

- Officials were eager to adopt electrocution as a means of execution, believing it would be much quicker and effective, countering arguments of those who opposed the death penalty on the grounds that it was cruel and inhumane.

Excerpt from "Far Worse Than Hanging"

Coterie of cranks: Promoters of the electric chair.

*Auburn, N.Y., Aug. 6.—A sacrifice to the whims and theories of the **coterie of cranks** and politicians who induced the Legislature of* *this State to pass a law supplanting hanging by electrical execution as offered today in the person of William Kemmler, the Buffalo murderer. He died this morning under the most revolting circumstances, and with his death there was placed to the discredit of the State of New York an execution that was a disgrace to civilization.*

Probably no convicted murderer of modern times has been made to suffer as Kemmler suffered. Unfortunate enough to be the first man convicted after the passage of the new execution law, his life has been used as the bone of contention between the alleged humanitarians who supported the law, on one side, and the electric-light interests, who hated to see the commodity in which they deal reduced to such a use as taking a life. For fifteen months they have been fighting as to whether he should be killed or not, and the question has been dragged through every court. He has been sentenced and resentenced to death, only to be dragged back from the **abyss** *by some* **intricacy** *of the law.*

The uncertainty in which he has so long lived would have driven any ordinary man insane. That suffering has culminated in a death so fearful that people throughout the country will read of it with horror and disgust.

The execution cannot merely be characterized as unsuccessful. It was so terrible that the word fails to convey the idea. It was, as those who advocated it desired that it should be, attended by men eminent in science and in medicine, and they almost unanimously say that this single experiment warrants the prompt repeal of the law. The opinion is further expressed that the public will demand its repeal, and that it is the first and last electrical execution that this State will ever witness. As might have been expected, such of the so-called humanitarians as witnessed Kemmler's fearful death still insist that their hobby will be a success "under proper conditions." The publication of the scenes that were enacted in the death room will probably prevent them from ever having another opportunity to prove their assertion.

Fortunately there was no difficulty in getting the full details of the affair, despite the fact that the advocates of the law attempted to do their work concealed from the eyes of the public.

WAITING FOR THE EVENT

By 4 o'clock this morning people were astir on the streets, and an hour later the street in front of the prison contained not less than 500 people. At 6 o'clock it was almost impossible to force a passage

Abyss: Bottomless depths.

Intricacy: Detail.

through the throng. Every eye that could be pressed to the openings between the bars of the gate was directed toward the window which lighted Kemmler's cell. . . .

As the morning wore on and the time for the execution drew near, the trees and housetops in the vicinity began to be peopled. Young men climbed telegraph poles and gazed eagerly toward the vine-clad prison. Men and women on their way to their daily labor joined the crowd at the entrance. The platform of the railway station across the street was black with people, and the temporary office of the Western Union Telegraph Company, which had been established in the freight station directly opposite the prison, showed many expectant faces. Just before 7 o'clock it seemed as if all Auburn had congregated in the immediate neighborhood of the prison. . . .

KEMMLER SAYS HE IS READY

In the meantime Warden Durston had arisen and had gone to the cell of the condemned man. He carried with him the death warrant, and he read it to Kemmler as the latter sat on the side of his bunk. Kemmler's sole remark when the Warden had finished reading was: "All right, I am ready." The Warden then left the cell, and in the entrance hall above met the witnesses who had accepted his invitation. . . .

There was a very apparent nervousness among the men, used as most of them are to sights that would chill ordinary men's blood. The uncertainty of what was to come filled them with awe. Somebody attempted to speak, but his voice was lost in its own faintness. A step was heard outside. All eyes turned toward the door leading into the chamber. Warden Durston appeared, and beside him was the man who stood on the verge of an awful death. Yet there was nothing in his appearance to suggest this. His face was composed and he walked in an easy manner as though he were entering a room to receive a party of friends.

After he had crossed the threshold there was for an instant the deadest silence. It was broken by Warden Durston.

"Gentlemen," he said, "this is William Kemmler." And Kemmler bowed.

"Gentlemen," [Kemmler] said, "I wish you all good luck. I believe I am going to a good place, and I am ready to go. I want only to say that a great deal has been said about me that is untrue. I am bad enough. It is cruel to make me out worse."

As he finished this little speech, he bowed again, and was about to sit down in a chair which had been placed beside the death chair. Warden Durston, seeing this, stepped forward, and Kemmler, noticing his action, saw that the time had come, and instead of sitting where he had intended, turned and easily dropped into the seat. Still he did it much as one might after a long walk fall into the welcome arms of an easy chair. He sat with the light from the window streaming full on his face, and immediately in front of him was the semicircle of witnesses. Warden Durston stepped to the chair, and at his request Kemmler arose. It was desired to see whether his clothing had been so cut away at the base of the spine as to allow of a clean contact between the electrode and the flesh. It was found that the outer garments had been cut, but the lower clothing had not been so. Durston took out a pocket knife and cut two small triangular pieces out of the shirt.

Then Kemmler easily settled back into the chair again. As he did so Durston started to get the rear piece in position. A murmur of surprise passed among the witnesses when Kemmler turned calmly to the Warden and in such tones as one might speak to a barber who was shaving him, said calmly: "Now take your time and do it all right, Warden. There is no rush. I don't want to take any chances on this thing, you know."

"All right, William," answered Durston, and then began to adjust the headpiece. It looked horrible with its leather bands crossing the doomed man's forehead and chin and partially concealing his features. When the job was finished Durston stepped back. Kemmler shook his head as one might when trying on a new hat, and then just as coolly as before said; "Warden, just make that a little tighter. We want everything all right, you know."

The Warden did as requested and then started to fix the straps around the body, arms, and legs. There were eleven of them. As each was buckled Kemmler would put some strain on it so as to see if it was right enough. . . . The last minute had come.

THE FATAL CURRENT TURNED ON

Standing on the threshold he turned and said quietly: "Is all ready?" Nobody spoke. Kemmler merely lifted his eyes and for a moment turned them enough to catch a glimpse of the bright, warm sunlight that was streaming through the window of the death chamber.

"Goodbye, William," said Durston, and a click was heard. The "good-bye" was the signal to the men at the lever. The great

experiment of electrical execution had been launched. New York State had thrown off forever the barbarities, the inhumanities of hanging its criminals. But had it? Words will not keep pace with what followed. Simultaneously with the click of the lever the body of the man in the chair straightened. Every muscle of it seemed to be drawn to its highest tension. It seemed as though it might have been thrown across the chamber were it not for the straps which held it. There was no movement of the eyes. The body was as rigid as though cast in bronze, save for the index finger of the right hand, which closed up so tightly that the nail penetrated the flesh on the first joint, and the blood trickled out on the arm of the chair. Drs. Spitzka and Macdonald stood in front of the chair, closely watching the dead or dying man. Beside them was Dr. Daniels, holding a stop-watch.

After the first convulsion there was not the slightest movement of Kemmler's body. An ashen pallor had overspread his features. What physicians know as the "death spots" appeared on his skin. Five seconds passed, ten seconds, fifteen seconds, sixteen, and seventeen. It was just 6:43 o'clock. Dr. Spitzka, shaking his head, said: "He is dead." Warden Durston pressed the signal button, and at once the **dynamo** was stopped. The assembled witnesses who had sat as still as mutes up to this point gave breath to a sigh. The great strain was over. Then the eyes that had been momentarily turned from Kemmler's body returned to it and gazed with horror on what they saw. The men rose from their chairs impulsively and groaned at the agony they felt. "Great God! He is alive!" someone said: "Turn on the current," said another; "See, he breathes," said a third: "For God's sake kill him and have it over,' said a representative of one of the press associations, and then, unable to bear the strain, he fell on the floor in a dead faint. District Attorney Quimby groaned audibly and rushed from the room.

Drs. Spitzka and Macdonald stepped toward the chair. Warden Durston, who had started to loosen the electrode on the head, raised it slightly and then hastily screwed it back into place. Kemmler's body had become limp and settled down in the chair. His chest was raising and falling and there was a heavy breathing that was perceptible to all. Kemmler was, of course, entirely unconscious. Drs. Spitzka and Macdonald kept their wits about them. Hastily they examined the man, not touching him, however. Turning to Warden Durston, who had just finished getting the head electrode back in place, Dr. Spitzka said: "Have the current turned on again, quick—no delay.' Durston sprang to the door, and in an instant had sounded the two

Dynamo: Electric generator.

bells, which informed the man at the lever that the current must be turned on.

THE CURRENT TURNED ON AGAIN

Again came that click as before, and again the body of the unconscious wretch in the chair became as rigid as one of bronze. It was awful, and the witnesses were so horrified by the ghastly sight that they could not take their eyes off it. The dynamo did not seem to run smoothly. The current could be heard sharply snapping. Blood began to appear on the face of the wretch in the chair. It stood on the face like sweat.

The capillary or small blood vessels under the skin were being ruptured. But there was worse than that. An awful odor began to permeate the death chamber, and then, as though to cap the climax of this fearful sight, it was seen that the hair under and around the electrode on the head and the flesh under and around the electrode at the base of the spine was singeing. The stench was unbearable.

How long this second execution lasted—for it was a second execution, if there was any real life in the body when the current was turned on for the second time—is not really known by anybody. Those who held watches were too much horrified to follow them. Some said afterward that it lasted a minute. One said it lasted fully four minutes and a half. Opinions ranged all the way between those figures. Dr. Spitzka, who was as cool as any man could be under such circumstances, says it was not more than a minute. It was 6:51 o'clock when the signal went to the man at the lever to shut off the current. Kemmler had been in the chair just eight minutes from the time the current was first turned on. There is nobody among the witnesses present who can tell just how much of that time the current was passing through the body of Kemmler.

As soon as the current was off again Warden Durston rapidly unscrewed the electrodes and unbuckled the straps. Kemmler's body again was limp. This time he was surely dead. There was no doubt of that. The body was left sitting upright in the chair, and the witnesses of the tragedy that had been enacted passed out into the stone corridors as miserable, as weak-kneed a lot of men as can be imagined. It had nauseated all but a few of them, and the sick ones had to be looked out for. They were all practically silent for some time. Their minds were too busy to enable them to talk. They all seemed to act as though they felt that they had taken part in a scene that would be told to the world as a public shame, as a legal crime. . . .

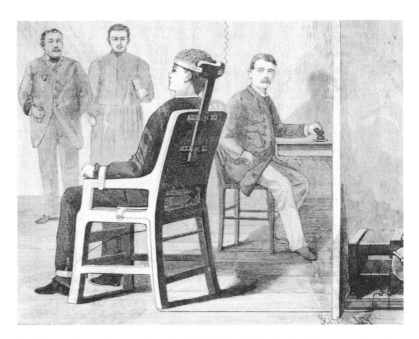

An illustration of execution by electricity. This illustration was done in 1888—two years before William Kemmler was to be the first person executed by such means. *(© Bettmann/Corbis)*

DR. JENKINS'S DESCRIPTION.

There can be no doubt that the result was unsatisfactory to Deputy Coroner Jenkins of New York. He was one of the first to leave the prison for the Osborne House, and when THE TIMES's correspondent talked with him he was visibly unnerved by his recent experience. . . .

"How did it compare with a hanging?"

"I would rather see ten hangings than one such execution as this. In fact I never care to witness such a scene again. It was fearful. No humane man could witness it without the keenest agony. I am not an electrician, but I have a considerable insight into electrical matters. Electricity applied as it was today will never serve as an executioner, and yet it is my honest belief that things might have been a thousand times worse than they were, though it seems almost impossible that they could be. Today the apparatus was defective to a standpoint that approached carelessness. Even had it been perfect, we cannot say now any better than we could a week or a year ago that it would do its work as it should be done. I don't think that

Kemmler was dead when the current was applied the second time, but he was unconscious."

"Do you think that electrical executions will continue?"

"That is not for me to say. We shall be able to tell pretty quick when the facts concerning Kemmler's death are read by the public.". . .

Dr. Lewis Balch, Secretary of the State Board of Health, said: "With many others I was asked by the commission to give my views as to the best of the modes of execution—electricity, hanging, or guillotine. Personally I was in favor of hanging, but having seen the absolute certainty, rapidity, and painlessness with which death can be caused by electricity, my opinions have been changed to favor that mode of legal execution. I do not consider that the failure of the first shock to cause instant death is any proof that this method of execution is futile, for from the first shock the prisoner was virtually dead, suffered no pain, and had no return to consciousness. I think there should be one electrician appointed who would attend all executions and have charge of all electrical apparatus, under the supervision of the officers delegated by law to carry the sentence into effect."

What happened next . . .

A number of witnesses to Kemmler's execution were deeply troubled and shaken by what they saw. The media coverage of the execution was extensive and portrayed a wide range of emotions. Some were sensational, even falsely reporting that flames shot from Kemmler's mouth. As a result, a public push in New York for prohibiting electrocutions rose but proved ineffective. The state legislature stood behind the new law. Thomas Edison and others claimed that more powerful generators in future executions would avoid the problems of Kemmler's execution.

The next execution by electric chair came soon in the spring of 1891. Four convicted murders, each for a different crime, were executed at New York's Sing Sing Prison. The revamped generator was able to produce a steady high voltage current. The lower electrodes were placed on the inmates'

Capital Punishment Around the World

By the early 2000s the United States was the only Western democracy and one of only two highly developed countries in the world maintaining the death penalty. Japan was the other. Western European countries began abolishing capital punishment in the 1940s through the 1970s. Eastern and Central European countries abolished capital punishment in the 1990s as the control of the Soviet Union ended. The newly established European Union in the 1990s required that countries abolish capital punishment in order to qualify for membership. Other developed countries abolishing capital punishment in the late twentieth century included Australia, Canada, and New Zealand. Nations still using the death penalty, in addition to the United States and Japan, include China, Middle Eastern countries, and African countries.

calves rather than on their spines. With much smoother operation in these executions, acceptance of the electric chair grew.

New York State used the electric chair for seventy-two more years, executing 695 convicts. Other states adopted electrocution as well to carry out death sentences. The change over to electric chairs, however, was not uniform. Some states still used hanging into the 1950s.

Other states, including California and Arizona, never adopted the electric chair. They eventually switched to use of cyanide gas in gas chambers to replace hanging. Delaware, New Hampshire, and Washington still offered hanging as an option at the end of the twentieth century. Through early 2003 a total of 4,458 people had been executed in the electric chair after Kemmler.

Did you know . . .

- More problems occurred while conducting electrocutions through the years. As late as March 1997 flames actually spewed out from under the electrode helmet on a convict's head, lasting for ten seconds to the horror of witnesses.

- The first woman executed in the electric chair was Martha Place on March 20, 1899, in New York's Sing Sing Prison for the murder of her stepdaughter. Twenty-three more women were executed in the electric chair through the twentieth century.

- In 1977 executions by lethal injection (an injection of powerful drugs) began with Texas carrying out the first execution of this means. By the early 1980s more states switched to lethal injections, claiming it was more humane than electrocutions.

- By the end of the twentieth century the number of electrocutions had dwindled but still persisted in some states. Three of ninety-eight executions in 1999 involved the electric chair as did five out of eighty-five executions in 2000. No electrocutions occurred in 2001 and only one in 2002.

- In the early 2000s only Alabama and Nebraska had electrocution as their only means of execution.

- New medical evidence in the late twentieth century indicated that death by electrocution was not as immediate and painless as thought in 1890.

Consider the following . . .
- The electric chair replaced hanging as the preferred method of execution. Divide the class into two groups and debate the merits of both in regard to the Eighth Amendment banning cruel and unusual punishment.

- Is the death penalty used in your state? If so, what are the capital punishment laws? How many executions have there been in the past twenty years and what means of execution was used?

- At the end of the excerpt, two contrasting opinions were reported in the news article. What are they and which prevailed through time?

For More Information

Books

Baird, Robert M., and Stuart E. Rosenbaum. *Punishment and the Death Penalty: The Current Debate.* Amherst, NY: Prometheus Books, 1995.

Bedau, Hugo A., ed. *Death Penalty in America: Current Controversies.* New York: Oxford University Press, 1997.

Brandon, Craig. *The Electric Chair: An Unnatural American History.* Jefferson, NC: McFarland & Company, 1990.

Web Sites

"Death Penalty." *American Civil Liberties Union.* http://www.aclu.org/DeathPenalty/DeathPenaltyMain.cfm (accessed on August 19, 2004).

Death Penalty Information Center. http://www.deathpenaltyinfo.org (accessed on August 19, 2004).

Clarence Darrow

Excerpt from "The Plea of Clarence Darrow"
Reprinted from *The Amazing Crime and Trial of Leopold and Loeb,*
edited by Maureen McKernan
Published in 1996

"When the public is interested and demands a punishment, no matter what the offense, great or small, it thinks of only one punishment, and that is death."

Richard Loeb and Nathan Leopold were nineteen years old, exceptionally bright students, and from wealthy families. Loeb was a handsome University of Chicago student and Leopold an ornithologist (person who studies birds). The Leopolds were wealthy German Jewish immigrants who made their fortune shipping grains and minerals on the Great Lakes.

Nathan entered college at age sixteen and graduated from University of Chicago in 1923 with high honors. He was taking law classes with plans to attend Harvard Law School. Richard's father was a millionaire executive in charge of the massive Sears-Roebuck mail order business. Richard was a brilliant child, graduating from high school at age fourteen and becoming one of the youngest graduates in University of Michigan history, at age seventeen.

Their lives, however, would take a dramatic and tragic turn on Wednesday, May 21, 1924. That afternoon Bobby Franks, fourteen years of age, was walking home from school when Richard Loeb and Nathan Leopold pulled up in a rental car and offered him a ride. Bobby knew both the nineteen-year-olds since they all three lived in a wealthy neighborhood of

118

Nathan Leopold (center left) and Richard Loeb (center right), convicted of kidnapping and murdering a fourteen-year-old, leave the county jail in Chicago, January 28, 1936. *(AP/Wide World Photos)*

Chicago known as Kenwood, and Loeb was Bobby's neighbor. As soon as Bobby was in the car they hit him over the head with a heavy metal chisel and stuffed a piece of cloth down his throat suffocating him.

While waiting for dark Leopold and Loeb had dinner at a hotdog stand. They then drove to Wolf Lake, took the boy's clothes off, poured hydrochloric acid over him to obscure his identity, and dumped the body in a culvert. On their way back to town, they mailed a ransom note to Franks home demanding $10,000. The note provided instructions on how to deliver the money. They warned about contacting authorities and not following instructions. They went to Loeb's house where they burned bloodstained clothes and tried taking any bloodstains out of their rental car. The two young men then stayed up late that night playing a game.

The special delivery ransom letter arrived the following morning at the Franks' residence. A phone call from Loeb and Leopold to Bobby's father Jacob gave further instructions on how to deliver the money to a particular drugstore address. In the confusion, Jacob forgot the address of the drugstore mentioned and was unable to carry through with the delivery. Later that same day the body of a boy, identified as Bobby, was found in a culvert at Wolf Lake.

Rewards for the capture of the murderer quickly mounted. Police investigators and newspaper reporters searched for clues. It was discovered that a pair of glasses found near the body of Franks had an unusual hinge. Sales records showed that only three had been sold in the Chicago area, one to Leopold. When approached by authorities, however, he explained that he often bird-watched in the area and the glasses had recently fallen out of his pocket there.

On May 29, 1924, both Leopold and Loeb were detained and questioned separately by authorities at the La Salle Hotel. They avoided the police station because of the intense media coverage. Though their stories did not match perfectly, police were unable to build a case and finally let them go. Newspaper investigators discovered much more substantial evidence. The type on the ransom note matched a portable typewriter that Loeb had sometimes used.

Faced with the new evidence, Leopold and Loeb confessed to the murder and kidnapping, and told their story. They

Nathan Leopold (left) and Richard Loeb (right) with attorney Clarence Darrow (center). Seeking life in prison instead of death, the two men hired Darrow, a staunch opponent of the death penalty, after confessing to the abduction and brutal murder of fourteen-year-old **Bobby Franks.** *(© Bettmann/Corbis)*

readily revealed the kidnapping had been planned for months as a legal challenge to the two bored students. Through the following days the two young men took police to locations where they found various pieces of evidence including the chisel.

The case was a major story in the newspapers. The public demanded swift trials and executions. To this point, the boys were not represented by lawyers during the questioning. Albert Loeb went to sixty-seven-year-old Clarence Darrow, known for his personal opposition to the death penalty. Loeb sought a life sentence rather than death penalties.

On June 5, 1924, a grand jury indicted Leopold and Loeb for murder and kidnapping. The following day their full confessions were published in the Chicago newspapers. The trial began on July 21. Darrow immediately stunned the court by changing their pleas from not guilty to guilty. Everyone had assumed he would be using a defense of not guilty by reason of insanity. Darrow knew a not guilty plea would lead to a trial by jury; given the confessions and evidence, he figured a jury would be more likely to sentence his clients to death than Judge John R. Caverly. On August 22, 1924, Darrow made his impassioned two hour speech against the death penalty.

Things to remember while reading excerpts from "The Plea of Clarence Darrow":

- The fact that Leopold and Loeb had already confessed and told their stories in detail to the police, including leading them to evidence, already established that they had indeed killed Franks.

- The public and the media were strongly pressing for a quick trial and execution.

- A key reason famed attorney Clarence Darrow accepted the case was because it gave him a unique opportunity to present his arguments against the death penalty before the media.

- The two young men were pampered while in jail awaiting trial. A local restaurant provided catering service including food, cigarettes, and even liquor though this was in the midst of Prohibition when the possession and sale of alcoholic beverages was illegal.

- Hanging was the key means of execution in Illinois where the trial was being held.

Excerpt from "The Plea of Clarence Darrow"

Your Honor, it has been almost three months since the great responsibility of this case was assumed by my associates and myself. I am willing to confess that it has been three months of great anxiety. . . .

*Our anxiety over this case has not been due to the facts that are connected with this most unfortunate affair, but to the almost unheard of publicity it has received; to the fact that newspapers all over this country have been giving it space such as they have almost never before given to any case. The fact that day after day the people of Chicago have been **regaled** with stories of all sorts about it, until almost every person has formed an opinion.*

And when the public is interested and demands a punishment, no matter what the offense, great or small, it thinks of only one punishment, and that is death.

*It may not be a question that involves the taking of human life; it may be a question of pure **prejudice** alone; but when the public speaks as one man it thinks only of killing. . . .*

I told your Honor in the beginning that never had there been a case in Chicago, where on a plea of guilty a boy under twenty-one had been sentenced to death. I will raise that age and say, never has there been a case where a human being under the age of twenty-three has been sentenced to death. And, I think I am safe in saying, although I have not examined all the records and could not—but I think I am safe in saying—that never has there been such a case in the State of Illinois.

And yet this court is urged, aye, threatened, that [it] must hang two boys contrary to precedents, contrary to the acts of every judge who ever held court in this state.

Why?

Tell me what public necessity there is for this.

Why need the State's Attorney ask for something that never before has been demanded?

Why need a judge be urged by every argument, moderate and immoderate, to hang two boys in the face of every precedent in Illinois, and in the face of the progress of the last fifty years?. . .

You may stand them up on the trap-door of the scaffold, and choke them to death, but that act will be infinitely more cold-blooded whether justified or not, than any act that these boys have committed or can commit.

Cold-blooded!

Regaled: Amused.

Prejudice: Opinion already established.

Let the State, who is so anxious to take these boys' lives, set an example in consideration, kindheartedness and tenderness before they call my clients cold-blooded.

I have heard this crime described; this most distressing and unfortunate homicide, as I would call it—this cold-blooded murder, as the State would call it.

I call it a homicide particularly distressing because I am defending.

They call it a cold-blooded murder because they want to take human lives.

Call it what you will. . . .

They say that this was a cruel murder, the worst that ever happened. I say that very few murders ever occurred that were as free from cruelty as this.

There ought to be some rule to determine whether a murder is exceedingly cruel or not. . . .

But I would say the first thing to consider is the degree of pain to the victim.

Poor little Bobby Franks suffered very little. There is no excuse for his killing. If to hang these two boys would bring him back to life, I would say let them go, and I believe their parents would say so, too. . . .

Robert Franks is dead, and we cannot call him back to life. It was all over in fifteen minutes after he got into the car, and he probably never knew it or thought of it. That does not justify it. It is the last thing I would do. I am sorry for the poor boy. I am sorry for his parents. But, it is done. . . .

This is a senseless, useless, purposeless, motiveless act of two boys. Now, let me see if I can prove it. There was not a particle of hate, there was not a grain of malice, there was no opportunity to be cruel except as death is cruel—and death is cruel. . . .

Three hundred and forty murder cases in ten years with a plea of guilty in this county. All the young who pleaded guilty—every one of them, three hundred and forty in ten years with one hanging on a plea of guilty, and that a man forty years of age. And yet they say we come here with a preposterous plea for mercy. When did any plea for mercy become preposterous in a tribunal in all the universe?. . .

I have faith that this court [the judge] will take this case, with his conscience, and his judgment and his courage and save these boys' lives. . . .

What about this matter of crime and punishment, anyhow? I may know less than the rest, but I have at least tried to find out, and I am fairly familiar with the best literature that has been written on that subject in the last hundred years. The more men study, the more they doubt the effect of severe punishment on crime. And yet Mr. Savage [the prosecutor] tells this court that if these boys are hanged, there will be no more murder.

Mr. Savage is an optimist. He says that if the defendants are hanged there will be no more boys like these.

I could give him a sketch of punishment. . . . You can trace it all down through the history of man. You can trace the burnings, the boiling, the drawings and quarterings, the hanging of people in England at the crossroads, carving them up and hanging them as examples for all to see.

We can come down to the last century when nearly two hundred crimes were punishable by death, and by death in every form; not only hanging—that was too humane—but burning, boiling, cutting into pieces, torturing in all conceivable forms.

You can read the stories of the hangings on a high hill, and the populace for miles around coming out to the scene, that everybody might be awed into goodness. Hanging for picking pockets—and more pockets were picked in the crowd that went to the hanging than had been known before. Hangings for murder—and men were murdered on the way there and on the way home. Hangings for poaching, hangings for everything and hangings in public, not shut up cruelly and brutally in a jail, out of the light of day, wakened in the night time and led forth and killed, but taken to the shire town on a high hill, in the presence of a multitude, so that all might see that the wages of sin were death. . . .

Gradually the laws have been changed and modified, and men look back with horror at the hangings and the killings of the past. What did they find in England? That as they got rid of these barbarous statutes crimes decreased instead of increased; as the criminal law was modified and humanized, there was less crime instead of more. I will undertake to say, your Honor, that you can scarcely find a single book written by a student—and I will include all the works on criminology of the past—that has not made the statement over and over again that as the penal code was made less terrible crimes grew less frequent. . . .

If these two boys die on the scaffold, which I can never bring myself to imagine—if they do die on the scaffold, the details of this will be spread over the world. Every newspaper in the United States will carry a full account. Every newspaper of Chicago will be filled with the gruesome details. It will enter every home and every family.

Will it make men better or make men worse? I would like to put that to the intelligence of man, at least such intelligence as they have. I would like to appeal to the feelings of human beings so far as they have feelings—would it make the human heart softer or would it make hearts harder? How many men would be colder and crueler for it? How many men would enjoy the details, and you cannot enjoy human suffering without being affected for better or for worse; those who enjoyed it would be affected for the worse.

What influence would it have upon the millions of men who will read it? What influence would it have upon the millions of women who will read it, more sensitive, more impressionable, more imaginative than men? Would it help them if your Honor should do what the state begs you to do? What influence would it have upon the infinite number of children who will devour its details as Dicky Loeb has enjoyed reading detective stories? Would it make them better or would it make them worse? The question needs no answer. You can answer it from the human heart. What influence, let me ask you, will it have for the unborn babes still sleeping in their mother's womb? And what influence will it have on the psychology of the fathers and mothers yet to come? Do I need to argue to your Honor that cruelty only breeds cruelty?—that hatred only causes hatred; that if there is any way to soften this human heart which is hard enough at its best, if there is any way to kill evil and hatred and all that goes with it, it is not through evil and hatred and cruelty; it is through charity, and love and understanding. . . .

We have raised the age of hanging. We have raised it by the humanity of courts, by the understanding of courts, by the progress in science which at last is reaching the law; and in ninety men hanged in Illinois from its beginning, not one single person under twenty-three was ever hanged upon a plea of guilty—not one. If your Honor should do this, you will violate every precedent that had been set in Illinois for almost a century. There can be no excuse for it, and no justification for it, because this is the policy of the law which is rooted in the feelings of humanity, which are deep in every human being that thinks and feels. There have been two or three cases where juries have convicted boys younger than this, and where courts on convictions have refused to set aside the sentence because a jury had found it. . . .

I do not know how much salvage there is in these two boys. I hate to say it in their presence, but what is there to look forward to? I do not know but what your Honor would be merciful if you tied a rope around their necks and let them die; merciful to them, but not merciful to civilization, and not merciful to those who would be left behind. To spend the balance of their days in prison is mighty little to look forward to, if anything. Is it anything? They may have the hope that as the years roll around they might be released. I do not know. I do not know. I will be honest with this court as I have tried to be from the beginning. I know that these boys are not fit to be at large. I believe they will not be until they pass through the next stage of life, at forty-five or fifty. Whether they will be then, I cannot tell. I am sure of this; that I will not be here to help them. So far as I am concerned, it is over.

I would not tell the court that I do not hope that some time, when life and age has changed their bodies, as it does, and has changed their emotions, as it does—that they may once more return to life. I would be the last person on earth to close the door of hope to any human being that lives, and least of all to my clients. But what have they to look forward to? Nothing. . . .

Criminal defense lawyer Clarence Darrow outside the White House in 1927. With his clients having already confessed to murder, Darrow, known for his oratory skills, successfully pleaded with the judge to refrain from sentencing Loeb and Leopold to death. *(AP/Wide World Photos)*

I care not, Your Honor, whether the march begins at the gallows or when the gates of Joliet close upon them, there is nothing but the night, and that is little for any human being to expect.

But there are others to be considered. Here are these two families, who have led honest lives, who will hear the name that they bear, and future generations must carry it on.

Here is Leopold's father—and this boy was the pride of his life. He watched him, he cared for him, he worked for him; the boy was brilliant and accomplished, he educated him, and he thought that fame and position awaited him, as it should have awaited. It is a hard thing for a father to see his life's hopes crumble into dust.

Should he be considered? Should his brothers be considered? Will it do society any good or make your life safer, or any human being's life safer, if it should be handed down from generation to generation, that this boy, their kin, died upon the scaffold?

And Loeb's, the same. Here is the faithful uncle and brother, who have watched here day by day, while Dickie's father and his mother are too ill to stand this terrific strain, and shall be waiting for a message which means more to them than it can mean to you or me. Shall these be taken into account in this general **bereavement***?*

Have they any rights? Is there any reason, your Honor, why their proud names and all the future generations that bear them shall have this **bar sinister** *written across them? How many boys and girls, how many unborn children will feel it? It is bad enough as it is, God knows. . . . But it's not yet death on the scaffold. It's not that. And I ask your honor, in addition to all that I have said, to have two honorable families from a disgrace that never ends, and which could be of no avail to help any human being that lives. . . .*

I am pleading for life, understanding, charity, kindness, and the infinite mercy that considers all. I am pleading that we overcome cruelty with kindness and hatred with love. I know the future is on my side. Your Honor stands between the past and the future. You may hang these boys; you may hang them by the neck until they are dead. But in doing it you will turn your face toward the past. . . . I am pleading for the future; I am pleading for a time when hatred and cruelty will not control the hearts of men. When we can learn by reason and judgment and understanding and faith that all life is worth saving, and that mercy is the highest attribute of man.

What happened next . . .

The small, stuffy courtroom holding some two hundred news media members and another seventy spectators had just witnessed what many historians regarded the finest oration by Clarence Darrow in his career though he had long been noted for his oratory skills. On September 19 Judge Caverly announced his decision. He accepted Darrow's arguments. Based on the young age of the defendants, Caverly sentenced them to life in prison and recommended no possibility of future parole.

In 1932 Leopold and Loeb opened a school for prisoners making use of their educations and talents in a constructive way. On January 28, 1936, Loeb's cellmate attacked him with a razor blade slashing him over fifty times. He died from loss of blood at thirty-two years of age. Leopold dedicated himself to learning. He learned twenty-seven languages, raised canaries, worked in the prison library, and volunteered for medical experiments. In 1953 he was given a parole hearing but was denied. A second time, however, was successful.

Leopold was paroled in March 1958 after thirty-three years in prison. Also during that year he published an autobiography titled *Life Plus 99 Years*. He moved to Puerto Rico where he obtained a master's degree from the University of Puerto Rico, married, and worked at various jobs. Leopold published a book titled *The Birds of Puerto Rico*. He died of a heart attack in 1971 at the age of sixty-six.

Despite Darrow's pleas against use of the death penalty, capital punishment continued in the United States even though almost all other developed countries had banned capital punishment by the late twentieth century. Over seven thousand executions occurred in the United States during the twentieth century. Some six hundred took place after 1977 with over 80 percent in southern states and 35 percent in Texas alone.

By 2000 two-thirds of all executions were in three states— Texas, Oklahoma, and Virginia. To guarantee fairness, an extensive system of court reviews is provided making the execution process long and complex. Supporters of the death penalty are as dissatisfied with it as opponents; because of the lengthy process inmates sentenced to die sit for years on death row. For this reason the number of death row inmates grew from 220 in 1960 to 3,500 in 2000.

Did you know . . .
- The effect of the trial to participants was pronounced. Judge Caverly and his wife entered a hospital immediately afterwards to recover from exhaustion and strain. He only heard divorce cases in the future.

- The crime and trial took a huge toll on the families; the fathers of Franks, Loeb, and Leopold all died within a few years time by 1929.

- Two of Nathan Leopold's older brothers changed their names to separate themselves from the crime.

- Clarence Darrow went from the fame of this case to his most famous case of all, the Scopes "Monkey' trial in which he defended a Tennessee schoolteacher charged with teaching evolution (that mankind was descended from ape-creatures rather than created by a supreme being) in the classroom.

Consider the following . . .

- Divide the class into two groups and debate the merits of capital punishment. Does it serve a useful purpose in deterring future crime? Use the Internet in your research, using Web sites to support and oppose the death penalty.

- What organizations in your state or community support the death penalty? Which ones oppose the death penalty?

- What is the perception of the death penalty in other countries? How do Europeans view the death penalty?

For More Information

Books

Higdon, Hal. *Crime of the Century: The Leopold & Loeb Case.* New York: G. P. Putnam's Sons, 1975.

Leopold, Nathan F., Jr. *Life Plus 99 Years.* New York: Doubleday, 1958.

McKernan, Maureen. *The Amazing Crime and Trial of Leopold and Loeb.* Holmes Beach, FL: Gaunt, Inc., 1996.

Tierney, Kevin. *Darrow, A Biography.* New York: Thomas Y. Crowell, Publishers, 1979.

Web Sites

"Illinois v. Nathan Leopold and Richard Loeb." *University of Missouri Faculty: Famous Trials.* http://www.law.umkc.edu/faculty/projects/ftrials/leoploeb/leopold.htm (accessed August 19, 2004).

White-Collar and Organized Crime

Two major categories of crime attracted considerable attention from the U.S. criminal justice system during the twentieth century and posed far greater costs to society than usual street crime. They were white-collar crime and organized crime. Both involved illegal activities through enterprises. An enterprise is a group of associated individuals such as a business partnership, corporation, or union. The key difference between the two is that white-collar criminals try to profit off of legitimate businesses in a nonviolent way, while organized crime seeks profits through illegal businesses and frequently employs physical intimidation and violence. In addition, white-collar crime can involve one person or a group of individuals. Organized crime usually employs a large number of crime bosses and members.

White-collar crime is one of the most costly crimes to society. Near the end of the twentieth century white-collar crime was costing U.S. businesses some $400 billion a year, or about 6 percent of total revenue in the nation. White-collar crime is illegal activity conducted within what are normally legal business transactions. They can involve banking, stock trad-

The Sherman Antitrust Act of 1890 was passed to eliminate the power large companies could enact by squashing competition, gaining monopolies, and fixing prices. (© Hulton Archive/Getty Images)

ing, or insurance claims. Unlike organized crime, white-collar crime is not carried out within the framework of illegal activities such as drug trafficking or smuggling. White-collar crime also includes illegal price-fixing.

During the late 1880s business leaders of several major industries brought their companies together to control competition by ruining smaller companies. They would fix prices so low it drove small competitors out of business, then set prices high again after their competitors were eliminated to make large profits. The organizations they formed were called "trusts." The public was outraged by this growing business practice. The first excerpt is from the first key white-collar crime legislation, the Sherman Antitrust Act of 1890. The legislation was effectively applied during the first decade of the twentieth century; the act remains the cornerstone of U.S. antitrust and price-fixing law.

Organized crime did not become high profile until the 1920s when the organizations became incredibly wealthy supplying illegal liquor during Prohibition (1920–33), the thirteen-year period when the distribution, production, sales, and possession of alcoholic beverages was illegal. U.S.-based organized crime continued to prosper for several decades following Prohibition.

In 1965 President Lyndon B. Johnson (1908–1973; served 1963–69) assembled the President's Commission on Law Enforcement and the Administration of Justice, or simply known as the President's Crime Commission. The commission's 1967 report revealed a behind-the-scenes look at the operations of organized crime for the first time.

A key focus was the La Costa Nostra, a network of some two dozen Italian and Sicilian crime families operating in a number of U.S. cities. Congress responded to the commission's findings and pleas from law enforcement authorities by passing legislation giving them the authority they needed to successfully fight organized crime.

The second excerpt is from the Racketeer Influenced and Corrupt Organizations (RICO) Act of 1970. RICO led to many successful prosecutions of crime bosses and members through the 1990s. Most of the U.S.-based organized crime organizations were significantly weakened.

Sherman Antitrust Act

Excerpt from the Sherman Antitrust Act of 1890

Reprinted from *The Statutes at Large and Proclamations of the United States of America from December, 1889, to March, 1891,* **Vol. XXVI**

Published in 1891

"Every contract, combination in the form of trust or otherwise . . . of trade or commerce among the several States, or with foreign nations, is hereby declared illegal."

Since 1890 the Sherman Antitrust Act has been the key law representing America's commitment to a free market economy. A free market economy, one where competition operates free from private or government restraints, assures the best goods and services at the lowest prices for consumers. The Sherman Antitrust Act outlaws any business "combination" or "conspiracy" that unreasonably restrains trade or commerce between states and foreign nations.

In the act, restraining trade or commerce means hindering or preventing competition. Agreements or "conspiracies" among competitors to fix prices, rig a bidding process for a contract, or divide up a customer base are all examples of illegal competition. The act also forbids a company to "monopolize or attempt to monopolize" a product or service by using unreasonable or unfair methods. A business monopoly is the complete control over the manufacture and distribution of a product, or control of a service by one company thereby eliminating competition.

Growth of a Trust in the Late Nineteenth Century

Businessman John D. Rockefeller established Standard Oil Company in 1870 in Cleveland, Ohio. At that time Standard Oil refined less than 4 percent of oil in the United States. More than 250 competitors also refined oil. Rockefeller entered into agreements with other oil companies to pool transportation of their oil to receive very cheap railroad transport rates. Only those who agreed to cooperate received the cheap rates. By 1873 through these various agreements Rockefeller managed to control 80 percent of the oil refining in Cleveland, which represented about one-third of the country's total refining ability.

By 1880 Standard Oil controlled most U.S. refineries. In 1882 the approximately forty companies that had entered into agreements with Standard Oil reorganized into Standard Oil Trust, the first large trust in America. The shareholders of those companies turned their shares over to nine individuals or trustees (hence the name trust) who ran all operations. In return shareholders received "trust certificates." The trustees paid out earnings to the holders of the trust certificates.

Later in 1882 the Ohio courts dissolved the huge oil trust but Standard merely reestablished in New Jersey, a state allowing trusts. When Congress passed the Sherman Antitrust Act in 1890, Standard again reformed calling itself a holding company, which again was allowable in New Jersey and allowed the firm to avoid the term "trust." By 1900 Standard Oil controlled 90 percent of U.S. oil refinery business and the Rockefeller family had become enormously wealthy.

In 1911 the U.S. Supreme Court in *Standard Oil of New Jersey v. United States* found Standard in violation of the Sherman Antitrust Act. The Court ordered the breakup of Standard Oil into smaller companies. The names of those companies included American Standard, Chevron, Esso, Exxon, and Mobil. Competition among the smaller oil companies resumed.

What is a trust?

In the twenty-first century the word "trust" in a business sense is generally thought of by the public as an arrangement where an individual or "trustee" is appointed to manage the affairs of a child or impaired adult. In the late nineteenth century and early twentieth century the word "trust" was commonly used to describe an arrangement where stockholders of several companies turned over their company shares to a single group of individuals called trustees who then administered

Senator John Sherman, after whom the 1890 legislation outlawing trusts and monopolies was named.

and controlled the affairs of the newly combined companies.

The combined companies were called a trust. The stockholders received trust certificates entitling them to receive earnings from the trust. The first large U.S. trust, Standard Oil Trust, was formed in 1882 in Ohio. Nine trustees ran the oil trust and monopolized the oil refinery business in America. The term monopoly is more commonly used and understood in the twenty-first century than the term trust. The two terms can be used interchangeably. Whenever the term antitrust appears in this chapter it could also read as antimonopoly.

Congress passes the Sherman Antitrust Act of 1890

By the late nineteenth century businesses producing refined oil, sugar, or providing services such as railroad transportation fought for market dominance by agreeing to become trusts. Both the government and public were becoming alarmed at the rapid growth of trusts and their power to limit competition. Limited competition results in higher prices, reduced availability, and lowered quality. Methods used to hinder competition included forcing rivals out of business through price fixing; buying out competitors; and, forcing customers to sign long-term contracts with one trust.

Congress passed the Sherman Antitrust Act in 1890 as the first federal legislation to prohibit trusts. The act was named after Senator John Sherman of Ohio. The act passed in the Senate on April 8, 1890, by a vote of 51 to 1 and in the House on June 20, 1890, by a vote of 242 to 0. The vote illustrated the high level of concern over trusts among lawmakers. President Benjamin Harrison (1833–1901; served 1889–93) signed the act into law on July 2, 1890.

The Sherman Antitrust Act allowed the federal government, under direction of the attorney general, to prosecute trusts and dissolve them (break them up). Any trust found to restrain trade—hamper or eliminate competition—was illegal. The original act allowed any person forming such an illegal trust to be subject to fines of up to $5,000 and a year in jail. Businesses as well as individuals who suffered economic losses due to trust actions could sue the trust for three times as much as they lost.

The following primary source is the entire Sherman Antitrust Act as approved and signed into law in 1890. Sections 1 and 2 prohibit the formation of trusts, monopolies, or conspiracy to restrain interstate (between states) or foreign trade, trade meaning competition. Section 3 is worded exactly as Section 1 and merely adds that restraint of trade is also illegal in territories of the United States and in the District of Columbia. Sections 4, 5, and 6 define legal procedures to be followed when an individual or company is suspected of restraint of trade. Section 7 allows for victims to recover damages. Section 8 defines the terms "person" and "persons" found in the act.

Things to remember while reading excerpts from the Sherman Antitrust Act of 1890:

- In 1890 industries in America were rapidly expanding; freedom of competition was vital to this growth.

- The American competitive business system works only when competitors set prices honestly and independently.

- The intent of antitrust law is to guard freedom of competition and opportunity in the marketplace, not to destroy businesses.

- Competition produces greater choice and better products at a lower cost for consumers.

- Antitrust legislation assures free, uninhibited competition, which results in stronger businesses. Competition constantly tests businesses and helps them become more successful in the worldwide marketplace.

Excerpt from the Sherman Antitrust Act of 1890

Be it enacted by the Senate and House of Representatives of the United States of America in Congress assembled,

*Sec. 1. Every contract, combination in the form of **trust** or otherwise, or **conspiracy**, in **restraint** of trade or commerce among the several States, or with foreign nations, is hereby declared to be illegal. Every person who shall make any such contract or engage in any such combination or conspiracy, shall be deemed, guilty of a **misdemeanor**, and, on conviction thereof, shall be punished by fine not exceeding five thousand dollars, or by imprisonment not exceeding one year, or by both said punishments, in the **discretion** of the court.*

Sec. 2. Every person who shall monopolize, or attempt to monopolize, or combine or conspire with any other person or persons, to monopolize any part of the trade or commerce among the several States, or with foreign nations, shall be deemed guilty of a misdemeanor, and, on conviction thereof, shall be punished by fine not exceeding five thousand dollars, or by imprisonment not exceeding one year, or by both said punishments, in the discretion of the court.

*Sec. 3. Every contract, combination in form of trust or otherwise, or conspiracy, in restraint of trade or commerce in any **Territory of the United States** or of the **District of Columbia**, or in restraint of trade or commerce between any such Territory and another, or between any such Territory or Territories and any State or States or the District of Columbia, or with foreign nations, or between the District of Columbia and any State or States or foreign nations, is hereby declared illegal. Every person who shall make any such contract or engage in any such combination or conspiracy, shall be deemed guilty of a misdemeanor, and, on conviction thereof, shall be punished by fine not exceeding five thousand dollars, or by imprisonment not exceeding one year, or by both said punishments, in the discretion of the court.*

*Sec. 4. The several circuit courts of the United States are hereby **invested with jurisdiction** to prevent and restrain violations of this act; and it shall be the duty of the several district attorneys of the*

Trust: A company that controls other companies and unfairly limits competition.

Conspiracy: A scheme or agreement to work together.

Restraint: To reduce or inhibit.

Misdemeanor: A lesser or minor crime.

Discretion: Choice.

Territory of the United States: Countries such as Puerto Rico and Guam.

District of Columbia: Washington, DC.

Invested with jurisdiction: Provided the legal authority.

United States, in their respective districts, under the direction of the Attorney-General, to **institute proceedings** . . . to prevent and restrain such violations. Such proceedings may be by way of **petition** setting forth the case and praying that such violation shall be **enjoined** or otherwise prohibited. When the parties complained of shall have been duly notified of such petition the court shall proceed, as soon as may be, to the hearing and determination of the case; and pending such petition and before final decree, the court may at any time make such **temporary restraining order** or prohibition as shall be deemed just. . . .

Sec. 5. Whenever it shall appear to the court before which any proceeding under section four of this act may be pending, that the ends of justice require that other parties should be brought before the court, the court may cause them to be summoned, whether they reside in the district in which the court is held or not; and subpoenas to that end may be served in any district by the marshal thereof.

Sec. 6. Any property owned under any contract or by any combination, or pursuant to any conspiracy (and being the subject thereof) mentioned in section one of this act, and being in the course of transportation from one State to another, or to a foreign country, shall be forfeited to the United States, and may be seized and condemned by like proceedings as those provided by law for the forfeiture, seizure, and condemnation of property imported into the United States contrary to law.

Sec. 7. Any person who shall be injured in his business or property by any other person or corporation by reason of anything forbidden or declared to be unlawful by this act, may sue therefore in any circuit court of the United States in the district in which the defendant resides or is found, without respect to the amount in controversy, and shall recover **threefold** the damages by him sustained, and the costs of suit, including a reasonable attorney's fee.

Sec. 8. That the word "person," or "persons," whenever used in this act shall be deemed to include corporations and associations existing under or authorized by the laws of either the United States, the laws of any of the Territories, the laws of any State, or the laws of any foreign country.

Institute proceedings: Begin legal action.

Petition: Legal document presented to the court starting legal action.

Enjoined: Stopped.

Temporary restraining order: A court order to stop the challenged activity until further legal decisions can be made.

Threefold: Three times the amount.

What happened next . . .

The wording of the Sherman Antitrust Act was not specific. It failed to define such key terms as "trust," "conspiracy," "restraint of trade or commerce," "monopolize," or "combine." As a result the U.S. courts struggled through the 1890s to give precise legal meaning to the law.

The first important case to be brought under Sherman was *U.S. v. E. C. Knight Company* in 1895. About 1890 the American Sugar Refining Company began purchasing stock in four competitors including E. C. Knight Company. By 1892 the resulting American Sugar trust controlled 98 percent of sugar refining in the United States. President Grover Cleveland's (1837–1908; served 1885–89 and 1893–97) administration charged American Sugar for illegal restraints of trade under the Sherman Act.

In 1895 the U.S. Supreme Court ruled the manufacturing (refining) of sugar was an activity that took place in facilities in specific states and was not a restraint of interstate trade. At the time, the decision seemed to end any thought that the provisions of the Sherman Act would actually be used to regulate the formation of trusts.

Little progress was made against trusts until the election of "trust-busting" President Theodore "Teddy" Roosevelt (1858–1919; served 1901–09). Roosevelt, who became president in March 1901, was as concerned as the public over the continued growth of powerful trusts. In 1903 Roosevelt convinced Congress to establish the first new government cabinet-level department since the Civil War (1861–65), the Department of Commerce and Labor. The new department would oversee the actions of business and labor unions. Within the department Roosevelt established the Bureau of Corporations to uncover violations of the Sherman Act. The bureau began to look into various businesses such as oil, tobacco, steel, and meatpacking.

Philander C. Knox, Roosevelt's attorney general, initiated forty-four antitrust suits during the Roosevelt administration. One of the earliest suits was against the Northern Securities Company (NSC). NSC was formed in New Jersey as a holding company, the name given trusts in New Jersey to avoid the Sherman Act. Monopolizing rail traffic between Chicago and the Northwest, NSC controlled railroad stock of the Great

Northern, Northern Pacific, and the Chicago, Burlington, and Quincy railroads.

Wealthy businessmen involved with NSC were J. P. Morgan, James J. Hill, and E. H. Harriman. In 1904 the U.S. Supreme Court found in favor of the government and ordered the breakup of NSC. The decision in *Northern Securities Company v. U.S* reversed the Court's position on trusts taken in the E. C. Knight case. The combining of railroads halted, and Roosevelt's popular approval rating hit an all-time high. Despite his aggression towards trusts, Roosevelt wanted only to regulate not destroy big business.

The Sherman Act was again used successfully by President William H. Taft (1857–1930; served 1909–13), when he took on the powerful Standard Oil Trust of New Jersey in 1911. In the same year, American Tobacco was broken up into smaller companies after being taken court under provisions of the Sherman Act.

Little progress was made against trusts until the election of "trust-busting" President Theodore "Teddy" Roosevelt. *(© Corbis)*

Congress strengthened U.S. antitrust legislation in 1914 by passing the Clayton Antitrust Act and the Federal Trade Commission (FTC) Act. The Clayton Act regulated mergers of companies to avoid the creation of monopolies. The act also required notification of any impending mergers, which had to be approved by the FTC. The second 1914 act created the FTC to enforce antitrust laws. In 1919 the Antitrust Division was formed within the Department of Justice.

For over eight decades the FTC and Antitrust Division worked together to enforce antitrust laws. The FTC is empowered to temporarily suspend anticompetitive activities of suspected companies while the Antitrust Division investigates and prosecutes. The division prosecutes serious and willful violations of antitrust laws but also, along with the FTC, gives guidance to the business community to help structure and organize operations in compliance with U.S. law.

The Microsoft Settlement—The Twenty-First Century's First Major Antitrust Settlement

In 1998 the Department of Justice (DOJ), twenty states, and District of Columbia charged computer software giant Microsoft in federal court of violating federal antitrust laws with its monopoly on personal computer (PC) operating systems. Netscape Communication, another software giant on the West Coast, had pioneered the web browser—a system allowing individual Internet users to search for information by using a key word. Microsoft, however, had begun to package a free browser with its Windows operating system, which was installed in many PCs. At issue was whether Microsoft could piggyback a free browser and other software onto its Windows system. These packages made Windows very attractive and it had become the dominant operating system installed by various PC manufacturers. Other companies with similar software were left out.

In 2000 U.S. District Judge Thomas Penfield Jackson found Microsoft guilty of antitrust violations. He ordered the soft-

ware giant to be broken apart. Microsoft appealed the decision to the U.S. Supreme Court but the Court refused to hear the case and sent it instead to the court of appeals. The appeals court upheld the Microsoft conviction. U.S. District Judge Colleen Kollar-Kotelly then received the case to consider Microsoft's punishment. The DOJ, states, and Microsoft entered negotiations on a settlement. Judge Kollar-Kotelly approved the settlement in November 2002. The settlement did not include the company's breakup. Instead Microsoft was required to treat all PC makers equally and to share technology so other products not made by Microsoft would work well within Windows. By June 2003 all states except Massachusetts had agreed to the settlement.

Contrary to other states, Massachusetts attorney general Tom Reilly refused to settle with Microsoft believing the agreement did not protect consumers and competitors from Microsoft's monopoly in the personal

The Sherman Act remained the cornerstone of U.S. antitrust law ensuring a competitive free market. Suits were brought under the act against offending corporations throughout the twentieth century. The Sherman Act has changed little over the last 110 years. The only major changes involved penalties. Individual offenders may be fined up to $350,000 and sentenced to three years in prison for each offense. Corporations can be fined up to $10 million, in some cases even more.

If a company is found guilty of antitrust violations the U.S. government may choose, in addition to fines, among sev-

Microsoft founder and CEO Bill Gates. In 1998 computer software giant Microsoft was charged in federal court of violating federal antitrust laws. *(AP/Wide World Photos)*

the entire settlement reached in November 2002 between the federal government, states, and Microsoft. Many believed the decision would have a major influence on U.S. antitrust law. Since the mid-1980s few companies found guilty of antitrust violations had been required to break apart. Prior to that time a common penalty was breaking up, the most infamous involved American Telephone and Telegraph (AT&T).

In 1983 AT&T was found guilty of being an illegal monopoly. It was broken up into one long distance company and seven "baby Bell" regional phone companies. The first ruling on Microsoft's antitrust case in 2000 called for Microsoft to be broken up into smaller companies but the final settlement did not require breakup, strengthening the trend away from forced corporate breakups. Further appeals appeared unlikely ending Microsoft's six years of litigation. A similar case against Microsoft in Europe, however, concerning its digital media players was working its way through the European court system in 2004.

computer software market. Massachusetts appealed further.

On June 30, 2004, the U.S. Court of Appeals for the District of Columbia upheld

eral consequences. Consequences include breaking up the monopoly into different smaller companies, or forcing offending businesses to inform customers about competitors' products and services.

Throughout the twentieth century many major U.S. corporations have been involved in antitrust cases—U.S. Steel, International Business Machines (IBM), American Telephone & Telegraph (AT&T), General Electric, Yellow Cab Company, drug company Parke Davis & Company, General Motors Corporation, Pan American World Airways, Texaco, Exxon Corporation, Eastman Kodak Company, cellular phone company Verizon, and computer software giant Microsoft. In some cases the businesses were found guilty of antitrust violations, in others no illegal trust activities were found.

At the beginning of the twenty-first century there are three kinds of antitrust violations the Antitrust Division prosecutes most frequently—price-fixing, bid-rigging, and allocation of customers. Price-fixing means several competitors agree to raise, lower, or maintain prices. These activities inhibit price competition.

Bid-rigging involves competitors who conspire together when bidding on a contract for work, often a government contract. Bid-rigging takes many forms but almost always ends in increased costs for goods or services. Customer allocation schemes involve a few competitors conspiring to divide up markets among themselves to control prices or contracts.

These practices are carried out in secret and are difficult to detect. They cost consumers hundreds of millions of dollars every year. The Antitrust Division receives most of its tips about such activities from the public—customers, employees, and employers. Any possible violation can be reported to the New Case Unit of the Antitrust Division at the email address of newcase.atr@usdoj.gov.

Did you know . . .

- Section 1 outlaws "every contract, combination . . . or conspiracy, in restraint of trade—any scheme, or agreement to inhibit competition." By the early 1900s, however, the Supreme Court decided the intent of Congress was to outlaw only those agreements that restrained competition unreasonably. It would be left up to the courts to decide what agreements were unreasonable.

- Even if competition is limited, reasonable business practices are not illegal under antitrust laws. For example, according to the FTC, if a group of manufacturers all decide to make certain products with specific fire resistant materials, the decision will have reasonable justification. Even though it limits what materials can be used, and limits consumer choice, courts would see it as a standard adopted to provide for consumer safety.

- Section 2 makes it illegal for a company or companies to form or attempt to form a monopoly. Courts have interpreted this section to mean that only a monopoly reached by unreasonable practices is illegal. U.S. antitrust laws do not outlaw monopolies that companies establish by creating a superior product, vigorous competition including setting lower prices, efficient business practices, and excellent customer service. This is considered the American competitive spirit working in a proper manner. Only when a monopoly has been formed by suppressing competition through various anticompetitive schemes is the monopoly illegal.

Consider the following . . .

- During the 1890s a number of citizens suggested that while Congress passed the Sherman Act to appease the public clamoring for action against trusts, it also knew the law would be difficult to enforce and hoped it would not anger big business. Legislatures in the twenty-first century must also balance the interests of the public and big business. Decide on some key questions lawmakers should ask when deliberating the passage of any legislation that regulates big business.

- Research the Clayton Antitrust Act of 1914. How did it strengthen antitrust legislation?

- Go to the library reference section or to your favorite Internet search engine and find books or Web sites with information on Supreme Court cases. Find antitrust cases involving one of the companies listed in the "What happened next" section of this chapter. Carefully read the issues and outcome of the case.

For More Information

Books

Hovenkamp, Herbert. *Antitrust*. St. Paul, MN: West Group, 1999.

Shenefield, John H., and Irwin M. Stelzer. *Antitrust Laws: A Primer*. Washington, DC: AEI Press, 2001.

The Statutes at Large and Proclamations of the United States of America from December 1889 to March 1891, Vol. XXVI. Washington, DC: U.S. Government Printing Office, 1891.

Web Sites

"An Antitrust Primer." *Federal Trade Commission.* http://www.ftc.gov/bc/compguide/antitrst.htm (accessed on August 19, 2004).

"Price Fixing, Bid Rigging, and Market Allocation Schemes: What They Are and What to Look For." *U.S. Department of Justice.* http://www.usdoj.gov/atr/public/guidelines/primer-ncu.htm (accessed on August 19, 2004).

"Report Possible Antitrust Violations." *U.S. Department of Justice: Antitrust Division.* http://www.usdoj.gov/atr/contact/newcase.htm (accessed on August 19, 2004).

"The Sherman Act." *St. Olaf College.* http://www.stolaf.edu/people/becker/antitrust/statutes/sherman.html (accessed on August 19, 2004).

RICO

Excerpt from the Racketeer Influenced and Corrupt Organizations (RICO) Act of 1970
Reprinted from *United States Statutes at Large, 1970–1971,*
Volume 84, Part 1
Published in 1971

Organized crime is defined as any group that has an organized structure of bosses, advisors, and committed working members whose key goal is to obtain money and property through illegal activities. Organized crime groups thrive on supplying goods and services that are not legally available but for which a large number of people are willing to pay. Gambling, prostitution, pornography, and dealing in illegal drugs have long been moneymakers for organized crime.

At the beginning of the twenty-first century drug trafficking was the largest illegal organized crime activity in the United States and worldwide. The term "trafficking" means dealing in illegal drugs—smuggling, buying with the intent to sell, and selling. The money received is called "dirty" money and needs to be "laundered." Money laundering means banking and investing the dirty money through a complicated series of financial networks until it can no longer be traced and appears to be legally earned or "clean" money invested in legal businesses. Money laundering is another key activity of organized crime groups.

From the late 1920s through the mid-1980s, U.S. organized crime was dominated by the American Mafia or mob

> "It shall be unlawful for any person who has received income derived, directly or indirectly, from a pattern of racketeering activity."

Members of the Lucchese crime family arrested in 2002 under the Organized Crime Control Act of 1970. The legislation gave law enforcement much needed power to combat organized crime rings.
(AP/Wide World Photos)

families, descendants of the Italian and Sicilian Mafia. Many families have become legendary. New York City was divided amongst the Bonnano, Columbo, Gambino, Genovese, and Lucchese families. Approximately nineteen more prominent crime families were located in other U.S. cities. The highly popular movie *The Godfather* debuted in 1972 and popularized the notion of a secretive, tightly knit mob underworld.

To assist law enforcement in curtailing organized crime, the U.S. Congress passed the Organized Crime Control Act of 1970. The central part of the act is the Racketeer Influenced and Corrupt Organizations (RICO) section. RICO defines the term racketeering as the act of participating in a pattern (more than one action) of criminal offenses commonly engaged in by organized crime. RICO makes it illegal to receive an income from a racketeering activity and sets punishments. RICO is law enforcement's most powerful tool against organized crime. During the 1980s and 1990s many bosses and members of organized crime were convicted and sent to prison under RICO.

Section 1961 of RICO lists many criminal offenses that fall under the definition of racketeering activity. Some of these include murder, kidnapping, illegal gambling, arson (intentionally setting a fire), robbery, bribery (promising a person money or a favor in return for certain action), extortion (threatening harm if one does not comply with a crime group's request or plan), dealing in obscene matter (pornography), smuggling aliens (moving illegal immigrants across the nation's borders); counterfeiting, embezzlement (to secretly steal money or property for one's own use), mail fraud (fake offers through the mail between different states), obstructing criminal investigations, prostitution, sexual exploitation of children, theft, drug trafficking, and money laundering.

Things to remember while reading excerpts from the Racketeer Influenced and Corrupt Organizations (RICO) Act of 1970:

- By the time RICO was passed many different types of organized crime activities were well known. These activities were costing the U.S. economy billions of dollars each year.

- Racketeering crimes were hidden under many confusing layers of secrecy. They took years to investigate once RICO became law.

- Even though RICO required that all illegal gains from racketeering be turned over to authorities once a gangster was convicted, most was never recovered due to the "laundering" process.

Excerpt from the Racketeer Influenced and Corrupt Organizations (RICO) Act of 1970

Sec. 1962. Prohibited activities

Why RICO Was An Appropriate Name

On January 17, 1920, Prohibition became law in the United States. The states had ratified (passed) the Eighteenth Amendment to the U.S. Constitution banning the manufacture, sale, and distribution of alcoholic beverages in the United States. Only about one-third of the adult population was willing, however, to not drink alcoholic beverages. Americans remained thirsty and beating Prohibition became a national pastime.

Gangsters who before 1920 had limited their activities to gambling, thievery, and vendettas against rival gang members transformed into organized groups of "bootleggers." Bootlegging gangs illegally brought liquor into the country and sold it to eager Americans. The most prominent bootlegger was Alphonse "Al" Capone (1899–1947) who became a legendary character as a Chicago organized crime boss. His income in the late 1920s and early 1930s was over $100 million a year. By comparison the average American family's income was roughly $1,500 to $2,000 a year. Americans became fascinated with the powerful gangsters whose activities were often reported on the same newspaper pages with reports of glamorous Hollywood stars.

Unlawful debt: Money owed from illegal gambling activity.

Principal: A person highly involved in its operations.

Interest in: Ownership of.

Enterprise: A business partnership, corporation, or union.

Interstate or foreign commerce: Trade across state or national boundaries.

*(a) It shall be unlawful for any person who has received any income derived, directly or indirectly, from a pattern of racketeering activity or through collection of an **unlawful debt** in which such person has participated as a **principal** . . . to use or invest . . . any part of such income, or the proceeds of such income, in acquisition of any **interest in**, or the establishment or operation of, any **enterprise** which is engaged in, or the activities of which affect, **interstate or foreign commerce**. . . .*

(b) It shall be unlawful for any person through a pattern of racketeering activity or through collection of an unlawful debt to acquire or maintain, directly or indirectly, any interest in or control of any enterprise, which is engaged in, or the activities of which affect, interstate or foreign commerce.

(c) It shall be unlawful for any person employed by or associated with any enterprise engaged in, or the activities of which affect, interstate or foreign commerce, to conduct or participate, directly or indirectly, in the conduct of such enterprise's affairs through a pattern of racketeering activity or collection of unlawful debt.

Following the crash of the New York stock market in October 1929, Americans were thrown into an economic crisis known as the Great Depression. Banks failed, businesses folded, factories closed their doors, and increasing numbers of Americans lost their jobs or had their incomes severely cut.

During this time, approximately 60 percent of the population, 60 to 75 million people, paid a few pennies to enter movie houses and escape their desperate lives for a short time. In the early 1930s gangster films enjoyed incredible success. Surrounded by social and economic woes, these dynamic, successful, and flamboyant gangsters contrasted with the hardship and despair of most people. *Little Caesar*, produced by Warner Brothers Studios and re-leased in 1930, was the first great gangster "talkie," a movie with sound.

The film followed the story of Rico Bandello, or "Little Caesar," played by Edward G. Robinson as he climbed the ladder of the criminal underworld. Rico was a thinly disguised version of Al Capone. Rico's activities were obviously outside the law so the movie had to end his life to stay on high moral ground. Rico was a wildly popular character with Depression era audiences. Most all Americans were familiar with the character and the name Rico.

When Congress passed the Organized Crime Control Act forty years later in 1970, lawmakers cleverly named the central portion of the act the **R**acketeer **I**nfluenced and **C**orrupt **O**rganizations Act. Abbreviated, the title of the act is RICO.

---

*(d) It shall be unlawful for any person to **conspire** to violate any of the provisions of subsections (a), (b), or (c) of this section.*

Sec. 1963 Criminal penalties

(a) Whoever violates any provision of section 1962 of this chapter shall be fined not more than $25,000 or imprisoned not more than twenty years, or both, and shall forfeit to the United States (1) any interest he has acquired or maintained in violation of section 1962. . . .

*(b) In any action brought by the Untied States under this section, the district courts of the United States shall have **jurisdiction** to enter such **restraining orders** or prohibitions . . . in connection with any property or other interest subject to forfeiture under this section, as it shall deem proper.*

(c) Upon conviction of a person under this section, the court shall authorize the Attorney General to seize all property or other interest declared forfeited under this section upon such terms and conditions as the court shall deem proper. . . .

Conspire: Agree together.

Jurisdiction: The geographic area or type of crime that the court has legal authority to prosecute.

Restraining orders: Court orders to temporarily stop an activity being challenged.

Divest: To withdraw from.

Estop: Prohibit.

Essential allegations: Charges.

Civil proceeding: A lawsuit separate from the criminal prosecution seeking compensation.

Sec. 1964. Civil remedies

*(a) The district courts of the United States shall have jurisdiction to prevent and restrain violations of section 1962 of this chapter by issuing appropriate orders, including, but not limited to: ordering any person to **divest** himself of any interest, direct or indirect, in any enterprise; imposing reasonable restrictions on the future activities or investments of any person, including, but not limited to, prohibiting any person from engaging in the same type of endeavor as the enterprise engaged in, the activities of which affect interstate or foreign commerce; or ordering dissolution or reorganization of any enterprise, making due provision for the rights of innocent persons.*

(b) The Attorney General may institute proceedings under this section. In any action brought by the United States under this section, the court shall proceed as soon as practicable to the hearing and determination thereof. . . .

(c) Any person injured in his business or property by reason of a violation of section 1962 of this chapter may sue therefore in any appropriate United States district court and shall recover threefold the damages he sustains and the cost of the suit, including a reasonable attorney's fee.

*(d) A final judgment . . . in favor of the United States in any criminal proceeding brought by the United States under this chapter shall **estop** the defendant from denying the **essential allegations** of the criminal offense in any subsequent **civil proceeding** brought by the United States.*

What happened next . . .

Due to the complexity of bringing organized crime members to justice, ten years passed before the first RICO convictions were obtained. Throughout the 1970s crime families continually fought for power over the many racketeering enterprises that brought in huge sums of money. The National Conference on Organized Crime in 1975 estimated mob-related racketeering reached about $50 billion a year in the United States.

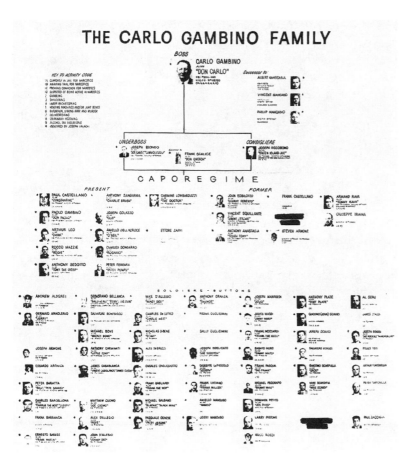

The Carlo Gambino family tree. The Gambino family was one of New York's most powerful in the American Mafia. It was successfully weakened by convictions obtained under the RICO Act of 1970.

(© Bettmann/Corbis)

Battles for power and control between crime families resulted in numerous murders. Members of one family would assassinate another's boss. The family of the assassinated boss sought revenge by murdering a member of the offending family. Murders were also committed to prevent a crime member from testifying in a trial.

The first convictions of American Mafia members under RICO began in 1980. Numerous gangsters were convicted for a variety of racketeering offenses. In 1985 the bosses of all five New York City Mafia families were convicted under RICO and each received at least one hundred years in prison.

In 1992 Salvatore "Sammy the Bull" Gravano testified in court against his boss John Gotti, head of the Gambino crime family. In doing so he broke the sacred code of the Mafia—the code of silence barring every Mafia member from ever testifying against another Mafia member. Gotti was sentenced to life in prison. His brother Peter Gotti took over the family but was sentenced in April 2004 to nine years in prison.

Three decades of arrests and convictions weakened the old American organized crime families, disrupting their criminal activities. RICO proved a powerful, effective law for convicting crime family members and for tough, long sentences. By 2000 criminal gangs of "bikers" (Hells Angels, Outlaws, and Bandidos), young Hispanics, and young black Americans had become organized, profitable, and rivaled the weakened American mob families.

International crime groups had also come to America, partnering with U.S. organized crime. They include the Russian Mafia, Japanese Yakuza, Chinese Triads, South American drug groups, West Africa crime groups, Mexican Mafia, and Southeast Asian crime groups.

Did you know . . .

- Organized crime family members who broke the code of silence and testified in RICO proceedings received much shorter prison sentences than if they had not cooperated.

- By the 1990s with many Mafia leaders convicted under RICO and in prison, the life of traditional organized crime members became less attractive. A considerable number of young people from Mafia families chose to attend college and adopt lawful careers and lifestyles. The face of American organized crime changed significantly as crime bosses were forced to recruit uneducated youth from impoverished backgrounds. These new recruits had neither loyalty to the crime families nor skilled leadership qualities.

- While drug trafficking continues to be a top moneymaker, weapons, diamonds, luxury cars, and even natural resources such as Russian oil are smuggled and illegally bought and sold by organized crime groups.

Consider the following . . .

- When passed, RICO was aimed at twentieth century organized crime groups. What major new challenges face law enforcement agencies at the beginning of the twenty-first century, considering the rise of the Internet and World Wide Web?

- Research one of the five New York City crime families from its beginnings. How has this family been affected by RICO by the end of the twentieth century?

- Go to the Web site of the Federal Bureau of Investigation (FBI) at http://www.fbi.gov. Research FBI units devoted to the investigation of organized crime in the United States and worldwide.

For More Information

Books

Lunde, Paul. *Organized Crime: An Inside Guide to the World's Most Successful Industry.* New York: DK Publishing, Inc., 2004.

Lyman, Michael D., and Gary W. Potter. *Organized Crime.* Upper Saddle River, NJ: Pearson Prentice Hall, 2004.

Sullivan, Robert, ed. *Mobsters and Gangsters: Organized Crime in America, from Al Capone to Tony Soprano.* New York: Life Books, 2002.

Thompson, Hunter S. *Hell's Angels: A Strange and Terrible Saga.* New York: Modern Library, 1999.

Web Sites

"Gangsters and Outlaws." *Court TV's Crime Library: Criminal Minds and Methods.* http://www.crimelibrary.com/gangsters-outlaws-gmen.htm (accessed on August 19, 2004).

"Investigative Programs: Organized Crime." *Federal Bureau of Investigation.* http://www.fbi.gov/hq/cid/orgcrime/ocshome.htm (accessed on August 19, 2004).

Protection of Minorities and Youth

The first portion of this chapter, historical in nature, deals with one of the most significant legal battles in the early twentieth century. The Scottsboro trials stood as examples of minority treatment in the criminal justice system. The second portion of the chapter deals with a highly significant child protection law, the PROTECT Act of 2003. PROTECT includes the AMBER Alert, used to rescue abducted children.

At the beginning of the 1930s most black Americans in the United States lived in extreme poverty, particularly in the South. Southern slavery had ended only a few generations earlier. Racism in the 1920s remained woven into every aspect of life in the United States and was freely expressed in public. What were known as Jim Crow laws were well entrenched. These state laws, predominantly found in the South, enforced racial segregation in almost every facet of life—restaurants, theaters, hotels, even water fountains and restrooms.

In 1897 the U.S. Supreme Court had put its approval on segregation by asserting that the required separation did not violate the constitutional rights of blacks as long as they were given access to equal facilities. In reality, the "separate but

Amber Alert provisions are a significant part of the PROTECT Act of 2003. *(AP/Wide World Photos)*

equal" approach did not translate into the equal quality of facilities, in fact far from it.

When the economic crisis of the Great Depression struck in 1929 hard times for blacks got even harder. While the 1933 national unemployment rate was over 25 percent, unemployment rates for various minorities ranged up to 50 percent or more. Racial discrimination was rampant as minority workers were normally the first to lose jobs at a business or on a farm. Jobs previously left to minorities, including elevator operators, field workers, street cleaners, garbage collectors, waiters, and bellhops, were suddenly needed by the larger white population.

Violence increased against minorities during the Depression, as whites now competed for jobs traditionally held by minorities. The lynching of blacks by white mobs increased, primarily in the South. Lynchings increased from eight in 1932 to twenty-eight in 1933, then fifteen in 1934, and twenty in 1935. Lynching is mob violence in which a group or mob murders a person (usually black and usually by hanging) who might have been accused of committing a crime.

Economic conditions and racial discrimination in every facet of American life put blacks at a severe social and political disadvantage. As with every other part of the society, the criminal justice system was also weighted against minorities. With the system dominated by whites in all positions of authority, blacks found themselves treated more harshly than other citizens, including more severe penalties for the same crimes. The inmate populations of Southern prisons were predominantly black.

The first excerpt "Scottsboro Case Goes to the Jury" is a newspaper accounting of the fourth trial of Haywood Patterson, one of the nine Scottsboro Boys. The Scottsboro Boys, all black youth, were charged with raping two white women from Alabama.

Some of the worst crimes committed in the United States are crimes against children. Kidnappers, child molesters, and child pornographers prey on the nation's young. The PROTECT Act of 2003 is the most comprehensive child protection legislation ever passed by the U.S. Congress. The act greatly strengthens law enforcement's ability to investigate, prosecute, and punish offenders who victimize children. Its provisions work to help law enforcement prevent crimes against children. Highlights of the lengthy PROTECT Act include increased penalties for those who harm children, better tools against those who prey on children over the Internet, and swift, coordinated law enforcement response when a child is abducted.

The most publicized provision of PROTECT is the AMBER Alert. The entire PROTECT Act is frequently referred to as the AMBER Alert bill. AMBER Alert provides coordination between law enforcement, media, and the general public to help quickly locate abducted children. The second excerpt in this chapter is from sections 301, 302, 303, and 304 of the PROTECT Act of 2003 that constitute the AMBER Alert. These sections were fought for by parents across the country whose children had been the victims of abduction.

Scottsboro Trial

Excerpt from "Scottsboro Case Goes to the Jury"
Reprinted from the *New York Times*
Published on January 23, 1936

"It takes courage to do the right thing in the face of public clamor for the wrong thing."

"It takes courage to do the right thing in the face of public clamor for the wrong thing, but when justice is not administered fairly, . . . there is no protection for any one, man or woman, black or white." These words were spoken in January 1936 by defense attorney C. L. Watts at the fourth trial of Haywood Patterson, one of nine young black men known as the Scottsboro Boys, accused of raping two white women. The words struck at the heart of a criminal justice system heavily biased against black Americans. Watts urged the all white jury "to do the right thing" in spite of heavy public pressure for a guilty decision. The "right thing" in Watts's thinking was to deliver a not-guilty verdict.

History of the Scottsboro Boys

In 1931 it was common for the unemployed to hitch rides on trains and travel from town to town in search of a job, adventure, or a way home. On March 25, nine young black men jumped on board a Southern Railroad pulling out of Chattanooga, Tennessee. Olen Montgomery, Clarence Norris, Haywood Patterson, Ozie Powell, Willie Roberson, Charles Weems,

160

Deputy Sheriff Charles McComb (left) and attorney Samuel Leibowitz (second from left) confer with seven of the nine youths held in the Scottsboro case, May 1, 1935. The nine black youths were charged with the rape of two white women of Scottsboro, Alabama.
(AP/Wide World Photos)

Eugene Williams, Andy Wright, and Roy Wright ranged in age from twelve to twenty years. Just after the train crossed into Alabama it stopped for water in Stevenson where a fight broke out between some of the black youths and white teenagers on board. Outnumbered, the white teens either jumped or were thrown from the train as it pulled from the station.

Seeking revenge, some of the white youth reported to the Stevenson train master that the black youth had assaulted two white women still on the train. The train master telegraphed ahead to the next station, Paint Rock, Alabama, where law enforcement officers boarded the train and rounded up every black youth they could find. The two white women emerged and accused the blacks of raping them.

The black boys were taken to a jail in Scottsboro, Alabama, hence the name Scottsboro Boys. The arrest of the nine was the beginning of repeated trials, convictions, appeals, and more trials over the next six years.

The alleged rape victims in the Scottsboro case were Victoria Price, age twenty-one, and teenager Ruby Bates. Price and Bates were from poor families who lived in the racially mixed town of Huntsville, Alabama. They, like the Scottsboro Boys, were riding the rails in search of work. When questioned by law enforcement officers they stated they had been beaten and raped by the black boys on the train.

Less than two hours after the alleged attack, however, Scottsboro physician Dr. R. R. Bridges examined Price and Bates and found no cuts, bruises, blood, or other injuries consistent with an attack. He reported the women were calm and did not appear to be under stress.

On March 31 all nine of the Scottsboro Boys were indicted for rape. Within weeks juries convicted and sentenced eight of the young men to death in the electric chair. Twelve-year-old Roy Wright's ordeal ended in a mistrial when eleven of the jurors held out for the death penalty but one juror disagreed.

Since the arrest of the Scottsboro Boys, anger and dismay had been growing across the United States and in other parts of the world over what appeared to be racially motivated arrests and prosecution of the boys. Demonstrations in support of the Scottsboro Boys occurred outside a number of U.S. embassies in Europe. In 110 American cities, 300,000 black and white workers gathered to protest the convictions on May 1.

On May 5 in Washington, D.C., some 200,000 supporters demanded freedom for the Scottsboro Boys. The International Labor Defense (ILD), the legal arm of the American Communist Party, declared the case a racial "frame-up" and example of the oppression of black people in the United States. ILD took over the legal appeal process for the boys when the National Association for the Advancement of Colored Persons (NAACP) withdrew from the case due to the nature of the charges.

In January 1932 the Alabama Supreme Court affirmed all the convictions and death sentences with the exception of Eugene Williams. In November, however, the U.S. Supreme Court ruled in *Powell v. Alabama* that Alabama had denied the defendants proper legal representation or due process guaranteed by the Fourteenth Amendment. The Fourteenth Amendment states that no state shall "deprive any person of life, liberty or property, without due process of law; nor deny to any person within its jurisdiction the equal protection of the laws." Due process means fair treatment in all phases of the criminal justice system.

For the second round of trials ILD called in a well-known criminal defense attorney, Samuel Leibowitz. The medical testimony of Dr. Bridges convinced Leibowitz of the boys' innocence. He had never before been associated with racial issues but was appalled at what he viewed as the extreme unjust prosecution of the Scottsboro cases. Leibowitz worked for several years on the cases but did not charge any fees.

Haywood Patterson's second trial was before Alabama judge James Horton in March 1933. The trial took a dramatic turn when Ruby Bates stated that she and Price had made up the entire story. Price, however, stayed with her original testimony that they were raped. The jury again delivered a guilty verdict and the death penalty. Judge Horton, believing the verdict unjustified, granted a motion for a new trial. In December 1933 a jury again found Patterson guilty and sentenced him to die. About the same time, Clarence Norris endured his second trial, which ended with a conviction and the death penalty.

Leibowitz, stunned by the verdicts, appealed unsuccessfully to the Alabama Supreme Court, but moved the cases on to the U.S. Supreme Court. In April 1935 the Supreme Court reversed both convictions in *Norris v. Alabama*. The Court found that black Americans had been excluded from serving on the juries; therefore neither Patterson nor Norris had been judged by their equals or peers. The ruling meant the trials violated the Fourteenth Amendment's guarantee to equal protection under the law.

The following excerpt reports on Patterson's fourth trial held in January 1936. The presiding judge was William W. Callahan. Attorneys prosecuting Patterson were Melvin C.

Protestors of the Scottsboro verdict march in Washington, D.C., January 1, 1934. After the nine black youths were falsely charged and convicted of rape, many demonstrated asking for the boys' freedom.
(© Bettmann/Corbis)

Hutson and Thomas E. Knight Jr., the lieutenant governor of Alabama. Defending Patterson were Leibowitz and C. L. Watts. Watts was an Alabama lawyer brought into the Scottsboro case by Leibowitz.

The jury again consisted of only whites, in this case twelve white farmers. The Supreme Court decision of *Norris v. Alabama* was dealt with by having five blacks in the pool from which the jury was selected. All five, however, were eliminated by the prosecution.

The defense charged numerous times during the two-day trial that Judge Callahan was impatient and acted annoyed by the defense. His comments repeatedly suggested the defense attorneys were wasting everyone's time. The defense moved several times for a mistrial since this conduct influenced the jurors against the defense. Judge Callahan denied all motions for a mistrial.

Judge Callahan went so far as to halt Patterson's trial for a few hours while jurors were chosen for the trials involving Andrew Wright and Charles Weems, which were to be held the following week. As described under the subtitle "Defense Objections Overruled" Wright and Weems sat "manacled" (shackled) in chains in full view of the Patterson jurors during this time. The sight of the black youth in chains, defense attorneys argued, would prejudice the jurors against them.

The defense was able to enter the previous testimony of Dr. R. R. Bridges, about his examination of Price and Bates hours after the alleged attack and how there was no evidence of such an attack. Patterson plus four other Scottsboro Boys were put on the stand and testified that they had not touched Price or Bates; the boys further testified they had never even seen the women. Discounting Dr. Bridges and the boys' words, prosecutor Hutson, in closing statements, emotionally pleaded with the jury to protect the "rights of womanhood of Alabama" and convict Patterson.

Things to remember while reading excerpts from "Scottsboro Case Goes to the Jury":

- The Scottsboro trials are considered one of the most significant legal battles of the twentieth century. Scottsboro resulted in two U.S. Supreme Court decisions that contributed to the start of the Civil Rights movement in the 1950s.
- The South at the time was completely racially segregated (blacks and whites kept separate in public places) with blacks treated as inferior humans of little worth.
- The prejudiced and impatient comments of Judge Callahan were typical of Southern judges hearing cases involving black Americans.
- The following excerpt is an account of the FOURTH trial that defendant Patterson endured.

Excerpt from "Scottsboro Case Goes to the Jury"

DECATUR, Ala., Jan. 22.—Haywood Patterson's fourth trial for his life on a charge of rape ended today, as have all the other trials in the famous Scottsboro case, with an appeal to the passions of the jury. Summing up for the **prosecution**, *Melvin C. Hutson, the* **local solicitor**, *told the jurors that the womanhood of Alabama was looking to them for "protection." If Patterson were not made to pay with his life for a crime of which he swore today that he was innocent, Mr. Hutson said, the women of the State would "have to go around with six-shooters" to protect themselves. . . .*

Defense Objections Overruled

A panel of 100 **talesmen** *has been drawn for the Norris trial and Judge Callahan yesterday interrupted Patterson's trial to draw* **veniremen** *to sit in judgment of Charlie* **Williams** *and Andy Wright next week. He did this in full view of the jury trying Patterson's case and this morning Mr. Watts asked Judge Callahan to declare a* **mistrial** *on the grounds that bringing the Negroes* **manacled** *into court was prejudicial.*

Angrily denying the motion, Judge Callahan pointed out that the defense had registered no objection when he announced what he was going to do. Mr. Watts quickly renewed his motion on the grounds that the mere announcement was sufficient basis for a mistrial and Judge Callahan, with rising **choler** *denied the motion.*

"I now move," began Mr. Watts, but Judge Callahan cut him short, declaring that he "did not want to hear any further argument," and that the court would "not be **tampered** *with." Twice later in the day the defense moved unsuccessfully for a mistrial because of comments by Mr. Hutson on the testimony of the Negro defendants.*

Before the closing arguments began, the defense succeeded in reading into the record the testimony of Dr. R. R. Bridges, a physician who examined Victoria Price, the complaining witness, within an hour after she was taken from the freight train on which she says she was assaulted by a dozen Negroes.

Physician Contradicts Woman

Prosecution: Those lawyers bringing legal action against the accused.

Local solicitor: Chief city government lawyer.

Talesmen: Individuals from which a jury is chosen.

Veniremen: Individuals chosen for the jury.

Williams: His name was actually Charlie Weems; the newspaper erred.

Mistrial: A trial declared invalid because of technical errors or misconduct that eliminated the possibility of a legal and just decision.

Manacled: Handcuffed and chained.

Choler: Anger.

Tampered: Interfered.

Dr. Bridges, a Scottsboro physician, was too ill to come to court, but he testified before Judge James E. Horton at one of Patterson's earlier trials that the woman's pulse and breathing were normal and that her body showed no sign of cuts and bruises with which she testified at this trial that she was covered.

The doctor had testified also that he found physical indications which Judge Callahan refused to permit the defense to prove might have been accounted for by events which happened in a **hobo jungle** in Chattanooga the night before Ruby Bates and Mrs. Price **hoboed** their way home to Huntsville with their **escorts**.

One of these, Lester Carter, testified today that he was with the girls aboard the freight train when a fight broke out between colored and white **vagrants** who were also on the train. It was **immaterial**, Judge Callahan ruled, whether he and Orville Gilley had spent the night with Ruby and Mrs. Price.

Later when Mr. Knight was extracting in detail from Carter the various stages of his wanderings from coast to coast, Samuel S. Leibowitz, **chief defense counsel**, protested. Judge Callahan held that the evidence was **admissible**. Mr. Leibowitz inquired why he had not been permitted to trace the movements of Victoria Price prior to the alleged attack and Judge Callahan threatened to cite him for **contempt**.

"I won't have **insinuations** that you were denied something that somebody else got," he shouted. Carter was permitted to testify, however, that he overheard Mrs. Price urge one of the white hoboes while she was in jail at Scottsboro to pretend that he was her brother.

Carter said he had given up hobo life and was now a laborer for the Board of Education in New York.

Patterson on the Stand

Patterson next took the stand. Over and over he denied that he had touched Mrs. Price or Ruby Bates, or that he had even seen any woman on the train. The white hoboes had been throwing stones at him and the "other colored," he explained, and he had fought with them "to make them stop bothering us."

Mr. Hutson, cross-examining the defendant, **blustered** and stormed about the courtroom, repeating the Negro's answers to his questions with obvious scorn and disbelief in his voice and manner. Sometimes he didn't wait for Patterson to answer one question before he asked another, and he frequently attributed words to the witness that the Negro had not uttered.

Hobo jungle: Hobo camps repeatedly used in the woods along railroad lines.

Hoboed: travel by hitching onto trains and living in hobo camps.

Escorts: Men accompanying the women, Lester Carter and Orville Gilley.

Vagrants: Individuals wandering about without an apparent permanent home or financial means of support.

Immaterial: Unimportant.

Chief defense counsel: Lawyer in charge of defending the accused.

Admissible: Allowed to be presented to the jury in the trial.

Contempt: Disrespect of the judge.

Insinuations: Suggestions.

Blustered: To talk or act noisily and in a pompous or self-important manner.

At last the local prosecutor fell back upon the record of the **original trials** at Scottsboro, although Mr. Leibowitz protested that the record was **inadmissible** on the grounds that the Supreme Court of the United States had declared the whole proceeding illegal because the defendants were not adequately represented there by counsel.

Patterson said he did not remember testifying as the record indicated he had done when he was asked what he saw aboard the freight train on March 25, 1931. According to the transcript from which Mr. Hutson read, the Negro had testified that he saw all but three of the nine Negroes in custody attack the white girls. Later, reading from another part of the same record, Mr. Leibowitz showed that Patterson had testified just as he had today.

Four of Patterson's co-defendants followed him on the witness stand. They were Olin Montgomery, Willie Roberson, Ozie Powell and Andy Wright, Negro boys who have grown to manhood in jail. All denied participating in any attack on the white women.

Hutson Addresses Jury

The State offered no **rebuttal**, and after a short recess Mr. Hutson began.

It was then that he made his appeal for the protection of womanhood, and he warned the jurors that when they had **rendered** their verdict and gone home they would have to face their neighbors. His voice rose to a **crescendo** as he choked back a sob evoked by his own eloquence in lauding the **martyrdom** of Victoria Price.

"She fights for the rights of womanhood of Alabama," he shouted.

Mr. Watts, a prominent attorney in the home town of Mrs. Price, made a calm and detailed analysis of the evidence submitted, asserting that the story told by Mrs. Price had been **refuted** by the State's own witnesses "and **contradicted** by the physical facts in the case." Rape was a crime of secrecy, not one committed in broad daylight in full view of the public highway by a dozen men strangers to each other.

Introducing himself as a "friend and neighbor" from Madison County, Mr. Watts criticized the State for not placing Orville Gilley, an eye-witness of the alleged crime, on the witness stand, and remarked that he could not refrain from wondering why the State had left it for the defense to present medical testimony which was in the State's possession.

He too urged the jurors to weigh the evidence with common sense, and in answer to Mr. Hutson's plea for the protection of womanhood appealed for "protection of the innocent."

Original trials: Patterson's first three trials.

Inadmissible: Not allowed to be used in the trial.

Rebuttal: Arguments against testimony.

Rendered: Delivered.

Crescendo: Reached a high volume.

Martyrdom: To suffer for a cause.

Refuted: Shown to be false.

Contradicted: The opposite was suggested.

"It takes courage to do the right thing in the face of public **clamor** for the wrong thing, but when justice is not administered fairly, governments disintegrate and there is no protection for any one, man or woman, black or white."

Mr. Knight, who had the last word for the prosecution, summed up briefly and with restraint, confining himself to the evidence and arguing that all the testimony submitted, save that of Patterson himself, tended to bear out the **complainant's** story.

Judge Charges the Jury

Two hours were consumed by Judge Callahan in charging the jury and court did not recess until 9:30 P.M. The judge dwelt at length on the legal definition of the crime charged, on the differences between **direct** and **circumstantial** evidence and on the meaning of such terms as **reasonable doubt**.

He said that in weighing the testimony of Patterson and Victoria Price, the jurors might regard them as "interested" witnesses and consider that in deciding what weight to give it. Since the complainant was a white woman, he said, they must assume she did not yield willingly to the Negro defendant.

As Judge Callahan continued Patterson's face was glum and he slumped lower and lower in his chair. He perked up a little, however, when the court began reading a score or specific charges, requested by the defense. These emphasized the fact that the defendant was presumed to be innocent until proved guilty and that he must be **acquitted** if the possibility of his innocence was compatible with reason.

After the reading of almost every one of these requested charges, Judge Callahan expressed a comment of his own such as:

"That's just saying what I said in another way," or "that just means all twelve of you have to agree on a verdict—well, of course you do."

Clamor: Insistence.

Complainant: Person making accusations, Mrs. Price.

Direct: Hard evidence supporting the charge.

Circumstantial: Indirect evidence, such as events surrounding the case, that suggest the charges are true.

Reasonable doubt: Uncertainty about the guilt of the accused.

Acquitted: Freed from charges; not guilty.

What happened next . . .

Haywood Patterson was once again found guilty. He received a sentence of seventy-five years imprisonment. This was the first time in Alabama history that a black man

Police escort Olen Montgomery (center, with glasses) and Eugene Williams (wearing suspenders) through Penn Station, New York, July 26, 1937. Williams and Montgomery were two of the five Scottsboro boys against whom charges were finally dropped. The other four endured two, three, even four trials for their lives. *(AP/Wide World Photos)*

convicted of raping a white woman had not been sentenced to death.

In July 1937 the last trials of the Scottsboro Boys came to a close. On July 12 Clarence Norris began his third trial, which ended three days later with a conviction and death sentence. Andrew Wright was convicted on July 22 and received a ninety-nine year imprisonment. Two days later Charles Weems received a seventy-five-year sentence. Ozie Powell had his charges dropped when he agreed to plead guilty to assault and received a twenty-year sentence.

In a surprise move, the State of Alabama dropped charges and announced freedom for Olen Montgomery, Willie Roberson, Eugene Williams, and Roy Wright. None of the four were ever tried a second time but had been in prison since 1931.

Agitation for the release of the other imprisoned Scottsboro Boys continued by various interested groups across the United States. Charles Weems was paroled in 1943, Ozie Powell in 1946, and Andrew Wright in 1950. Clarence Norris was the only defendant who lived to see an official pardon in 1976 by the State of Alabama.

Following Patterson's conviction in 1937 he was imprisoned in Alabama's Atmore Prison. An unpopular prisoner, he constantly had to defend himself from other prisoners and guards. In 1941 Patterson survived being stabbed twenty times by a friend who a guard had paid to kill him. He stated he lost faith in everything but his knife, which he said had saved him many times.

Patterson taught himself to read using a Bible and dictionary. Transferred to Kilby Prison, then a prison farm, Patterson managed to escape. He ended up in Detroit and the Michigan governor refused to allow him to be taken back to Alabama. While in Detroit, Patterson, aided by journalist Earl Conrad, completed his autobiography *Scottsboro Boy,* published in 1950. At the end of 1950 Patterson was again in trouble with the law. He was involved in a bar fight that resulted in a stabbing death. Convicted of manslaughter in 1951, Patterson died in jail of cancer on August 24, 1952.

Did you know . . .

- Nineteenth-century criminal laws were clearly racially discriminatory. For example, a Georgia law specified a mandatory death sentence for rape of a white woman by a black man. A white man raping a white woman led to a two- to twenty-year sentence. Rape of a black woman had no mandatory sentence. Versions of such laws particularly in the southern United States carried on into the twentieth century.

- The Scottsboro case divided the northern and southern states more sharply than any racial event since the American Civil War (1861–65; war in the United States between the Union [North], who was opposed to slavery, and the Confederacy [South], who was in favor of slavery).

- Ultimately, none of the Scottsboro Boys were executed. The application of the death penalty against blacks, however, has drawn much attention in the criminal justice system and in the general public. Nationwide over half—55 percent—of those individuals executed between 1930 and 1991 were black.

Consider the following . . .

- Find three instances in the news account where Judge Callahan acted with bias and prejudice against the defense.

- Why did denying proper counsel (attorneys) violate due process guaranteed by the Fourteenth Amendment (see U.S. Supreme Court case *Powell v. Alabama*, 1932)?

- Whey did excluding black Americans from juries deprive blacks of equal legal protection guaranteed by the Fourteenth Amendment (see U.S. Supreme Court case *Norris v. Alabama*, 1935)?

- The American Communist Party was thoroughly involved in the legal defense of the Scottsboro Boys. It cited the case as an example of the American justice system's failure. Research the Communist Party in the United States in the 1930s. During this time period, why were a significant number of Americans willing to listen to the Communist Party's arguments?

For More Information

Carter, Dan T. *Scottsboro: A Tragedy of the American South*. Baton Rouge, LA: Louisiana State University Press, 1969.

Goodman, James. *Stories of Scottsboro*. New York: Pantheon Books, 1994.

Patterson, Haywood, and Earl Conrad. *Scottsboro Boy*. Garden City, NY: Doubleday & Company, Inc., 1950.

Web Sites

"Scottsboro: An American Tragedy." *PBS Online*. http://www.pbs.org/wgbh/amex/scottsboro/index.html (accessed on August 19, 2004).

"Scottsboro Boys." *Decatur/Morgan County Convention & Visitors Bureau*. http://www.decaturcvb.org/Pages/Press/scotboy.html (accessed on August 19, 2004).

PROTECT Act

Excerpt from the PROTECT Act of 2003

Reprinted from the *U.S. Government Printing Office Access* Web site at
http://www.gpoaccess.gov/index.html

"No family should ever have to endure the nightmare of losing a child. Our nation grieves with every family that has suffered unbearable loss. And our nation will fight threats against our children. . . . And now it is my honor to sign the PROTECT Act of 2003." President George W. Bush (1946 ; served 2001) made this statement in the White House Rose Garden immediately before signing into law the Prosecutorial Remedies and Other Tools to End the Exploitation of Children Today Act of 2003. The short title of the law, Public Law 108-21, is the PROTECT Act of 2003. The PROTECT Act is the most far reaching child protection legislation signed in decades.

Looking on was Donna Hagerman Norris and Elizabeth Smart and her parents. Norris is the mother of Amber Hagerman (1986–1996) who was kidnapped and brutally murdered in 1996. Fifteen-year-old Elizabeth Smart was abducted from her bedroom in the middle of the night, but in a rare happy ending, had been found alive and returned to her family. Donna Norris and Ed Smart, Elizabeth's father, both had urged passage of PROTECT. They were particularly instrumental in

"No child should ever have to experience the terror of abduction, or worse. . . . This law marks important progress in the protection of America's children."

President George W. Bush

President George W. Bush signs the Protect Act of 2003 on April 30, 2003. Also known as the AMBER Alert legislation, the law provides for a national AMBER Alert system for finding abducted children.
(© Reuters/Corbis)

pressuring Congress for the passage of provisions found in Title 3 of the act known as the AMBER (America's Missing: Broadcasting Emergency Response) Alert.

The AMBER Alert is the legacy of Amber Hagerman who was nine-years-old when she was abducted and murdered. Amber was riding her bicycle outside her home in Arlington, Texas, a city located between Dallas and Ft. Worth, when in daylight and in full view of witnesses she was abducted. Her body was found four days later at the bottom of a creek bed, her throat slit. Amber's murderer has never been found.

After Amber's death her mother, Donna, began working with local police and the media to create a quick alert system to inform the general public when a child has been abducted. A voluntary association between law enforcement and the Dallas-Ft. Worth Association of Radio Managers resulted in the

Robbie Callaway, Chairman of the National Center for Missing and Exploited Children, displays an AMBER Alert Kit. AMBER Alerts became increasingly important tools in rescuing kidnapped children since thousands of citizens could quickly join law enforcement in the search. *(AP/Wide World Photos)*

nation's first AMBER Alert program in 1997. AMBER stood for America's Missing: Broadcasting Emergency Response. Information about a child's abduction is quickly broadcast to the surrounding communities so the public is on the lookout for the missing child.

The idea and establishment of AMBER Alert programs spread across the country at the end of the 1990s and into the early 2000s. Some states organized statewide AMBER Alert programs while cities and entire metropolitan areas also set up AMBER systems.

AMBER Alerts became increasingly important tools in rescuing kidnapped children. As much information as possible is quickly gathered and broadcast over radio and television stations by way of the Emergency Alert System (EAS) to the areas where and near where the abduction took place. The EAS is an updated version of the Emergency Broadcast System originally designed to broadcast national nuclear attack alerts should it become necessary.

In general, an AMBER alert gives a missing child's name and description, description of the abductor, and description and license plate of the suspected car. By getting information out quickly thousands of citizens can join law enforcement in the search. AMBER Alerts have already brought a large percentage of abducted children home safely.

As the number of AMBER programs increased, the need for coordination became apparent. Within the PROTECT Act, the AMBER Alert sections provide a means for national coordination of the "patchwork" of established programs. Under the act an official from the U.S. Department of Justice is assigned as national AMBER Alert coordinator. Although each state and locality is free to set their own guidelines, the national coordinator established a set of minimum standards to apply when deciding to issue an AMBER Alert.

These alert standards, which guide most programs, are as follows: (1) a law enforcement agency confirms an abduction has taken place of a child seventeen years of age or younger; (2) the law enforcement agency believes the child abducted is in danger of bodily harm or death; and, (3) there is enough descriptive information about the child and abductor or the abductor's vehicle that if made available to the public, the public could help in the child's recovery.

An AMBER Alert can only be activated by law enforcement for the most serious abduction cases where the child is in immediate danger. In 2004 AMBER Alerts were issued over radio, television (often on a "crawl" information strip at the bottom of the picture), the Internet, and, if available, on electronic traffic information signs along roadways.

Things to remember while reading excerpts from the PROTECT Act of 2003:

- A quick response is vital to save abducted children from harm. The Department of Justice reports 74 percent of children murdered by their abductors are killed within three hours of being taken.

- Section 301 requires the U.S. attorney general to name a national AMBER Alert coordinator and lists the duties of the national coordinator.

- Section 302 directs the coordinators to establish minimum standards for guidance as to when an AMBER alert should be issued. Although most follow the voluntary standards closely, state and local programs set their own requirements for issuing an alert.

- Section 303 involves the U.S. Department of Transportation's role in the AMBER Alert programs. The section requires the secretary of transportation to provide money grants to states for alert programs, including installation of electronic message signs or other motorist notification systems.

- Section 304 requires the attorney general to provide grants to states to develop support programs such as education and training programs to teach the public about AMBER Alerts and new technologies to aid the program's quick response.

- The following excerpt allows students to read a portion of a law as it is actually organized and worded.

Excerpt from the PROTECT Act of 2003

TITLE III—Public Outreach

SEC. 301. NATIONAL COORDINATION OF AMBER ALERT COMMUNICATIONS NETWORK.

*(a) Coordination Within Department of Justice.—The Attorney General shall assign an officer of the Department of Justice to act as the national coordinator of the AMBER Alert communications network regarding abducted children. The officer **so designated** shall be known as the AMBER Alert Coordinator of the Department of Justice.*

So designated: Appointed.

(b) Duties.—In acting as the national coordinator of the AMBER Alert communications network, the Coordinator shall—

*(1) seek to eliminate **gaps** in the network, including gaps in areas of interstate travel;*

(2) work with States to encourage the development of additional elements (known as local AMBER plans) in the network;

*(3) work with States to ensure appropriate regional coordination of various **elements** of the network; and*

(4) act as the nationwide point of contact for—

(a) the development of the network; and

(b) regional coordination of alerts on abducted children through the network.

(c) Consultation With Federal Bureau of Investigation.—In carrying out duties under subsection (b), the Coordinator shall notify and consult with the Director of the Federal Bureau of Investigation concerning each child abduction for which an alert is issued through the AMBER Alert communications network.

(d) Cooperation.—The Coordinator shall cooperate with the Secretary of Transportation and the Federal Communications Commission in carrying out activities under this section.

*(e) Report.—Not later than March 1, 2005, the Coordinator shall submit to Congress a report on the activities of the Coordinator and the effectiveness and status of the AMBER plans of each State that has **implemented** such a plan. The Coordinator shall prepare the report in consultation with the Secretary of Transportation.*

*SEC. 302. MINIMUM STANDARDS FOR ISSUANCE AND **DISSEMINATION** OF ALERTS THROUGH AMBER ALERT COMMUNICATIONS NETWORK.*

(a) Establishment of Minimum Standards.—Subject to subsection (b), the AMBER Alert Coordinator of the Department of Justice shall establish minimum standards for—

(1) the issuance of alerts through the AMBER Alert communications network; and

(2) the extent of the dissemination of alerts issued through the network.

*(b) Limitations.—(1) The minimum standards established under subsection (a) shall be adoptable on a **voluntary** basis only.*

Gaps: Areas where alert communications are lacking.

Elements: Local, regional, and state AMBER plans.

Implemented: Put into use.

Dissemination: Spreading the word of an alert.

Voluntary: The minimum standards are not required but may be used by local and regional plans at their choosing.

(2) The minimum standards shall, to the maximum extent practicable (as determined by the Coordinator in consultation with State and local law enforcement agencies), provide that appropriate information relating to the special needs of an abducted child (including health care needs) are disseminated to the appropriate law enforcement, public health, and other public officials.

*(3) The minimum standards shall, to the maximum extent practicable (as determined by the Coordinator in consultation with State and local law enforcement agencies), provide that the dissemination of an alert through the AMBER Alert communications network be limited to the geographic areas most likely to **facilitate** the recovery of the abducted child concerned.*

(4) In carrying out activities under subsection (a), the Coordinator may not interfere with the current system of voluntary coordination between local broadcasters and State and local law enforcement agencies for purposes of the AMBER Alert communications network.

(c) Cooperation.—(1) The Coordinator shall cooperate with the Secretary of Transportation and the Federal Communications Commission in carrying out activities under this section.

(2) The Coordinator shall also cooperate with local broadcasters and State and local law enforcement agencies in establishing minimum standards under this section.

SEC. 303. GRANT PROGRAM FOR NOTIFICATION AND COMMUNICATIONS SYSTEMS ALONG HIGHWAYS FOR RECOVERY OF ABDUCTED CHILDREN.

*(a) Program Required.—The Secretary of Transportation shall carry out a program to provide grants to States for the development or **enhancement** of notification or communications systems along highways for alerts and other information for the recovery of abducted children.*

(b) Development Grants.—

*(1) In general.—The Secretary may make a grant to a State under this subsection for the development of a State program for the use of changeable message signs or other motorist information systems to notify motorists about abductions of children. The State program shall provide for the planning, coordination, and design of systems, **protocols**, and message sets that support the coordination and communication necessary to notify motorists about abductions of children. . . .*

Facilitate: Bring about.

Enhancement: Improvement.

Protocols: Detailed plans for communication.

(c) Implementation Grants.—

(1) In general.—The Secretary may make a grant to a State under this subsection for the implementation of a program for the use of changeable message signs or other motorist information systems to notify motorists about abductions of children. A State shall be eligible for a grant under this subsection if the Secretary determines that the State has developed a State program in accordance with subsection (b). . . .

(d) Federal Share.—The Federal share of the cost of any activities funded by a grant under this section may not exceed 80 percent. . . .

(g) Definition.—In this section, the term "State"' means any of the 50 States, the District of Columbia, or Puerto Rico.

*(h) Authorization of **Appropriations**.—There is authorized to be appropriated to the Secretary to carry out this section $20,000,000 for **fiscal year** 2004. Such amounts shall remain available until expended.*

(i) Study of State Programs.—

*(1) Study.—The Secretary shall conduct a study to examine State **barriers** to the adoption and implementation of State programs for the use of communications systems along highways for alerts and other information for the recovery of abducted children. . . .*

SEC. 304. GRANT PROGRAM FOR SUPPORT OF AMBER ALERT COMMUNICATIONS PLANS.

(a) Program Required.—The Attorney General shall carry out a program to provide grants to States for the development or enhancement of programs and activities for the support of AMBER Alert communications plans.

(b) Activities.—Activities funded by grants under the program under subsection (a) may include—

(1) the development and implementation of education and training programs, and associated materials, relating to AMBER Alert communications plans;

(2) the development and implementation of law enforcement programs, and associated equipment, relating to AMBER Alert communications plans;

(3) the development and implementation of new technologies to improve AMBER Alert communications; and

(4) such other activities as the Attorney General considers appropriate for supporting the AMBER Alert communications program.

Appropriations: Funding.

Fiscal year: A twelve month period based on receipt of taxes and other revenues, extending from October 1 to September 30 of the following year.

Barriers: Things that would block or hinder use of the programs.

(c) Federal Share.—The Federal share of the cost of any activities funded by a grant under the program under subsection (a) may not exceed 50 percent. . . .

(f) Authorization of Appropriations.—(1) There is authorized to be appropriated for the Department of Justice $5,000,000 for fiscal year 2004 to carry out this section and, in addition, $5,000,000 for fiscal year 2004 to carry out subsection (b)(3).

What happened next . . .

In many instances AMBER Alerts have led to the quick rescue of abducted children. At the time of PROTECT's signing (April 30, 2003) forty-one states had established AMBER Alert programs and about forty-nine local and regional programs existed. These numbers were up from sixteen state and thirty-two local and regional programs in August 2002.

Regional plans are plans that cover a larger area than just one city such as the King County AMBER Alert Plan that covers the greater metropolitan Seattle, Washington, area. According to the National Center for Missing and Exploited Children, by June 4, 2004, all states except Hawaii had established statewide plans (Hawaii had local plans in both Honolulu and Maui County). Seventeen regional and thirty-two local plans were in operation.

Attorney General John Ashcroft had appointed Deborah J. Daniels, assistant attorney general for the Office of Justice programs, as the first national AMBER Alert Coordinator six months before PROTECT was signed into law. In 2003 and 2004 she was in the process of studying all AMBER plans across the country and coordinating their efforts nationwide. Daniels and her staff developed minimum standards for issuing alerts; developed federal, state, and local partnerships; evaluated improving technologies and their compatibility (ability to work together) with different systems; and developed programs to raise public awareness about abductions.

National advisory member groups contributing to the coordinated AMBER effort included, in addition to the U.S.

Meghan's Law

President Bill Clinton (1946–; served 1993–2001) signed Meghan's Law, also known as Megan's Law, on May 17, 1996. Megan's Law requires registration of convicted sex offenders and notification when a sex offender moves into a community. States are required to register sex offenders and to make public both private and personal information about the offender in the community where the offender lives.

States may establish their own standards for what information is disclosed about an offender. Megan's Law is named after seven-year-old Megan Kanka, who was the victim of a brutal rape and murder in 1994.

Registration and community notification of convicted sex offenders is required because of the high rate of repeat offenses by sex offenders after their release from custody. The government's first interest and responsibility is protection of the public. These interests come before the privacy interests of sex offenders. Registration allows law enforcement to immediately investigate known offenders when a crime is committed. Community notification allows citizens to better protect their children from sex offenders who might have moved into their community.

Department of Justice and Department of Transportation, the Federal Communications Commission (FCC), National Center for Missing and Exploited Children, broadcasters nationwide, and law enforcement agencies across the country.

Did you know . . .

- Canadian provinces have also been establishing AMBER Alert programs in 2003 and 2004.

- In some areas the AMBER system has been used to send alerts about people with Alzheimer's disease or other disabilities who are missing.

- AMBER alerts are generally given for children kidnapped by strangers since statistics show they are in the most serious danger. Child custody abductions and abductions by relatives usually do not qualify for an alert unless the child is likely to suffer physical harm.

- America Online (AOL), the Internet provider, issues AMBER Alerts to subscribers signed up by an AOL Alerts and Reminder service.

- Section 323 of the PROTECT Act created a cyber tip line so online users can report Internet-related child sexual activities.

- Child Abuse Prevention Month is in April of each year, the same month in which PROTECT was signed.

Consider the following . . .

- Rather than being the initiator of AMBER programs throughout the country, the AMBER Alert sections of PROTECT followed and further organized efforts of states and cities. Why do you think the establishment of AMBER programs progressed so rapidly that the federal government found itself having to catch up?

- Research the AMBER Alert program in your state or locality. What guidelines are followed for issuing an alert? How are alerts issued to the public? How successful have they been in safely recovering abducted children?

- What is the key reason for not issuing an AMBER Alert when the abductor is a relative?

For More Information

Books

Ramsey, Sarah H., and Douglas E. Adams. *Children and the Law in a Nutshell*. 2nd ed. St. Paul, MN: Thomson/West, 2003.

Web Sites

"AMBER Alert National Strategy." *U.S. Department of Justice, Office of Justice Programs*. http://www.ojp.usdoj.gov/amberalert/AMBERale.pdf (accessed on August 19, 2004).

Beyond Missing, Inc. http://www.beyondmissing.com (accessed on August 19, 2004).

"FCC Consumer Advisory: The Amber Plan." *Federal Communications Commission*. http://www.fcc.gov/cgb/consumerfacts/AMBERPlan.html (accessed on August 19, 2004).

National Center for Missing and Exploited Children. http://www.missingkids.com (accessed on August 19, 2004).

PROTECT Act of 2003. U.S. Government Printing Office Access. http://frwebgate.access.gpo.gov/cgi-in/getdoc.cgi?dbname=108_cong_public_laws&docid=f:publ021.108 (accessed on August 19, 2004).

Terrorism

Following the September 11, 2001 terrorist attack (known as 9/11) on the United States, the U.S. government named its number one mission as protecting the homeland from future terrorist actions. Prior to 9/11 there was no comprehensive plan for such a mission; immediately after the terrorist attacks the government began developing a plan and the practical steps needed to achieve it.

President George W. Bush (1945–; served 2001–) declared a "War on Terrorism." The American people, industry, and government leaders and agencies focused and cooperated to a degree not seen since World War II (1939–45). Congress passed the USA Patriot Act on October 25, 2001, to strengthen the ability of law enforcement agencies to investigate and prosecute terrorists and those who gave them support.

An unprecedented coordinated effort between local, state, and federal law enforcement agencies, intelligence agencies, and private industry to share information improved protection for the nation's infrastructure. This infrastructure includes both physical and virtual or electronic networks. Physical networks include airline transportation, energy pro-

Following the September 11, 2001, terrorist attacks on the Pentagon and the World Trade Center towers (seen here), national security became priority number one for the U.S. government. *(© Reuters/Corbis)*

duction facilities, seaports, highways, pipelines, railroads, and private industry and government buildings. Virtual networks include complex computer systems and the cyberspace of the Internet.

Many infrastructures function nationwide across the borders of every state and in many cases worldwide. In doing so they operate in multiple law enforcement jurisdictions (areas in which specific agencies have legal authority to make arrests) overseen by many different agencies.

Since the United States operates under a federal system, state governments share power with the federal government. In turn, state governments share power with local governments. The country has more than 87,000 different law enforcement jurisdictions at all levels. Examples of local and state law enforcement agencies are city, county, and state police, and district attorney (government lawyers) offices. The Federal Bureau of Investigation (FBI) is a federal law enforcement agency. Intelligence agencies include the Central Intelligence (CIA), FBI Counterintelligence Division, National Security Agency (NSA), and intelligence departments of the army, navy, air force, and marines.

President Bush created the Office of Homeland Security within the White House in October 2001. The office grew into the cabinet level Department of Homeland Security (DHS), which became fully functional in early 2003. The mission of DHS is to connect, streamline, and unify homeland protection efforts among law enforcement and intelligence agencies.

Protection of the homeland also relies by necessity on a global effort against terrorists. After 9/11 a global antiterrorism coalition was created to fight terrorism. This coalition involves countries in every corner of the world. As the first international action in the War on Terrorism, the U.S. military and coalition forces went to Afghanistan and forced out the oppressive Taliban government. The Taliban had been in close collaboration with Al Qaeda, the terrorist group responsible for 9/11.

The first excerpt in this chapter, "Speech by Louis J. Freeh, Director of the FBI" provides insight into U.S. worries about national security in the late 1990s before 9/11. The director of the FBI interestingly describes national security matters as on the "back burner," not law enforcement's number one priority. Freeh states the American people do not feel "imminently threatened with the collapse of infrastructures" and are "not seeing intrusions (attacks) that would alarm them."

Freeh's speech focuses on potential terrorist crimes against computer systems and warns of the potential for future terrorist actions. His heightened concern over criminals carrying out terrorist activities became apparent to all Americans on 9/11.

The next two excerpts, both post-9/11, illustrate how and why U.S. national priorities shifted dramatically by late 2001. "Patterns of Global Terrorism" is the 2002 U.S. State Department report on terrorism. "Patterns of Global Terrorism," the department's annual world terrorism assessment report, describes U.S. policy toward terrorism post-9/11. The third excerpt, "The Al Qaeda Training Manual," provides in chilling detail procedures on how to be a successful al Qaeda terrorist.

Louis J. Freeh

Excerpt from "Speech by Louis J. Freeh, Director of the FBI, 1997 International Computer Crime Conference, New York, New York, March 4, 1997"

Reprinted from *Cyber Terrorism and Information Warfare: 1. Assessment and Challenges,* edited by Yonah Alexander and Michael S. Swetnam

Published in 1999

"But we know with great certainty that of the problem [of cyber crime] is not dealt with very quickly, the time will come that . . . national security will clearly be at risk."

By the 1990s computer systems had become a critical operating component for governments and private business. The Internet, a computer network for information and electronic mail, allowed for almost instantaneous worldwide communication. Any disruption of a computer system in either governments or businesses brought a virtual halt to operations until the problems could be corrected.

The following excerpt is from "Speech by Louis J. Freeh, Director of the FBI, 1997 International Computer Crime Conference, New York, New York, March 4, 1997." Realizing that rapid advances in computer technology had not only benefited the world's population but also was an aid to those wishing to engage in criminal activity, Freeh praised leaders of private industry and law enforcement agencies for gathering together to discuss cyber crime issues. The conference involved individuals from the United States and from around the world.

Freeh's words give an interesting insight into thinking at the end of the twentieth century concerning the potential threats of cyber crime. The threats he predicted could affect a nation's national security by disrupting computer network systems. Increasingly, national infrastructures were being operated and controlled with complex computer technology. Examples include communication systems, 911 emergency lines, business transactions, power generation, and transportation systems such as air traffic control. Criminal computer specialists already had the ability to intrude into computer systems of both private corporations and governments with serious consequences.

Freeh notes that the science of law enforcement, how crimes are investigated and criminals pursued, was changing dramatically because of advancing computer technology. No longer were crimes always committed at a particular geographic location by a person with a specific street address. No longer could a single law enforcement agency with local jurisdiction investigate and make arrests.

Computer hacker "Mudge" testifying in 1998 that computer security is so careless that he and fellow hackers could disable the entire Internet in thirty minutes. *(AP/Wide World Photos)*

Internet crimes, Freeh pointed out, were committed in cyberspace. Local, state, national, or international jurisdictions did not exist for cyber crime. Instead local, state, and national law enforcement agencies would have to work together and with law enforcement agencies of different countries to both solve and prevent cyber crime. Since they knew their own systems thoroughly, computer specialists of international industries and businesses would also be required to aid law enforcement investigations.

Freeh called for those at the conference to begin thinking about pulling law enforcement and private business from all over the world into cooperative working groups to combat cyber crime. He called the cooperation a critical step toward designing systems and procedures to protect against and react to disruptions in computer networks.

Freeh describes measures the FBI had taken by 1997 to investigate the threat of cyber crime. The FBI Computer Investigations and Threat Assessment Center provided expertise in computer investigations and threat assessments. Three FBI computer squads had been organized to serve as a resource for other FBI divisions and other law enforcement agencies. Internationally, thirty countries had "Legats," FBI offices located abroad to provide "cop-to-cop bridges" in partnering with international law enforcement agencies.

Things to remember while reading excerpts from "Speech by Louis J. Freeh, Director of the FBI":

- In 1997 the potential for a direct terrorist action against the United States on U.S. soil did not worry many Americans. Neither did disruption of computer systems by terrorists. Aside from the occasional hacker entering a classified computer system, no such actions had been serious enough to cause much interest or concern. Freeh pointed out such national security matters were not a priority at the time.

- Freeh acknowledges that law enforcement has historically operated in a catch-up mode. Only once a crime is committed or new alarming information made public would Congress act to pass new laws enabling law enforcement agencies to act.

- Freeh gives examples of actual cyber crimes. He challenges both private industry and law enforcement agencies to begin thinking globally, in terms of worldwide cooperation. Calling for industry and law enforcement agencies all over the world to begin working together was a new concept.

Excerpt from "Speech by Louis J. Freeh, Director of the FBI"

Mideast: Region between Europe and Asia including northeastern Africa.

*I just returned from a very brief trip to the **Mideast** where I visited three countries and spent time with the leaders of all the coun-*

*tries involved in the current peace process. We met with **Yasser Arafat, the Prime Minister of Israel, King Hussein, President Mubarak**, and, over the course of several days, all of my **counterparts**, both in law enforcement services and security services.*

*And part of our agenda . . . did in fact deal with some of the issues that this conference is going to address—issues like **technology crimes**; law enforcement in the **information age**; threats to **infrastructure**; threats to national security; the new ways that criminals and terrorists have found to achieve their objectives; taking advantage of all of the technological changes; the **transparency of borders**; the ability to travel and send information instantaneously. . . .*

*It's an obvious point, but one which I think we need to make: in the United States also, these critical issues will continue to occupy industry and law enforcement, but they are not at this time on the front burners for law enforcement or for national security people. This should not be surprising. We are not imminently threatened with the collapse of infrastructures. We are not seeing **intrusions** at a frequent enough index that people are alarmed about them. . . .*

*Today this kind of debate continues in Washington and around the world on **encryption**. Again, at this point we can't point to a **proliferation** of examples where encryption, unbreakable encryption, has caused the loss of lives or shut down major investigations. But we know, with great certainty, that if that problem is not dealt with very quickly, the time will come that, as **robust encryption proliferates without any recovery systems**, law enforcement and national security will clearly be at risk.*

In a sense, this process really describes the history and the saga of law enforcement. In 1933, unarmed FBI agents transporting a prisoner were gunned down in a crossfire that became known as the Kansas City Massacre. Only then was Congress spurred to enact, within a week after that attack, the authority for FBI agents to carry firearms and make arrests.

*It took the chance discovery of the **Apalachin meeting** up in New York and subsequent investigations in the mid-60's to demonstrate the existence of **la Cosa Nostra** in the United States—and that spurred Congress to authorize court-authorized wiretapping in 1968.*

So we see, over the course of time, how law enforcement strives to catch up with technology. And I think that's where we are right now with computer crime, with the encryption issues, with the telecommunication issues, and with the wireless communication issues—all of which need to be addressed and solved.

Arafat, Hussein, Mubarak: Arafat, leader of Palestinian Authority; Hussein, king of Jordan; Mubarak, president of Egypt.

Counterparts: Government law enforcement directors of other countries.

Technology crimes: Disabling computer systems or using computers and the Internet for criminal activity.

Information age: Communications with high speed computers.

Infrastructure: Basic framework for systems, such as communications, bridges, railroads, roadways, airports.

Transparency of borders: Lack of geographical lines in cyberspace.

Intrusions: Terrorist threats or acts.

Encryption: Coded message systems that allow secret information to be sent.

Proliferation: Rapid increase.

Robust encryption proliferates without any recovery systems: Vigorous encryption continues without a way to retrieve the coded data.

Apalachin meeting: A historic gathering of numerous organized crime leaders.

La Cosa Nostra: The Mafia, an Italian and Sicilian crime organization.

Imperative: Essential.

So I really salute all of you—and the different countries and corporations that you represent—for putting together a conference which, for the first time, focuses internationally on this problem. Your lead is one that law enforcement must follow.

*Today when new FBI agents graduate from our training academy in Virginia, they leave with their firearms and their badges, but they also leave with a laptop computer. It's an excellent symbol of the changing environment in which these young men and women will function over the next 20 years. It is also **imperative** for the way they must conduct investigations. When they serve law enforcement search warrants, they seize hard drives and disks instead of the boxes and boxes of records and books and ledgers that their predecessors, myself included, used to seize to support our cases.*

Today, also, they chase fugitives over cyberspace as well as over fences. You may remember when we arrested Mr. Mitnik a year or so ago. He was found by the FBI, but he was found because we hired a 23-year-old computer specialist to locate exactly where he was and where he was transmitting from. That was the basis of effecting that arrest.

*I though also I would mention, very briefly, some of the cases where the technology of computers and cyber crime is evidencing itself, and then talk generally and briefly about recent **initiatives** undertaken between the FBI and other government organizations, in partnership with the private sector, to deal with some of these problems.*

*Clearly these problems and issues cannot be solved **unilaterally** by law enforcement, no more than they could be solved unilaterally by the **private sector**. If we are to identify and respond to these various problems, we have got to unite the efforts of industry and law enforcement on an international scale.*

*Let me mention very quickly a couple of cases; these are all public cases so I can comment on them. The Citibank case . . . was a case where someone with a laptop computer, sitting in an apartment in St. Petersburg, Russia, intrudes into a bank and attempts to move millions of dollars out of accounts to a place where they can be **exploited**.*

*We had a similar case recently with a so-called **"phone phreaker"** in Sweden—and because of the assistance we received from Swedish authorities, we were able to solve that case. There a young man, sitting in his own apartment, hacked his way across the Atlantic Ocean into U.S. telephone switching systems and worked his way down to*

Initiatives: Actions.

Unilaterally: Alone.

Private sector: Privately owned businesses and industry.

Exploited: Used by criminals for criminal activities.

Phone phreaker: A person who disrupts and causes confusion in a telephone system.

.

northern Florida, where over the course of several weeks, he interfered with 911 systems and had the capability to disable the system. It could have been disastrous, because 911 systems not only affect the police but also affect fire and emergency services.

Now **extrapolate** that to imagine if he had hit larger systems—banking systems, stock exchanges, or power grids in the northeast or northwest in the middle of winter.

We had another recent and continuing case in Baltimore, which we call the Innocent Images case. . . . It goes back to 1993 when we began investigating a kidnapping case. When we began to focus on several subjects, it became clear that they were using computers—computer telecommunications networks—to contact, identify and, in some cases, arrange for meetings with children.

In a sense, they were entering the homes of the children, not on the telephone or by a knock on the door, but through computer modems. That case, which has become a national initiative by the FBI, has resulted so far in approximately 88 arrests and 78 convictions. And the only people targeted in those cases are the individuals who are involved in large-scale distributions of **pornography**, and that's just, in our view, the tip of the iceberg.

FBI Director Louis Freeh testifies on Capitol Hill, April 27, 1995. With the rising possibility of cyber crimes and computer system terrorism affecting the entire nation in the 1990s, Freeh called for industry and law enforcement agencies across the world to work together—a new concept in law enforcement. *(AP/Wide World Photos)*

We had a recent terrorism case where an individual maintained plans in his laptop computer to attack airliners and other targets. Part of the files contained in that laptop is still encrypted and is still in need of being **deciphered** by the law enforcement authorities.

Those are just several cases on the menu—again, not representative of thousands of others, but all of a very serious nature and with **grave implications**. If you take the context of those cases and translate them to large scale industries, to infrastructure, and to informational systems, then you can see that the potential is **catastrophic**.

Extrapolate: Project to a larger situation.

Pornography: Videos, books, and photographs focusing on nudity and sexual activities.

Deciphered: Figured out.

Grave implications: Capable of doing great harm.

Catastrophic: Disastrous.

*Consider for example, a recent exercise by a government agency that is responsible for maintaining and transmitting secure information. This agency ran some computer attacks against its own very well defended systems, using people inside and outside the agency to perform them. The results of the test were that 88 percent of the attacks were successful. Again, the implications of that exercise, translated to all our informational systems, are **sobering**.*

*We have been trying to respond to the **prospective issues** involved in this issue in a number of different ways. In June last year the President signed an Executive Order that asked all government agencies, coordinated by the FBI, to do a critical infrastructure study over a one-year period that would focus on the **vulnerabilities** of the systems—both physical and informational security—and that would compose and design **protocols of plans and systems** to protect key areas of government, as well as private industry infrastructure.*

That process has been ongoing now for several months. We have enlisted the assistance of many agencies, particularly Department of Defense agencies, which have great expertise in this area. We have also heavily relied upon private industry and private consultants to supply some of the necessary expertise for analysis and planning.

*In addition, **pursuant to** the Executive Order and to a Presidential Directive on terrorism, we established an FBI Computer Investigations and Threat Assessment Center in our headquarters, which we call CITAC. The purpose of that center is two-fold: one, to develop and provide expertise in computer investigations; secondly, to do **threat assessments** with respect to computer crime infrastructure defenses. This ties in as best it can with the infrastructure analysis program which is ongoing at the same time.*

*We have established three FBI computer crime squads in the field now, one is there in New York; two, in others cities around the country. These are very different animals in terms of our FBI structure. Most FBI squads are **programmatic squads**, dealing with bank robbery or with theft from interstate shipment. These new computer crime squads, however, are disciplinary squads—nonprogrammatic and specifically designed and ordered to gather up, within a particular division, all of the computer investigative expertise that we have both from an analytic and an operational point of view. We then use them as a resource for all other programs, criminal programs, or national security matters. We also use them to assist our partners in other law enforcement agencies.*

Sobering: Makes one think more serious consequences would be likely.

Prospective issues: Potential criminal activity.

Vulnerabilities: Weaknesses.

Protocols of plans and systems: Defense strategies.

Pursuant to: In direct response to.

Threat assessments: Determine weak areas that could be hit.

Programmatic squads: Groups of agents that deal with certain types of criminal activity.

*Part of our CITAC program also requires the **SACs** in all our 56 field divisions to form working groups with local industry—banking, utilities, energy, whatever the framework may be for that particular location—and put together working groups that will serve both to advise and respond to a crisis that threatens infrastructure, whether it be a criminal or a national security matter. To date, those advisory working groups are working very well around the country.*

Again, the real key to success here—and I don't think it can be repeated too much—is the critical partnership of government with the private sector and private industry. . . . It is critical that, prior to an emergency, we develop the contacts, the associations, and the working groups to deal with some of those problems.

*We have worked very hard, as you know, in the legislation area to obtain the **authorities** that not only enable us to continue our investigative programs and techniques, but also help us anticipate some of the emerging problems. Last year, for instance, the FBI worked very hard with private industry and with many distinguished **academics**, to propose and ultimately to see pass the economic espionage statute, which is really a **trade secrets** act.*

The interesting thing behind that initiative, however, was the fact that it was computer crime—particularly computer intrusions into major companies to valuable trade secrets—that focused our efforts to protect commerce and industry here in the United States. We found, for instance, that the traditional theft statutes, like the transportation of stolen property, just didn't apply to the situations where an intruder into or an employee of a corporation quickly downloads an important trade secret and transports that information on a disk either locally or globally.

*The courts had said in many cases that **intellectual property** or knowledge of a trade secret was not really a "good" or "ware" as intended by the Congress in the interstate transportation of stolen property act. So we found we had a large area of criminal activity legally exempted from the FBI's program.*

*A major **impetus** for this trade secrets act was thus the ability of computer criminals to steal valuable intellectual property that doesn't quite fit the 1930s definition of "goods, wares, and merchandise." This is just one example of our legislative initiatives directed towards those technology problems.*

Encryption is another important one. We realize that the need for robust encryption is critical for the health of our national economy and

SACs: Security assessment centers.

Authorities: Legal responsibility.

Academics: Scholars, such as university professors, who were experts in trademark, copyright, and patent issues.

Trade secrets: Business secrets.

Intellectual property: A creation of someone's mind, such as a poem, song, story, or play.

Impetus: Incentive.

for American competitiveness, here and overseas. As a law enforcement agency that wears a national security hat, however, we also realize that we need encryption with some **exempted or court-authorized recovery mechanism** for those very rare instances when encrypted channels are used to either transmit or store information relative to a crime, an act of terror, or a national security matter. Of course such a mechanism would be available to us only under court orders and very **stringent requirements**, as with the 1968 court-authorized wiretapping statute. . . .

Another FBI initiative that deals with the cyber crime and global crime issue is the expansion of our Legal Attaché program. As many of our international friends here know, the FBI has had, for many, many years a "Legat" program, as well call it, where FBI agents are assigned to various embassies to engage in **liaison functions** with the **host** law enforcement authorities. They deal exclusively in law enforcement-related activities. They do not engage in any other non-criminal activities except as liaison.

We have Legats now in 30 countries. On my last trip, in fact, I dedicated an office in Tel Aviv, which will also serve as liaison with Jordan, with the Palestinian authority, and with the office in Cairo. Over the next two years, pursuant to a plan approved by the Congress, we will open another 16 Legats which will take us to the places like Beijing, South Africa, and Buenos Aires—places where law enforcement needs cop-to-cop bridges and the police-to-police contacts that are necessary to deal with crimes like computer crime and others that have no boundaries and that are committed in the twinkling of a eye. These crimes absolutely require us to work with our partners in order to identify and solve them.

We are **behind the eight ball**, I think, in our efforts to deal both with cyber crime and global crime. But the initiatives I have mentioned—including infrastructure initiatives, training initiatives, the Legat programs—are all certainly moving in the right direction. My concern is that we are moving too slowly and that the pace of change is so rapid that, despite our best efforts and our resources, we will still remain a little bit behind the curve.

If you think about what's happening now with respect to cyber crime and global crime, it's not unfair to compare it to the advent of the automobile back in the early part of the century. Easy automobile use then changed everything. It didn't just change the economy, it also had an immense impact on law enforcement, which had been dealing with crime on a localized basis.

Exempted or court-authorized recovery mechanism: Legal authority to retrieve information stored in computers like legal authority to wiretap telephone lines.

Stringent requirements: Strict guidelines for information gathering to avoid invasion of privacy of individuals or groups.

Liaison functions: Cooperating and coordinating.

Host: The country where Legat is located.

Behind the eight ball: Needing to act and react defensively.

Today the change is from national to international borders. I remember when I was a new FBI agent here in New York in 1975. It was an **anomaly** to have a lead in your case which went overseas to a foreign bank account, or to need to speak to a witness who was outside our jurisdiction, or to need records from an offshore location where we had no jurisdiction.

Now in 1997, that's all changed. It is probably rare when we don't have an international connection in a drug case or an economic crime case, or a fugitive case or a national security matter. Just like the automobile back in the 1920s and the 1930s, the computer is impacting the economy and the science of law enforcement today, except, probably, with a tenfold greater impact.

It is affecting everything we do in law enforcement. It is changing the rules of the game with respect to how we prepare for and deal with national security issues. And it will continue to do that at an even more alarming rate.

U.S. Department of Homeland Security secretary Tom Ridge speaks at the National Cyber Security Summit in Santa Clara, California, December 3, 2003. *(AP/Wide World Photos)*

Remember the old gangster movies where somebody robbed a bank, got in an old Model T, and raced away from the police to a state line—where the police had to stop because they didn't have jurisdiction to take the bank robbers over the state line? Congress **intervened** when that happened. It established interstate banking authority for the FBI with respect to the bank robbery jurisdiction. And everybody thought we had solved the problem. In today's world, though, we are dealing with global borders and economic borders that have ceased to exist. We now need to have authorities from Congress, and we also need technological means to deal with a problem that is getting increasingly more complex and global. We need to draw on your expertise and advice and partner our efforts.

So, let me just close by again thanking you all for your attendance and participation here. We certainly appreciate your interest. We thank your chiefs and director generals for approving this. And

Anomaly: Unusual.

Intervened: Took action on.

we ask that you help us to combat these new crime phenomena. A critical part of our success will come from industry and from you. Thank you very much.

What happened next . . .

On September 11, 2001, nineteen terrorists, all members of al Qaeda, a terrorist organization based in Afghanistan, hijacked four fully fueled U.S. airliners. Two were flown into the twin towers of the World Trade Center in New York City, one into the Pentagon in Washington, D.C., and the fourth, presumably heading for Washington, D.C., crashed in Pennsylvania. A total of 3,047 people died and the issue of national security immediately went to the "front burner" as the nation's number one priority.

Cooperation between law enforcement agencies, private businesses, and Americans in general became crucial. Just as Freeh predicted, computers had become vital to terrorists and criminals as communication and planning tools. Computer systems themselves became the target of criminal activity when terrorists made efforts to disrupt key communication networks, or extract sensitive information from company or military files. Since cyber crimes are carried out over worldwide computer linkages, U.S. and international law enforcement agencies had to work together, ignoring traditional jurisdictional boundaries.

In 2004 the FBI and Computer Criminal Intellectual Property Section (CCIPS), both within the U.S. Department of Justice, were the lead law enforcement agencies dealing with cyber crime. The FBI Investigative Programs, Cyber Investigations Unit has the responsibility of protecting the nation from cyber crime, from both terrorist activities and cyber criminals such as sexual predators or those stealing from U.S. businesses. All information about terrorist threats goes to the Terrorist Threat Integration Center (TTIC) in Northern Virginia. Representatives of all U.S. counterterrorist agencies work together at the TTIC.

The CCIPS employs a team of about forty lawyers to prosecute cyber criminal cases. CCIPS also oversees the National Cybercrime Training Partnership (NCTP) that provides education to local state and federal agencies in the latest law enforcement techniques for fighting cyber crime.

There are forty-nine FBI Legal Attachéor Legats offices in the world. The FBI special agents assigned to Legats work side by side with other countries to prevent terrorism.

Did you know . . .
- By 1977 new graduating FBI agents were trained and armed with firearms but their most important piece of equipment was a laptop computer.

- Encryption, or coded messages, used in computer communications benefited law enforcement agencies and businesses but also benefited criminals. For example, a business might code the credit card numbers of its customers so the numbers cannot be stolen. Criminals, too, send information in code so law enforcement is unable to decipher it. Just as encrypted message codes of the Japanese and Germans were broken by U.S. intelligence agents in World War II, Freeh believed further efforts in the study of encryption were essential.

Consider the following . . .
- Historically law enforcement agencies stayed within their jurisdictions for investigative work and arrests. For example, state police did not move across state boundaries. Why does Freeh say crime can no longer be solved "unilaterally" by a single agency? Why are traditional jurisdiction boundaries, in some cases, obsolete?

- Why was Freeh so determined to involve private industry in combating cyber crime? Think in terms of an industry as the victim and their computer specialists having expert knowledge of their computer systems.

- What single event in U.S. history put national security and cyber terrorist crime on the "front burner?"

- Research and list at least five types of cyber crime.

For More Information

Books

Alexander, Yonah, and Michael S. Swetnam, eds. *Cyber Terrorism and Information Warfare: 1. Assessment and Challenges.* Dobbs Ferry, NY: Oceana Publications, Inc., 1999.

Sherman, Mark. *Introduction to Cyber Crime.* Washington, DC: Federal Judicial Center, 2000.

Web Sites

"Computer Crime and Intellectual Property Section (CCIPS) of the Criminal Division." *U.S. Department of Justice.* http://www.cybercrime.gov (accessed on August 19, 2004).

"The Electronic Frontier: The Challenge of Unlawful Conduct Involving the Use of the Internet." *U.S. Department of Justice.* http://www.usdoj.gov/criminal/cybercrime/unlawful.htm (accessed on August 19, 2004).

Internet Crime Complaint Center. http://www.ic3.gov (accessed on August 19, 2004).

"Investigative Programs, Cyber Investigations." *Federal Bureau of Investigation.* http://www.fbi.gov/cyberinvest/cyberhome.htm (accessed on August 19, 2004).

U.S. State Department

Excerpt from "Patterns of Global Terrorism—2002"

Reprinted from *Terrorism: Documents of International and Local Control, Volume 39, U.S. Perspectives,* edited by James Walsh

Published in 2003

Although post-9/11 many important reports on terrorism have been issued, the U.S. State Department's annual assessment has long been considered the government's most important public report on terrorism. U.S. law requires the Department of State to provide Congress with an annual report on global terrorism. The report must give a complete assessment of foreign countries where significant terrorist actions occurred, must report on countries known to support terrorism, and must assess worldwide terrorist organizations. U.S. law also requires the report to describe how countries cooperate with the United States to apprehend, convict, and punish terrorists who attack U.S. citizens or interests, as well as how countries attempt to prevent future terrorist acts.

The following excerpt from "Patterns of Global Terrorism—2002" is part of the introduction written by Cofer Black, State Department coordinator for counterterrorism. The impact of 9/11 on this report is obvious. His introduction, which precedes the lengthy country-by-country reports and assessment of each terrorist organization, is a summary of the actions taken by the U.S. government against terrorism since

"The world is fighting terrorism on five fronts: diplomatic, intelligence, law enforcement, financial, and military."

9/11. It also includes U.S. terrorism policy and strategy, and the four powerful guiding principles President Bush laid out for U.S. counterterrorism.

Things to remember while reading excerpts from "Patterns of Global Terrorism—2002":

- "Patterns of Global Terrorism—2002" is especially notable because it was the first State Department annual report on terrorism since 9/11.

- Congress and Americans were now totally aware that terrorism could reach the U.S. homeland. Preventing future terrorist attacks and bringing those responsible to justice was the number one priority of everyone.

- Following the 9/11 attacks President Bush had declared a "War on Terrorism."

Ambassador Francis X. Taylor discusses the 2001 "Patterns of Global Terrorism" report, which documented 2001 as the deadliest year for terrorist attacks because of 9/11. *(© Reuters/Corbis)*

- The crimes of terrorism had to be dealt with on a global basis.

- Preventing future crimes of terrorism requires a multiple front offensive. Note the five key fronts explained by the State Department.

Bali to Grozny to Mombasa: The island of Bali in Indonesia to the capital city of Grozny in Chechnya (a province of Russia) to the port city of Mombassa in Kenya.

Excerpt from "Patterns of Global Terrorism—2002"

*The evil terrorism continued to plague the world throughout 2002, from **Bali to Grozny to Mombasa**. At the same time, the global* war against the terrorist threat was waged intensively in all regions with encouraging results.

The year saw the **liberation** of Afghanistan by Coalition forces, the **expulsion** of **al-Qaida** and the oppressive **Taliban** regime, the destruction of their terrorist training **infrastructure**, and the installation of a **transitional government** committed to democracy and economic development.

Al-Qaida terrorists are on the run, and thousands of them have been **detained**. More than one third of al-Qaida's top leadership has been killed or captured, including some who conspired in the September 11 attacks, the 2000 attack on the **USS Cole**, and the 1998 bombings of **two US Embassies** in East Africa.

Moreover, the **global antiterrorism coalition** that was forged in the immediate aftermath of the September 11 attacks in the United States remains united.

The world is fighting terrorism on five fronts: **diplomatic, intelligence**, law enforcement, **financial**, and military.

Diplomatic

The progress that has been achieved in the global war on terrorism would not have been possible without intense diplomatic engagement throughout the world. Diplomacy is the backbone of the campaign, building the political will, support, and mechanisms that enable our law enforcement, intelligence, and military communities to act effectively.

The web of relationships we have **cultivated** has borne fruit in countless ways, from increasing security at home and abroad to bringing wanted terrorists to justice in the United States and elsewhere.

All our friends have stood with us multilaterally—at the United Nations, in NATO, ANZUS, EU, G-7, G-8, OAS, ASEAN, APEC, OIC, OECD, OSCE—and bilaterally in virtually every corner of the world.

New counterterrorism relationships with Russia, China, India, Pakistan, Central Asian republics, and others have shown results and hold promise for continued engagement in the future. **Collaboration** in combating terrorism has deepened with partners such as Algeria, Bahrain, Egypt, Morocco, Tunisia, and the United Arab Emirates.

The Coalition's objectives are clear: to eliminate the threat posed by international terrorism and to deter states from supporting or harboring international terrorist groups.

Liberation: Free from harsh rule.

Expulsion: Forced out.

al-Qaida: Islamic terrorist group led by Osama bin Laden.

Taliban: Radical Islamic religious and political group in Afghanistan.

Infrastructure: Network of camps and training facilities.

Transitional government: Temporary appointed rulers preparing the country for a permanent government.

Detained: Held in custody.

USS Cole: U.S. naval ship attacked by a small boat full of explosives while docked at a port in Yemen, killing 17 sailors and injuring 39.

U.S. Embassies: U.S. embassies in Tanzania and Kenya attacked with explosives, killing 378.

Global antiterrorism coalition: Alliance of nations worldwide that cooperates to fight terrorism.

Diplomatic: Skilled handling of relations between countries.

Intelligence: Gathering information on an enemy.

Financial: Halting the flow of money to terrorists.

Cultivated: Grown and nurtured.

Collaboration: Cooperation.

Intelligence

The gathering of intelligence about al-Qaida's infrastructure in Afghanistan helped enable us to dismantle or scatter much of its membership and organization.

Information gained from captured enemy combatants and imprisoned terrorists is being exploited effectively around the world.

The expansion of intelligence sharing and cooperation among nations since September 11 is preventing attacks, saving lives, and exposing the hiding places of terrorists.

Law Enforcement

An impressive global dragnet has tightened around al-Qaida. Since September 11 more than 3,000 al-Qaida operatives or associates have been detained in more than 100 countries, largely as a result of cooperation among law enforcement agencies.

Entire cells have been wrapped up in nations such as Singapore, Italy, and elsewhere. In all these cells, deadly attacks on U.S. interests or our allies were being planned.

In the United States, the rule of law is being applied relentlessly against terrorists. For example, U.S. Attorney General John Ashcroft called October 4 "a defining day in America's War on Terrorism." On that day, the United States convicted would-be shoe bomber Richard Reid; sentenced American Taliban John Walker Lindh; and neutralized a suspected al-Qaida terrorist cell in Portland, Oregon. Another alleged al-Qaida cell was uncovered and its members arrested in Lackawanna, New York, during the summer.

Since the previous Patterns of Global Terrorism *report was issued, the United States designated several additional groups as Foreign Terrorist Organizations (FTOs), including the Communist Party of the Philippines/New People's Army, Jemaah Islamiya, and Lashkar I Jhangvi. The Lashkar I Jhangvi was responsible for the kidnapping and murder of American journalist Daniel Pearl in 2002. The FTO designation carries several legal consequences: it is unlawful for U.S. persons to knowingly provide funds and other material support to designated groups; members of these groups are ineligible for U.S. visas; and U.S. financial institutions must block the funds of the groups.*

Financial

More than 166 countries have issued orders freezing more than $121 million in terrorist-related financial assets.

Enemy combatants: Term used by U.S. authorities for individuals engaged in battle against the United States.

Exploited: Used.

Dragnet: Network for police to find a criminal.

Operatives: Active members.

Cells: Groups or units.

Richard Reid: Person who attempted to blow up a commercial airliner with explosives hidden in his shoe.

John Walker Lindh: American who was captured in Afghanistan fighting against American forces.

Jemaah Islamiya: A radical Islamic group in Egypt.

Lashkar I. Jhangvi: A radical Islamic group based in India.

Daniel Pearl: American journalist captured and killed by terrorists in Pakistan.

Visas: Documents a person must have to enter a country.

Financial assets: Money and property.

Nearly all countries around the world have submitted reports to the United Nations [UN] on actions they have taken to comply with the requirements of UN Security Council Resolution (UNSCR) 1373, which includes obligations to freeze the assets of terrorists and to prohibit anyone in the country from providing financial or other material assistance to terrorists or their supporters.

The Financial Action Task Force—a 29-nation experts' group dedicated to the establishment of legal and regulatory standards and policies to combat **money laundering**—is working to deny terrorists access to the world financial system.

The European Union (EU) and the United States have worked closely together to ensure that nearly every terrorist individual or group designated by one . . . is also designated by the other. The Netherlands took effective action to freeze the financial assets of José Maria Sison, leader of the Communist Party of the Philippines/New People's Army terrorist group, and then asked the EU to freeze the assets of Sison and his group; the EU did so. In August, Italy joined the United States in submitting the names of 25 individuals and companies linked to al-Qaida to the UN, so their assets could be frozen worldwide.

The **G-8** nations have committed themselves to a range of measures aimed at seizing terrorist assets. The Asia Pacific Economic Cooperation group, APEC, has adopted an ambitious antiterrorist finance action plan. The United States joined with Kyrgyzstan, Afghanistan, and China in including the Eastern Turkestan Islamic Movement on the UN's list of organizations affiliated with al-Qaida.

In the United States, the Foreign Terrorist Asset Tracking Center, Operation Green Quest, and the Terrorist Financing Task Force are facilitating information sharing between intelligence and law enforcement agencies and helping other countries to improve their legal and regulatory systems so they can more effectively identify, disrupt, and defeat terrorist financing networks.

More than 250 terrorist groups and entities have been designated under **Executive Order 13224**, which freezes their U.S.-based assets.

In November, the United States blocked the assets of the Benevolence International Foundation, which for years misused its status as a charity by funneling money to al-Qaida. Its CEO is closely associated with **Usama Bin Ladin** and has helped his cause financially.

Also in November, the State and Treasury Departments announced a $5-million reward program that will pay for information leading to the disruption of any terrorism financing operation.

Money laundering: Placing money gained through crime into financial institutions where it is concealed from authorities.

G-8: A group of eight industrialized nations coordinating worldwide economic development.

Executive Order 13224: Presidential directive authorizing law enforcement agencies to tie up any terrorist money held in U.S. financial institutions.

Usama Bin Ladin: Leader of the Al-Qaeda terrorist network.

The USA Patriot Act

Six weeks after the September 11, 2001, terrorist attacks, Congress passed and President George W. Bush signed the USA Patriot Act, more formally labeled Uniting and Strengthening America by Providing Appropriate Tools Required to Intercept and Obstruct Terrorism Act. The act was passed by a 98 to 1 vote in the U.S. Senate and 357 to 66 vote in the U.S. House of Representatives. The U.S. Department of Defense, charged with preventing future terrorists attacks, lists four significant areas in which the Patriot Act strengthened their efforts against terrorism.

1) The act gave law enforcement more investigative tools to target terrorists. Section 201 allows the use of electronic surveillance methods (wiretaps) for investigation of specific terrorism-related crimes as the potential use of weapons of mass destruction like chemical weapons, the financing of terrorism, and killing Americans abroad. In the past wiretaps were allowed for crimes such as drug trafficking, or mail and passport fraud, but not on all of the crimes terrorists could commit.

Section 206 allows federal agents to use "roving wiretaps" against terrorists, which apply to a suspect rather than one particular phone line. Roving wiretaps had been used in other crime cases, but did not legally apply to terrorism. Using cell phones, terrorists are well trained in constantly changing communication devices and locations. Obtaining a court order to tap a specific phone at a specific location had become an obsolete, ineffective tool.

Section 213 allows courts to give permission to law enforcement agents to delay notice that a search warrant has been approved and about to be used. Delayed notification search warrants give officers time to search a number of individuals without tipping them off ahead of time. Delayed notice prevents escape from the investigative scene, evidence destruction, or tipping off other criminal associates their activities are under investigation. Delayed notification has long been used in drug cases, fighting organized crime, and child pornography.

The Patriot Act also allows federal agents to ask for a court order to acquire business records in national security terrorism cases. This ability is granted in Section 215. The Department of Defense reports that they look not only for bank records to see who sends money to terrorists but records from hardware stores, booksellers, chemical suppliers, and weapons manufacturers. Although highly controversial, an individual's library checkout records can also be obtained.

2) The act allows for better sharing of information and cooperation between government agencies. Sections 203 and 218 breaks down the so-called "Wall" halting the flow of information and evidence-sharing between agencies. Section 203 allows police officers, FBI agents, intelligence officers, immigration officers, and federal prosecutors to share information gained by wiretaps and from grand juries who gather information on specific cases. Section 218 allows full coordination between intelligence and law enforcement to protect against threats from a foreign agent. An often used phrase by law enforcement agencies to describe this aspect of the Patriot Act is that they are better able to "connect the dots."

3) The Patriot Act recognizes that new technologies like computer systems are used by terrorists allowing them to plan terrorist activities from various locations and frequently switch locations. Previously search warrants had to be obtained for each site, which was time consuming and ineffective. Sections 219 and 220 allow warrants to be issued by a judge in any district where terrorist activities occur then used in any district necessary nationwide.

4) The act clearly defines "material support" for terrorists. All support activities are federal crimes. Section 805, "Material support of terrorism" identified what "support" encompassed. Section 805 includes any act specifically intended to support terrorism such as people who raise and move funds, open bank accounts, recruit terrorists, provide training, provide weapons and supplies, buy airline tickets, lease cars, and rent apartments. Also included are those who offer terrorists expert advice and assistance as how to destroy bridges, buildings, make bombs, or acquire deadly chemical or biological agents. The Department of Defense rates this section as vital to keeping terrorists out of U.S. communities. They list terrorism support as the most frequently encountered terrorist activity on U.S. soil.

A number of Patriot Act sections will expire on December 31, 2005, if not renewed by Congress. Those include Sections 201, 206, 215, and 220. Groups such as the American Civil Liberties Union (ACLU) oppose renewal of various sections unless they are altered to better protect civil liberties. For example, the ACLU opposes renewing Section 206 "roving wiretaps" because it believes the wiretaps infringe on every American's privacy.

The ACLU predictably opposes Section 215 as well, which allows law enforcement access to an individual's various records including library checkout and business records. A number of bills were in Congress in mid-2004 to make changes to the Patriot Act in an effort to better protect the civil liberties of all U.S. citizens.

*As a result of all these efforts, it is much harder today for terrorists to raise and move money. Many who formerly provided financial support for terrorism seem to have backed away. Some **facilitators** have been captured and arrested. The international banking system is no longer safe for terrorists to use.*

*Future progress will not be measured in millions of dollars worth of frozen assets, as the amount of such funding is **finite**, but rather in terms of nations' efforts to prevent terrorist financing. Fundamentally, terrorists must now look over their shoulders, wondering whether it is safe to move, raise funds, plan, and conduct operations.*

Military

Operation Enduring Freedom was launched on 7 October 2001. It comprises some 90 nations, nearly half of the world's countries. It is the largest military coalition ever assembled in all of human history. Its successes have also been historic. The bulk of Afghan territory was liberated from Taliban control within a matter of weeks. With our Coalition partners, the United States is helping to train the Afghan National Army so that Afghans can once again provide for their own security and the stability of the country. Schools have been rebuilt, teachers trained, and textbooks supplied. Land mines are being cleared. Hundreds of thousands of refugees have returned.

In Afghanistan and elsewhere, military action continues to be waged against terrorists with global reach. More than 500 suspected terrorists are being detained at the U.S. facility at Guantánamo Bay, Cuba.

Conclusion

Despite solid progress, the danger persists.

*Al-Qaida is still planning attacks. Every al-Qaida operations officer captured so far was involved in some stage of preparation for a terrorist attack at the time of capture. Recent audiotapes by al-Qaida leaders contain **exhortations** to further violence and threaten the United States and our Coalition allies.*

These threats must be regarded with utmost seriousness. Additional attacks are likely.

*I have focused on our many accomplishments—diplomatic, intelligence, law enforcement, financial, and military. As significant as those have been, however, it is important not to think that victory is on the horizon. Far from it. Indeed, the ultimate success of this campaign will hinge in large part on two factors—sustained international political will and effective **capacity building**.*

Facilitators: Those who provide support to terrorists enabling them to carry out actions.

Finite: Limited.

Exhortations: Encouragement for.

Capacity building: Increasing the ability of nations to fight terrorism.

First, *we must sustain and enhance the political will of states to fight terrorism. The secret of maintaining a coalition is demonstrating daily to its members that the fight is not over and that sustained effort is clearly in their long-term interests. My meetings with government officials in every region of the world have convinced me that we have made tremendous progress on that score.*

Second, *we have to bolster the capacity of all states to fight terrorism. Despite our unmatched power, we recognize that the United States will not be able to win without the help of others. The United States cannot investigate every lead, arrest every suspect, gather and analyze all the intelligence, effectively sanction every sponsor of terrorism, prevent the* **proliferation** *of weapons of mass destruction, or find and fight every terrorist cell.*

Simply put, this is a global fight that requires a global system to defeat it.

President Bush has stressed from the beginning that "the defeat of terror requires an international coalition of **unprecedented** *scope and cooperation." So our effort must also be truly* international. . . .

Around the world, we are working to build up the capability of nations' forces so that they can take the fight to the terrorists from the streets of Sanaa in Yemen to Pankisi Gorge in Georgia, from the island of Basilan in the Philippines to the jungles of Colombia.

These posters in downtown Rome, Italy, show the Italian and American flags promoting an upcoming rally against terrorism and in solidarity with the U.S., November 8, 2001. After 9/11 President Bush called upon all nations to come together to fight terrorism. *(AP/Wide World Photos)*

Our goal is to assist governments to become full and self-sustaining partners in the fight against terrorism.

As President Bush said at the end of 2002: "In the new year, we will prosecute the war on terror with patience and focus and determination. With the help of a broad coalition, we will make certain that terrorists and their supporters are not safe in any cave or corner of the world."

Proliferation: Rapid increase in number.

Unprecedented: Never before experienced.

Ransom: Payment of money for the return of a hostage.

State sponsors: Those countries that actively support terrorists in some way; restrictions include bans of arms sales to the countries, no economic assistance from the United States, and international trade restrictions.

Financial underpinnings: Monetary support.

Vulnerabilities: Weaknesses.

U.S. Policy

President Bush has laid out the scope of the war on terrorism. Four enduring policy principles guide U.S. counterterrorism strategy:

*First, make no concessions to terrorists and strike no deals. The U.S. Government will make no concessions to individuals or groups holding official or private U.S. citizens hostage. The United States will use every appropriate resource to gain the safe return of U.S. citizens who are hostage. At the same time, it is U.S. Government policy to deny hostage takers the benefits of **ransom**, prisoner releases, policy changes, or other acts of concession.*

Second, bring terrorists to justice for their crimes. The United States will track down terrorists who attack Americans and their interests, no matter how long it takes.

*Third, isolate and apply pressure on states that sponsor terrorism to force them to change their behavior. There are seven countries that have been designated **state sponsors** of terrorism: Cuba, Iran, Iraq, Libya, North Korea, Sudan, and Syria.*

*Fourth, bolster the counterterrorist capabilities of those countries that work with the United States and require assistance. Under the Antiterrorism Assistance program, the United States provides training and related assistance to law enforcement and security services of selected friendly foreign governments. Courses cover such areas as airport security, bomb detection, hostage rescue, and crisis management. A recent component of the training targets the **financial underpinnings** of terrorists and criminal money launderers. Counterterrorist training and technical-assistance teams are working with countries to identify **vulnerabilities**, enhance capacities, and provide targeted assistance to address the problem of terrorist financing.*

What happened next . . .

The United States continued to stabilize Afghanistan and disrupt remaining al Qaeda cells hiding in the rugged mountains between Afghanistan and Pakistan. As of June 2004, however, Osama bin Laden had not been captured. The U.S.

government continued to strengthen counterterrorism programs both at home and in cooperation with other nations. Weaknesses in U.S. infrastructure continued to be remedied. For example, the federal government took over the screening of all passengers boarding commercial airliners.

Internationally, the United States continued to help nations working to defeat terrorism by assisting their law enforcement and security agencies, in finding and freezing money for terrorist support, and in emergency response improvement.

On March 1, 2003, the cabinet level Department of Homeland Security (DHS) became operational. DHS has the tremendous responsibility of ensuring the protection of the country's critical infrastructure and to have coordinated and effective response policies in place. Over one hundred different government agencies have various responsibilities for homeland security; all report to the DHS, which must coordinate and evaluate their responses.

The United States pursued its War on Terrorism by attacking the nation of Iraq and ousting its tyrannical dictator Saddam Hussein. Hussein was later captured in December 2003. President Bush listed Iraq's support of international terrorists, including ties to al Qaeda, and the potential use of its arsenal of weapons of mass destruction (WMD)—biological, chemical, and possibly nuclear—as primary reasons for going to war with Iraq.

Prior to the March invasion, Secretary of State Colin Powell presented evidence before the United Nations of the existence of these weapons of mass destruction. Nevertheless many of the world's nations including France, Germany, and Russia did not believe war was the answer. The strong international cooperative spirit following 9/11 was damaged by disagreement about Iraq.

As of June 2004 no WMDs had been found and the official U.S. 9/11 Commission examining the entire 9/11 tragedy announced they found no connection between the attack by al Qaeda and Iraq. As the United States handed over all governing responsibilities to Iraq in late June, terrorist activities continued on a daily basis in the country, killing Iraqi citizens and U.S. soldiers.

Did you know . . .

- In 2002 no successful attacks by foreign terrorist groups occurred in the U.S. homeland.

- The 2002 "Patterns" report included a section on weapons of mass destruction and terrorists entitled "Chemical, Biological, Radiological, Nuclear (CBRN) Terrorism." It reported while terrorists will continue to use traditional tactics such as bombing, abductions, and murder, they increasingly seek WMDs. The section quotes the leader of al Qaeda, Osama bin Laden, as saying he sees acquiring WMDs for use in terrorist actions as a "religious duty."

- U.S. counterterrorism assistance to other countries attempting to improve counterterrorism capabilities includes a wide variety of programs. Some of these programs are: (1) training foreign police and security forces in airport security and bomb blast investigation; (2) holding seminars on how to write effective counterterrorism laws; (3) conferences on how to investigate and halt financial support to terrorists; and, (4) policy workshops building relationships and cooperation between counterterrorism agencies from different nations.

- Another vital report on terrorism issued in July 2002 was the National Strategy for Homeland Security. It was produced by the Office of Homeland Security within the White House (which later grew into the Department of Homeland Security). The report served as the overall policy statement for the U.S. government's counterterrorism efforts.

Consider the following . . .

- List and briefly describe the State Department's five fronts of terrorism.

- Consider the first principle used in fighting terrorism: "make no concessions to terrorists and strike no deals." Do you think since terrorist attacks continue this policy is effective? Either agree or disagree with this principle and explain your reasoning.

- As a class activity make a pro/con chart concerning the effects of the U.S.–Iraq war (2003–04) on worldwide terrorism. Is the United States and its interests less likely or more likely to suffer terrorists attacks?

For More Information

Books

Walsh, James, ed. *Terrorism: Documents of International and Local Control.* Vol. 39, *U.S. Perspectives.* Dobbs Ferry, NY: Oceana Publications, Inc., 2003.

Web Sites

"Patterns of Global Terrorism." *U.S. Department of State.* http://www.state.gov/s/ct/rls/pgtrpt. (accessed on August 19, 2004).

"Significant Terrorist Incidents, 1961–2003: A Brief Chronology." *U.S. Department of State.* http://www.state.gov/r/pa/ho/pubs/fs/5902.htm (accessed on August 19, 2004).

"Terrorism." *Federal Bureau of Investigation (FBI).* http://www.fbi.gov/terrorinfo/terrorism.htm (accessed on August 19, 2004).

U.S. Department of Health and Human Services, Centers for Disease Control. http://www.cdc.gov (accessed on August 19, 2004).

U.S. Department of Homeland Security. http://www.dhs.gov (accessed on August 19, 2004).

Al Qaeda

Excerpt from "The Al Qaeda Training Manual"

Reprinted from *Terrorism: Documents of International and Local Control,*
Volume 39, U.S. Perspectives, **edited by James Walsh**
Published in 2003

"Islamic governments have never and will never be established through peaceful solutions. . . . They are established as they [always] have been by pen and gun, by word and bullet."

At the beginning of the twenty-first century, following the September 11, 2001 attacks, the United States was involved in a long struggle to protect the nation's homeland and American interests abroad from terrorism. The threat of terrorism was an ever-changing enemy involving America in a new kind of war. The enemy was not a specific government of a specific country. Terrorist threats take many forms and aim at many different targets. The enemy has many hiding places and, more often than not, is invisible. Terrorist threats have only one common element, they aim at America's "vulnerabilities," weaknesses they find in U.S. defenses or in U.S. preparedness.

Since 9/11 the U.S. government's top priority has been the prevention of terrorist attacks. The United States has had to plan defenses for many types of terrorist methods—bombings, hostage taking, assassinations, and even cyber attacks. The U.S. government treats all terrorist threats or action as criminal activity.

The targets are as varied as the methods—individuals, structural facilities of businesses and government, airlines, rail-

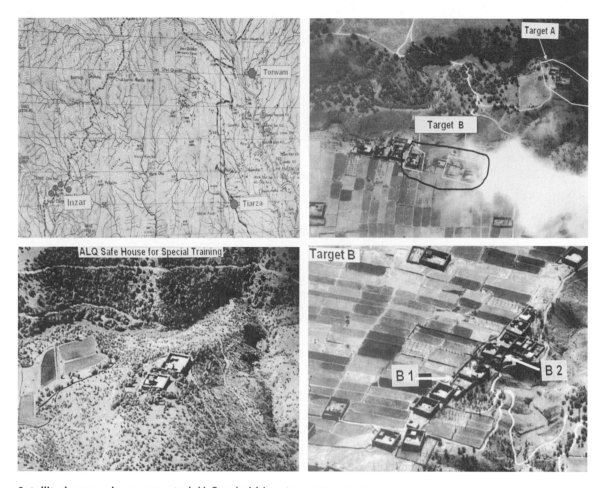

Satellite images show suspected Al Qaeda hideouts. *(AP/Wide World Photos)*

roads, subways, seaports, power generation systems, large gatherings at entertainment and sports venues, and computer networks. Threats or actual attacks are meant to instill fear in not only those directly involved but also in all who learn about them through media coverage. Terrorist actions are planned for maximum surprise, shock, and destruction. The goal is to so alarm individuals, groups, or governments that they give into terrorists demands.

Al Qaeda, the Islamic terrorist group responsible for 9/11, remains America's most serious threat despite the disruption of its central base in Afghanistan by U.S. troops. The following excerpt comes from "The Al Qaeda Training Manual."

British law enforcement discovered the training manual when searching a home in Manchester, England.

With great detail, clear instructions, and extensive warnings about not being discovered, the manual teaches how to operate as an al Qaeda terrorist. Included in the manual are such topics as the principles of military organization; qualifications for members; counterfeit currency and forged documents; hiding places; training; weapons; security plans; and espionage.

The thorough nature of the manual and its attention to detail illustrate how highly organized al Qaeda had become. It also reveals the determination of terrorist groups to further their cause by violent criminal acts.

Things to remember while reading excerpts from "The Al Qaeda Training Manual":

- The United States government considers radical Islamic religious terrorism the most serious form of all terrorism worldwide.

- The major or overall theme of the manual is that every movement and action of an al Qaeda operative must be done only after careful planning and in total secrecy.

- The well written manual reflects the organizational capabilities of the terrorist group to plan and carry out its terrorist acts.

Excerpt from "The Al Qaeda Training Manual"

Islamic governments have never and will never be established through peaceful solutions and cooperative councils. They are established as they [always] have been by pen and gun by word and bullet. . . .

*The young men returning to **Allah** realized that Islam is not just performing rituals but a complete system: Religion and government,*

Allah: Term for God in Islamic religion.

worship and Jihad [holy war], ethics and dealing with people, and the **Koran** and sword. The **bitter situation** that the nation has reached is a result of its **divergence** from Allah's course and His righteous law for all places and times. That [bitter situation] came about as a result of its children's love for the world, their loathing of death, and their abandonment of Jihad [holy war]. . . .

These young men realized that an Islamic government would never be established except by the bomb and rifle. Islam does not coincide or make a truce with **unbelief** but rather confronts it.

The confrontation that Islam calls for with these godless and **apostate** regimes, does not know **Socratic debates, Platonic ideals nor Aristotelian diplomacy**. But it knows the dialogue of bullets, the ideals of assassination, bombing, and destruction, and the diplomacy of the cannon and machine-gun.

The young came to prepare themselves for Jihad [holy war], commanded by the majestic Allah's order in the holy Koran. . . .

I present this humble effort to these young Moslem men who are pure, believing, and fighting for the cause of Allah. It is my contribution toward paving the road that leads to majestic Allah and establishes a **caliphate** according to the prophecy. . . .

FIRST LESSON GENERAL INTRODUCTION. . . .

Principles of Military Organization:

Military Organization has three main principles without which it cannot be established:

1. Military Organization commander and advisory council

2. The soldiers (individual members)

3. A clearly defined **strategy**

Military Organization Requirements:

The Military Organization dictates a number of requirements to assist it in confrontation and endurance. These are:

1. **Forged** documents and counterfeit currency

2. Apartments and hiding places

3. Communication means

4. Transportation means

5. Information

6. Arms and ammunition

Koran: The holy book of Islam, like the Bible in Christian religions.

Bitter situation: Following worldly ways of desiring material goods rather than strictly following Islamic ways.

Divergence: Separate path.

Unbelief: Not believing in Islam.

Apostate: Those who reject religion or another set of guiding principles.

Socratic debates, Platonic ideals nor Aristotelian diplomacy: The thought processes of Western world societies such as the United States and Europe in which citizens are free to debate and explore basic ideas about the natural world and society.

Caliphate: A spiritual leader in Islam.

Strategy: Overall planning and objectives.

Forged: Illegal copies.

7. Transport

Missions Required of the Military Organization:

The main mission for which the Military Organization is responsible is:

The overthrow of the godless regimes and their replacement with an Islamic regime. Other missions consist of the following:

1.Gathering information about the enemy, the land, the installations, and the neighbors.

2. Kidnapping enemy personnel, documents, secrets, and arms.

3. Assassinating enemy personnel as well as foreign tourists.

4. Freeing the brothers who are captured by the enemy.

5. Spreading rumors and writing statements that instigate people against the enemy.

6. Blasting and destroying the places of amusement, immorality, and sin. . . .

7. Blasting and destroying the embassies and attacking vital economic centers.

Blasting and destroying bridges leading into and out of the cities. . . .

SECOND LESSON NECESSARY QUALIFICATIONS AND CHARACTERISTICS FOR THE ORGANIZATION'S MEMBER

Necessary Qualifications for the Organization's members

1-Islam:

*The member of the Organization must be **Moslem**. How can an unbeliever, someone from a revealed religion [Christian, Jew], a **secular** person, a **communist**, etc. protect Islam and Moslems and defend their goals and secrets when he does not believe in that religion [Islam]? The Israeli Army requires that a fighter be of the Jewish religion. Likewise, the command leadership in the Afghan and Russian armies requires anyone with an officer's position to be a member of the communist party.*

*2—Commitment to the Organization's **Ideology**:*

*This commitment frees the Organization's members from **conceptional** problems.*

Moslem: One who follows the Islamic religion.

Secular: Apart from religion.

Communist: An economic theory that the state owns all production and profits are shared equally among the people; rejects religion.

Ideology: Beliefs and goals.

Conceptional: Questioning the ideology of the Organization.

3—Maturity:

The requirements of military work are numerous, and a **minor** cannot perform them. The nature of hard and continuous work in dangerous conditions requires a great deal of psychological, mental, and intellectual fitness, which are not usually found in a minor. . . .

4—Sacrifice

He [the member] has to be willing to do the work and undergo **martyrdom** for the purpose of achieving the goal and establishing the religion of majestic Allah on earth.

5—Listening and Obedience:

In the military, this is known today as discipline. It is expressed by how the member obeys the orders given to him. That is what our religion urges. . . .

6—Keeping Secrets and Concealing Information

[This secrecy should be used] even with the closest people, for deceiving the enemies is not easy. . . .

7—Free of Illness. . . .

8—Patience

[The member] should have plenty of patience for [enduring] **afflictions** if he is overcome by the enemies. He should not abandon this great path and sell himself and his religion to the enemies for his freedom. He should be patient in performing the work, even if it lasts a long time.

9—Tranquility and "Unflappability"

[The member] should have a calm personality that allows him to endure psychological traumas such as those involving bloodshed, murder, arrest, imprisonment, and reverse psychological traumas such as killing one or all of his Organization's comrades. [He should be able] to carry out the work.

10—Intelligence and Insight. . . .

11—Caution and **Prudence**. . . .

12—Truthfulness and **Counsel**. . . .

13—Ability to Observe and Analyze. . . .

14—Ability to Act, Chan ge Positions and Conceal Oneself. . . .

Minor: Commonly a person under eighteen years of age.

Martyrdom: Honored for dying for a cause.

Afflictions: Great suffering.

Prudence: Using good judgment.

Counsel: Giving good advice.

U.S. Attorney General John Ashcroft shows off an Al Qaeda training manual, Washington, D.C., December 6, 2001. Ashcroft used this to champion military tribunals and other legal weapons to protect Americans from terrorism. *(© Reuters/Corbis)*

FOURTH LESSON ORGANIZATION MILITARY BASES "APART-MENTS—HIDING PLACES"

Definition of Bases

These are apartments, hiding places, command centers, etc. in which secret operations are executed against the enemy.

These bases may be in cities, and are [then] called homes or apartments. They may be in mountainous, harsh terrain far from the enemy, and are [then] called hiding places or bases.

During the initial stages, the Military Organization usually uses apartments in cities as places for launching assigned missions, such as collecting information, observing members of the ruling regime, etc.

Hiding places and bases in mountains and harsh terrain are used at later stages, from which Jihad [holy war] groups are dispatched to execute assassination operations of enemy individuals, bomb their centers, and capture their weapons. In some Arab countries such as Egypt, where there are no mountains or harsh terrain, all stages of Jihad work would take place in cities. . . .

Security Precautions Related to Apartments:

1. Choosing the apartment carefully as far as the location, the size for the work necessary (meetings, storage, arms, fugitives, work preparation).

2. It is preferable to rent apartments on the ground floor to facilitate escape and digging of trenches.

3. Preparing secret locations in the apartment for securing documents, records, arms, and other important items.

4. Preparing ways of vacating the apartment in case of a surprise attack (stands, wooden ladders).

5. Under no circumstances should anyone know about the apartment except those who use it.

6. Providing the necessary cover for the people who frequent the apartment (students, workers, employees, etc.)

7. Avoiding seclusion and isolation from the population and refraining from going to the apartment at suspicious times.

8. It is preferable to rent these apartments using false names, appropriate cover, and non-Moslem appearance. . . .

11. Avoiding police stations and government buildings. Apartments should not be rented near those places. . . .

13. It is preferable to rent apartments in newly developed areas where people do not know one another. Usually, in older quarters people know one another and strangers are easily identified, especially since these quarters have many informers. . . .

15. Agreement among those living in the apartment on special ways of knocking on the door and special signs prior to entry into the building's main gate to indicate to those who wish to enter that the place is safe and not being monitored. Such signs include hanging out a towel, opening a curtain, placing a cushion in a special way, etc.

16. If there is a telephone in the apartment, calls should be answered in an agreed-upon manner among those who use the apartment. That would prevent mistakes that would, otherwise, lead to revealing the names and nature of the occupants. . . .

FIFTH LESSON: MEANS OF COMMUNICATION AND TRANS-PORTATION. . . .

First Means: The Telephone:

Because of significant technological advances, security measures for monitoring the telephone and broadcasting equipment have increased. Monitoring may be done by installing a secondary line or wireless broadcasting device on a telephone that relays the calls to a remote location. . . . That is why the Organization takes security measures among its members who use this means of communication (the telephone).

1. Communication should be carried out from public places. One should select telephones that are less suspicious to the security apparatus and are more difficult to monitor. It is preferable to use telephones in booths and on main streets.

2. Conversation should be coded or in general terms so as not to alert the person monitoring [the telephone].

3. Periodically examine the telephone wire and the receiver.

4. Telephone numbers should be memorized and not recorded. If the brother has to write them, he should do so using a code so they do not appear as telephone numbers (figures from a shopping list, etc.).

5. The telephone caller and person called should mention some words or sentences prior to bringing up the intended subject. The brother who is calling may misdial one of the digits and actually call someone else. The person called may claim that the call is for him, and the calling brother may start telling him work-related issues and reveal many things because of a minor error.

6. In telephone conversations about undercover work, the voice should be changed and distorted. . . .

Facsimile and Wireless:

*Considering its **modest capabilities** and the pursuit by the **security apparatus** of its members and forces, the Islamic Military Organization cannot obtain these devices. In case the Organization is able to obtain them, firm security measures should be taken to secure communication between the members in the country and the command outside. These measures are:*

1. The duration of transmission should not exceed five minutes in order to prevent the enemy from pinpointing the device location.

Facsimile: Electronically transmitting a document through telephone lines.

Modest capabilities: Lack of money.

Security apparatus: Law enforcement and intelligence agencies.

2. The device should be placed in a location with high wireless frequency, such as close to a TV station, embassies, and consulates in order to prevent the enemy from identifying its location.

3. The brother, using the wireless device to contact his command outside the country, should disguise his voice.

4. The time of communication should be carefully specified.

5. The frequency should be changed from time to time.

6. The device should be frequently moved from one location to another.

7. Do not reveal your location to the entity from which you report.

8. The conversation should be in general terms so as not to raise suspicion. . . .

SEVENTH LESSON: WEAPONS: MEASURES RELATED TO BUYING AND TRANSPORTING THEM

Prior to dealing with weapons, whether buying, transporting, or storing them, it is essential to establish a careful, systematic and firm security plan that deals with all stages. It is necessary to divide that task into stages: First Stage: Prior to Purchase; Second Stage: Purchasing; Third Stage: Transport; Fourth Stage: Storage.

1. Prior to Purchase Stage: *It is necessary to take the following measures:*

a. In-depth knowledge of the place where weapons will be purchased, together with its entrances and exits.

b. Verifying there are no informants or security personnel at the place where purchasing will take place.

c. The place should be far from police stations and government establishments.

d. Not proceeding to the purchasing place directly by the main road, but on secondary streets.

e. Performing the exercises to detect the surveillance.

f. One's appearance and clothing should be appropriate for the place where purchasing will take place.

g. The purchasing place should not be situated in such a way that the seller and buyer can be seen from another location. To the contrary, the purchasing place should be such that the seller and buyers can see the surrounding area.

h. Determining a suitable cover for being in that place.

i. The place should not be crowded because that would facilitate the police hiding among people, monitoring the arms receiving, and consequently arresting the brother purchasing.

j. In case one of the parties is unable to arrive, it is essential to prearrange an alternative place and time with the seller.

k. Selecting a time suitable for the purchase so that it does not raise suspicion.

l. Prior to purchasing, the seller should be tested to ensure that he is not an agent of the security apparatus.

m. Preparing a place for storage prior to purchasing.

2. The Purchase Stage:

a. Verifying that the weapons are in working condition.

b. Not paying the seller the price for the weapons before viewing, inspecting, and testing them.

c. Not telling the seller about the mission for which the weapons are being purchased.

d. Extreme caution should be used during the purchasing operation in the event of any unnatural behavior by the seller or those around you.

e. Not lengthening the time spent with the seller. It is important to depart immediately after purchasing the weapons.

3. The Transport Stage:

a. Avoid main roads where checkpoints are common.

b. Choose a suitable time for transporting the weapons.

c. Observers should proceed on the road ahead of the transportation vehicle for early warning in case of an emergency.

d. Not proceeding directly to the storage place until after verifying there is no surveillance.

*e. During the transport stage, weapons should be hidden in a way that they are **inconspicuous** and difficult to find.*

f. The route for transporting the weapons should be determined very carefully.

Inconspicuous: Not easily seen.

g. Verifying the legality of the vehicle, performing its maintenance, checking its gasoline and water levels, etc.

h. Driving the car normally in order to prevent accidents.

4. The Storage Stage:

*a. In order to avoid repeated transporting, suitable storage places should be selected. In case the materials are bombs or **detonators**, they should be protected from extreme heat and humidity.*

b. Explosive materials and detonators should be separated and stored apart from each other.

c. Caution should be exercised when putting detonators in the arsenal.

d. Lubricating the weapons and placing them in wooden or plastic crates. The ammunition should be treated likewise.

*When selecting an **arsenal**, consider the following:*

1. The arsenal should not be in well-protected areas, or close to parks or public places. . . .

3. The arsenal should not be in an apartment previously used for suspicious activities and often frequented by security personnel.

4. The arsenal should not be a room that is constantly sued and cannot be given up by family members who do not know the nature of the father or husband's work.

5. The apartment selected as an arsenal should be owned by the Organization or rented on a long-term basis.

6. The brother responsible for storage should not visit the arsenal frequently, nor toy with the weapons.

7. The arsenal keeper should record in a book all weapons, explosive materials, and ammunition. That book should be coded and well secured.

8. Only the arsenal keeper and the commander should know the location of the arsenal.

9. It is necessary to prepare alternative arsenals and not leave any leads in the original arsenals to the alternative ones.

***ELEVENTH LESSON: ESPIONAGE—(1) INFORMATION— GATHERING USING** OPEN METHODS. . . .*

Principle of Moslems Spying on their Enemies:

Spying on the enemy is permitted and it may even be a duty in the case of war between Moslems and others. Winning the battle is dependent on knowing the enemy's secrets, movements, and plans.

Detonators: Devices used to explode a bomb.

Arsenal: Storage place for weapons.

Open methods: not undercover intelligence gathering.

The prophet—Allah bless and keep him—used that method. He would send spies and informants. . . . Since Islam is superior to all human conditions and earthly religions, it permits spying for itself but not for others. . . . The prophet says, "Islam is supreme and there is nothing above it." Islam, therefore, fights so the word of Allah can become supreme. Others fight for worldly gains and lowly and inferior goals.

An Important Question:

How can a Muslim spy live among enemies if he maintains his Islamic characteristics? How can he perform his duties to Allah and not want to appear Muslim?

Concerning the use of clothing and appearance. . . . The [Muslim] man may prefer or even be **obligated** *to look like* **them***, provided his action brings a religious benefit of preaching to them, learning their secrets and informing Muslims, preventing their harm, or some other beneficial goal. . . ."*

As for the visible duties, like fasting and praying, he can fast by using any justification not to eat with them. . . . As for prayer . . . "he [the Moslem] may combine the noon and afternoon [prayers], sunset and evening [prayers]. That is based on the fact that the prophet—Allah bless and keep him—combined [prayers] . . . without fear or hesitation.". . .

Guidelines for Beating and Killing Hostages:

Religious scholars have permitted beating. . . .

In this tradition, we find permission to interrogate the hostage for the purpose of obtaining information. It is permitted to strike the nonbeliever who has no **covenant** *until he reveals the news, information, and secrets of his people.*

The religious scholars have also permitted the killing of a hostage if he insists on withholding information from Moslems. They permitted his killing so that he would not inform his people of what he learned about the Muslim condition, number, and secrets. . . .

The scholars have also permitted the exchange of hostages for money, services, and expertise, as well as secrets of the enemy's army, plans, and numbers. . . .

TWELFTH LESSON: ESPIONAGE—(2) INFORMATION—GATHERING USING COVERT METHODS

Information needed through covert means: *Information needed to be gathered through covert means is of only two types:*

Obligated: Committed or required.

Them: Those being spied on.

Covenant: An agreement between humans and God.

Covert: Hidden, undercover.

Britain's Defense Secretary Geoff Hoon stands next to a map illustrating the location of Al Qaeda training camps in Afghanistan destroyed by U.S. air strikes, London, October 23, 2001. The strikes were part of Operation Enduring Freedom in Afghanistan, the first military action in the "war against terrorism." *(© Reuters/Corbis)*

First: *Information about government personnel, officers, important personalities, and all matters related to those (resident, work place, times of leaving and returning, wives and children, places visited).*

Second: *Information about strategic buildings, important establishments, and military bases. Examples are important ministries such as those of Defense and Internal Security, airports, seaports, land border points, embassies, and radio and TV stations.*

General security measures that should be taken by the person gathering information: *During the process of gathering information, whether about governing personalities or establishments, the person doing the gathering must take the following security measures:*

1. Performing the exercises to detect surveillance while executing the mission. These exercises are not well defined, but are dependent on the time, place, and the ability to be creative. These exercises include the following:

a. Walking down a dead-end and observing who is walking behind you. Beware of traps.

b. Casually dropping something out of your pocket and observing who will pick it up.

c. Walking fast then stopping suddenly at a corner and observing who will be affected.

d. Stopping in front of store windows and observing who is watching you.

e. Getting on a bus and then getting off after it departs and observing who will be affected.

f. Agreeing with one of your brothers to look for whoever is watching you.

Surveillance by car:

Surveillance by car requires taking certain measures:

1. Inspecting the car's fuel, water, and lights.

2. The car should be of a common type so it would not attract people's attention.

3. The car should be in good condition and the driver should be experienced.

4. The car plates should not contain real numbers. It is important to use a false license plate and small numbers in order to prevent anyone from spotting and memorizing it.

5. The car's interior light should be disabled in order to hide the identity of the surveillance team members sitting inside. . . .

A. Surveillance, Intelligence, and Observation *(Information about the enemy places)*

The Organization's command needs detailed information about the enemy's vital establishments, whether civilian or military, in order to make safe plans, reach firm decisions, and avoid surprises. Thus, the individual who gathers information about a desired location should, in addition to drawing a diagram, describe it and all its details.

The Drawing: *The brother should draw a diagram of the area, the street, and the location which is the target of the information-gathering. He should describe its shape and characteristics. The drawing should be realistic so that someone who never saw the location could visualize it. It is preferable to also put on the drawing the directions of traffic, police stations, and security centers. . . .*

Recruitment Stages: *Suppose the Islamic Organization, with its **modest** capabilities, wants to obtain information about an important target (important personality, building, camp, agency, ministry). It has to do the following:*

1. Finding the **Agent**: *In this stage, the Organization picks the suitable person for supplying the information. The Organization learns about that person: His financial condition, his family status, his position regarding the government, and his weaknesses and strengths.*

2. Evaluating the Agent: *In this stage, the agent is placed under continuous observation to learn the times of his departure to and return from work, the places he visits, the individuals he meets, and his social interaction with those that he meets in coffee shops, clubs, etc.*

3. Approaching the Agent: *After gathering information about him, a relationship with him is developed under a certain cover, such as:*

a. Family connection and tribal relations.

*b. Developing a friendship with him in the club, coffee shop, and workers union. The [recruiting] brother develops the friendship as if it were **unpretentious** and unplanned. The relationship should develop naturally and gradually in order not to attract the target's attention.*

Important Note: *In case the first brother fails to develop a friendship with the target, another brother takes over after learning from the first about the target's weaknesses (motives that can be exploited) such as his love for money, opposition to the government, love for adventure. . . .*

4. Recruiting the Agent: *After finding, evaluating, and approaching a target, comes the second stage of recruiting him. Recruiting may be direct, that is, telling the agent frankly about working for the Organization for a specific and agreed-upon salary. A promise is secured in writing or verbally.*

Or recruitment may be indirect, that is, information may be taken from the target without informing him that he is an agent. That may

Modest: Limited money or equipment or available members.

Agent: A person Al Qaeda wants to recruit.

Unpretentious: Simple, not complex.

be accomplished by giving him gifts, sharing his joys and sorrows, and attempting to solve his problems.

Testing the Agent: In this stage, the agent is assigned certain tasks in order to test his ability, loyalty, and dependability. The agent does not know that the Organization already has the sought information. If the information supplied by the agent does not match the Organization's existing information, then the agent may be an unreliable source of information or may be trying to mislead the Organization. During the testing stage, the agent should remain under careful observation to spot all his movements. . . .

What happened next . . .

The U.S. Central Intelligence Agency (CIA) reports since 9/11 thousands of al Qaeda terrorists have been arrested and a considerable number of the top leaders killed or captured. Osama bin Laden had not been captured as of late spring 2004. Although severely disrupted by U.S. military operations in Afghanistan and worldwide efforts against al Qaeda by many governments, al Qaeda persists.

Groups of al Qaeda terrorists, called cells, are located worldwide. The global efforts to eliminate them have caused the cells to diversify and regroup into smaller cells. The cells, knowing their terrorist training manual directives well, operate independently to carry out strikes. While much of the funding that moved through financial institutions has been cut off, cells rely on informal person-to-person money transfers called "hawalas" that leave no electronic or paper trail and are untraceable. The threat of al Qaeda to U.S. interests abroad and to the U.S. homeland continued to be of major concern in mid-2004.

Did you know . . .

• Only the most dedicated, well-trained recruits are allowed to become full al Qaeda members. Osama bin Laden hand-picked the operatives used to hijack U.S. planes in the 9/11 attack.

- In 2002 and 2003 no successful attacks occurred on U.S. soil but attacks against U.S. interests worldwide continued. In 2002 of all anti-U.S. attacks carried out by various terrorist organizations, the most—forty-six—occurred in Latin America followed by sixteen in the Middle East and ten in Asia. The type of facilities targeted most were U.S. businesses. Most terrorist threats and attacks involved bombings.

- Each year the U.S. State Department compiles a list of Foreign Terrorist Organizations known as FTOs. Compiled since 1997, the list took on a new sense of urgency since 9/11. In 2004 the list included thirty-six terrorist organizations. The U.S. government may freeze any FTO assets in U.S. financial institutions, may deny entry of a FTO member into the United States, and may prosecute any U.S. citizen or person in the United States who supports an FTO in any way.

Consider the following . . .

- The current FTO list and information about each terrorist organization is available at the Center for Defense Information (CDI) Web site at http://www.cdi.org/terrorism/terrorist.cfm or the U.S. State Department Web site at http://www.state.gov.

- After reading this chapter's sidebar on the USA Patriot Act, find a number of investigative tools allowed by the act that should be helpful in uncovering al Qaeda cells.

- Research al Qaeda in depth. For what purpose was it originally created? Why did the United States and U.S. interests become a focus of its terrorist activities?

For More Information

Books

Walsh, James, ed. *Terrorism: Documents of International and Local Control.* Vol. 39, *U.S. Perspectives.* Dobbs Ferry, NY: Oceana Publications, Inc., 2003.

Web Sites

Center for Defense Information (CDI). http://www.cdi.org (accessed on May 28, 2004).

"Significant Terrorist Incidents, 1961–2003: A Brief Chronology." *U.S. Department of State.* http://www.state.gov/r/pa/ho/pubs/fs/5902.htm (accessed on August 19, 2004).

U.S. Department of Homeland Security. http://www.dhs.gov (accessed on August 19, 2004).

Where to Learn More

Books

Abadinsky, Howard. *Drug Abuse: An Introduction.* Chicago, IL: Nelson-Hall Publishers, 1997.

Acker, James R., Robert M. Bohm, and Charles S. Lanier, eds. *America's Experiment with Capital Punishment: Reflections on the Past, Present, and Future of the Ultimate Penal Sanction.* Durham, NC: Carolina Academic Press, 1998.

Anderson, Elijah. *Streetwise: Race, Class and Change in an Urban Community.* Chicago, IL: University of Chicago Press, 1990.

Arrigo, Bruce A., ed. *Social Justice, Criminal Justice.* Belmont, CA: Wadsworth, 1999.

Austern, David. *The Crime Victims Handbook: Your Rights and Role in the Criminal Justice System.* New York: Viking, 1987.

Bachman-Prehn, Ronet D. *Death and Violence on the Reservation: Homicide, Violence, and Suicide in American Indian Populations.* New York: Auburn House, 1992.

Baum, Lawrence. *American Courts.* 5th ed. Boston: Houghton Mifflin, 2001.

Belknap, Joanne. *The Invisible Woman: Gender, Crime, and Justice.* Toronto: Wadsworth Thomson Learning, 2001.

Benjamin, William P. *African Americans in the Criminal Justice System*. New York: Vantage Press, 1996.

Besharov, Douglas J. *Recognizing Child Abuse: A Guide for the Concerned*. New York: Free Press, 1990.

Burns, Ronald G., and Michael J. Lynch. *Environmental Crime: A Source Book*. New York: LFB Scholarly Publishing, 2004.

Burrough, Bryan. *Public Enemies: America's Greatest Crime Wave and the Birth of the FBI, 1933–34*. New York: Penguin Press, 2004.

Buzawa, Eve, and Carl Buzawa. *Domestic Violence: The Criminal Justice Response*. Thousand Oaks, CA: Sage, 1996.

Carp, Robert A., and Ronald Stidham. *Judicial Process in America*. 5th ed. Washington, DC: CQ Press, 2001.

Chase, Anthony. *Law and History: The Evolution of the American Legal System*. New York: The New Press, 1997.

Clement, Mary. *The Juvenile Justice System*. 3rd ed. Woburn, MA: Butterworth Heinemann, 2002.

Clifford, Mary. *Environmental Crime: Enforcement, Policy, and Social Responsibility*. Gaithersburg, MD: Aspen Publishers, Inc., 1998.

Clifford, Ralph D., ed. *Cybercrime: The Investigation, Prosecution, and Defense of a Computer-Related Crime*. Durham, NC: Carolina Academic Press, 2001.

Cohn, Marjorie, and David Dow. *Cameras in the Courtroom: Television and the Pursuit of Justice*. New York: McFarland & Company, 1998.

Coloroso, Barbara. *The Bully, the Bullied, and the Bystander: From Pre-School to High School, How Parents and Teachers Can Help Break the Cycle of Violence*. New York: HarperResource, 2003.

Conser, James A., and Gregory D. Russell. *Law Enforcement in the United States*. Gaithersburg, MD: Aspen, 2000.

Cromwell, Paul, Lee Parker, and Shawna Mobley. "The Five-Finger Discount." In *In Their Own Words: Criminals on Crime*, edited by Paul Cromwell. Los Angeles, CA: Roxbury, pp. 57–70.

Curran, Daniel J., and Claire M. Renzetti. *Theories of Crime*. Boston: Allyn & Bacon, 2001.

Davidson, Michael J. *A Guide to Military Criminal Law*. Annapolis, MD: Naval Institute Press, 1999.

Dummer, Harry R. *Religion in Corrections*. Lanham, MD: American Correctional Associates, 2000.

Dunne, Dominick. *Justice: Crimes, Trials, and Punishment*. New York: Three Rivers Press, 2002.

Federal Bureau of Investigation. *Crime in the United States, 2002: Uniform Crime Reports*. Washington, DC: U.S. Department of Justice, 2003.

Felson, Marcus. *Crime and Everyday Life*. 2nd ed. Thousand Oaks, CA: Pine Forge Press, 1998.

Frank, Nancy, and Michael Lynch. *Corporate Crime, Corporate Violence*. Albany, NY: Harrow and Heston, 1992.

Friedman, Lawrence M. *Crime and Punishment in American History*. New York: Basic Books, 1993.

Garbarino, James. *Lost Boys: Why Our Sons Turn Violent and How We Can Save Them*. New York: Free Press, 1999.

Gordon, Margaret, and Stephanie Riger. *The Female Fear*. New York: Free Press, 1989.

Hirsch, Adam Jay. *The Rise of the Penitentiary: Prisons and Punishment in Early America*. New Haven, CT: Yale University Press, 1992.

Hoffer, Peter C. *Law and People in Colonial America*. Baltimore: Johns Hopkins University Press, 1998.

Jones-Brown, Delores. *Race, Crime, and Punishment*. Philadelphia: Chelsea House, 2000.

Karmen, Andrew. *Crime Victims: An Introduction to Victimology*. 4th ed. Belmont, CA: Wadsworth, 2001.

Lane, Brian. *Crime and Detection*. New York: Alfred A. Knopf, 1998.

Levin, Jack. *The Violence of Hate: Confronting Racism, Anti-Semitism, and Other Forms of Bigotry*. Boston: Allyn and Bacon, 2002.

Lunde, Paul. *Organized Crime: An Inside Guide to the World's Most Successful Industry*. New York: DK Publishing, Inc., 2004.

Lyman, Michael D., and Gary W. Potter. *Organized Crime*. Upper Saddle River, NJ: Pearson Prentice Hall, 2004.

Mones, Paul. *When a Child Kills*. New York: Simon & Schuster, 1991.

Oliver, Willard M. *Community-Oriented Policing: A Systematic Approach to Policing*. Upper Saddle River, NJ: Prentice Hall, 2001.

Patrick, John J. *The Young Oxford Companion to the Supreme Court of the United States*. New York: Oxford University Press, 1998.

Ramsey, Sarah H., and Douglas E. Adams. *Children and the Law in a Nutshell*. 2nd ed. St. Paul, MN: Thomson/West, 2003.

Renzetti, Claire M., and Lynne Goodstein, eds. *Women, Crime, and Criminal Justice*. Los Angeles: Roxbury, 2001.

Russell, Katheryn. *The Color of Crime*. New York: New York University Press, 1998.

Sherman, Mark. *Introduction to Cyber Crime*. Washington, DC: Federal Judicial Center, 2000.

Siegel, Larry J. *Criminology: The Core*. Belmont, CA: Wadsworth/Thomson Learning, 2002.

Silverman, Ira. *Corrections: A Comprehensive View.* 2nd ed. Belmont, CA: Wadsworth, 2001.

Situ, Yingyi, and David Emmons. *Environmental Crime: The Criminal Justice System's Role in Protecting the Environment.* Thousand Oaks, CA: Sage Publications, 2000.

Smith, Helen. *The Scarred Heart: Understanding and Identifying Kids Who Kill.* Knoxville, TN: Callisto, 2000.

Stark, Rodney, and Williams Sims Bainbridge. *Religion, Deviance, and Social Control.* New York: Routledge, 1997.

Sullivan, Robert, ed. *Mobsters and Gangsters: Organized Crime in America, from Al Capone to Tony Soprano.* New York: Life Books, 2002.

Sutherland, Edwin H. *White-Collar Crime: The Uncut Version.* New Haven, CT: Yale University Press, 1983.

Walker, Samuel. *The Police in America: An Introduction.* New York: McGraw-Hill, 1992.

Wilkinson, Charles F. *American Indians, Time, and the Law: Native Societies in a Modern Constitutional Democracy.* New Haven, CN: Yale University Press, 1987.

Wright, Richard, and Scott Decker. *Armed Robbers in Action: Stickups and Street Culture.* Boston: Northeastern University Press, 1997.

Yalof, David A., and Kenneth Dautrich. *The First Amendment and the Media in the Court of Public Opinion.* Cambridge: Cambridge University Press, 2002.

Web Sites

"Arrest the Racism: Racial Profiling in America." *American Civil Liberties Union (ACLU).* http://www.aclu.org/profiling (accessed on September 20, 2004).

Center for the Prevention of School Violence. http://www.ncdjjdp.org/cpsv/ (accessed on September 20, 2004).

"Computer Crime and Intellectual Property Section (CCIPS) of the Criminal Division." *U.S. Department of Justice.* http://www.cybercrime.gov (accessed on September 20, 2004).

"Counterfeit Division." *United States Secret Service.* http://www.secretservice.gov/counterfeit.shtml (accessed on September 20, 2004).

Court TV's Crime Library. http://www.crimelibrary.com (accessed on September 20, 2004).

"Criminal Enforcement." *U.S. Environmental Protection Agency.* http://www.epa.gov/compliance/criminal/index.html (accessed on September 20, 2004).

Death Penalty Information Center. http://www.deathpenaltyinfo.org (accessed on September 20, 2004).

Department of Homeland Security. http://www.dhs.gov (accessed on September 20, 2004).

Federal Bureau of Investigation (FBI). http://www.fbi.gov (accessed on September 20, 2004).

McGeary, Johanna. "Who's the Enemy Now?" *Time,* March 29, 2004. http://www.time.com/time/classroom/glenfall2004/pg28.html (accessed on September 20, 2004).

Mothers Against Drunk Driving (MADD). http://www.madd.org (accessed on September 20, 2004).

National Alliance of Crime Investigators Associations. http://www.nagia.org (accessed on September 20, 2004).

National Center for Juvenile Justice. http://www.ncjj.org (accessed on September 20, 2004).

National Center for Victims of Crime. http://www.ncvc.org (accessed on September 20, 2004).

National Child Abuse and Neglect Data System (NCANDS). http://nccanch.acf.hhs.gov/index.cfm (accessed on September 20, 2004).

"National Institute of Corrections (NIC)." *U.S. Department of Justice.* http://www.nicic.org (accessed on September 20, 2004).

National Institute of Military Justice. http://www.nimj.com/Home.asp (accessed on September 20, 2004).

National Organization for Victim Assistance (NOVA). http://www.try-nova.org (accessed on September 20, 2004).

Uniform Crime Reporting Program. http://www.fbi.gov/ucr/ucr.htm (accessed on September 20, 2004).

United Nations Office for Drug Control and Crime Prevention, Organized Crime. http://www.undcp.org/organized_crime.html (accessed on September 20, 2004).

U.S. Courts. http://www.uscourts.gov (accessed on September 20, 2004).

U.S. Department of Justice. http://www.usdoj.gov (accessed on September 20, 2004).

U.S. Drug Enforcement Administration. http://www.dea.gov (accessed on September 20, 2004).

U.S. Securities and Exchange Commission. http://www.sec.gov (accessed on September 20, 2004).

Index